Don Carlos and Company

CHRISTOPHER MORGAN

Oxford   New York

OXFORD UNIVERSITY PRESS

1996

Oxford University Press, Walton Street, Oxford OX2 6DP

Oxford New York
Athens Auckland Bangkok Bogota Bombay
Buenos Aires Calcutta Cape Town Dar es Salaam
Delhi Florence Hong Kong Istanbul Karachi
Kuala Lumpur Madras Madrid Melbourne
Mexico City Nairobi Paris Singapore
Taipei Tokyo Toronto
and associated companies in
Berlin Ibadan

Oxford is a trade mark of Oxford University Press

First published by Julia MacRae 1994
First issued as an Oxford University Press paperback 1996

British Library Cataloguing in Publication Data
Data available

Library of Congress Cataloging in Publication Data
Data available
ISBN 0–19–288009–8

1 3 5 7 9 10 8 6 4 2

Printed in Great Britain by
Biddles Ltd.
Guildford and King's Lynn

Contents

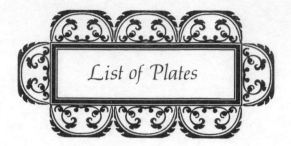

List of Plates

Introduction

Curiosity inspired this book, my own curiosity which came in two forms. First, after a lifetime of enjoying the opera, I was curious to know how much truth there was in apparently historical operas like *Don Carlos* or *Un Ballo in Maschera*. Their general contexts may be familiar to anyone with a basic knowledge of history, but they usually deal with some detail within that context. I was taught quite a lot about Philip II of Spain, that he married our Queen Mary, burnt heretics and sent the Armada against us, but virtually nothing about his other wives or his first son Carlos. Carlos and Elizabeth live off the main track of history, down a little byway which few are likely to explore without a special interest in the subject. Operatically, one can see the wisdom of this. Verdi's opera about Joan of Arc reduces her to a Mills and Boon heroine, the object of a tug of-love between her austere father and a mawkish Dauphin, while her Voices act as a sort of heavenly agony aunt. We all know that that is a travesty, but I, for one, was less certain about just what did go on between Carlos and Elizabeth. I wanted to find out.

Secondly, I was also curious to know why these particular minor incidents had found their way onto the opera stage. History teems with spear-carriers and walk-on parts. What was it about some of them that had attracted an author's and then a composer's attention? I suspected that their stories, like Joan's, had been somewhat adapted for the stage. Life does not often divide itself neatly into a soprano, a tenor, a mezzo and a baritone role. I believed that if, like an archaeologist, I could scrape away what had been overlaid, I might find an even better story underneath.

Why else would it have been chosen in the first place? I hoped that its discovery might add a new dimension to my appreciation of the opera. The stage Manrico might be even more moving if I knew that there had been a real Manrico who had serenaded ladies, fought the King and his evil servant di Luna, and died a hero's death.

My first thought was to find the book already written by someone else that would satisfy my curiosity, and it was only when I discovered that there did not seem to be one that it occurred to me to do some research myself. It was not long before I began to understand why no such book existed. Being concerned with rather obscure incidents, each opera requires a specialist in its period and place to know the truth about it. But the stories are scattered about the centuries and around Europe with no regard for such specialisations. This book starts in fourteenth century Genoa and ends in nineteenth century Paris. Some stories concern kings and others prostitutes. There are no doubt historians who have so comprehensive a grasp of their subject as to take such variety in their stride, but if so, I would hope that they were engaged on some more serious project. Although an amateur myself, I felt there was a small gap that I might fill.

The operas more or less selected themselves. I rejected some, like *Andrea Chenier* or *Rienzi*, because, sadly, they are so seldom staged. Perhaps a second volume, dealing with them, might encourage someone to put them on. Other works, like *Tosca*, though popular and full of historical signposts, proved to have too thin a historical basis. Yet others, though certainly true, are impossible to research. For example, the author Bouilly assures us that *Fidelio* is about "one of our brave Touraine women" during the Terror. He knew her, but he gives us no other lead as to who she was or where. Finally, I have avoided operas like *Giovanna d'Arco* or *Samson and Delilah*, about characters with whose stories readers will be thoroughly familiar.

Each story is accompanied by a synopsis of the opera, in case readers wish to cross-reference some detail that occurs both in real life and in the opera. Libretti sometimes quote things that someone actually said or represent on stage a real incident. The book does not attempt any musicological insights, nor does it search for the sort of political symbolisms and psychological angles which intrigue modern opera directors. The stories are told as simply as possible in the hope that they will entertain in their own right as well as enhance the reader's appreciation of each opera.

I include a bibliography for each story from which it will be seen that I have not been to the Archives at Simancas or the Vatican Library in search of primary sources. I have relied on the books of others who have. My concern has been to steer a sensible course between their often violently conflicting interpretations of the same material. I only quote my sources where I have borrowed a significant passage from a particular work.

Everything in the stories came from one source or another, and I felt it would be distracting to clutter the text with continual references. Only where I indulge in a philosophical aside is it my own. With the important exception of Swedish, the translations are also my own, unless it is indicated otherwise.

ACKNOWLEDGEMENTS

I would like to thank many people who have helped me to research and write this book. I received great help from the staffs of all the libraries I have used, but wish to mention, in particular, the British Library, the London Library, Wandsworth Library, the Bibliothèque Nationale in Paris, the Biblioteca del Museo Histórico de la Ciudad in Barcelona and the Biblioteca del Università in Genoa.

In addition, I am grateful for the particular contributions of the following: Concerning *Simon Boccanegra*, I was much helped by Prof. Giovanna Petti Balbi, the Hon. Edmund Howard and Mr Michael Wicks, the British Consul in Genoa. I would like to thank Mr Anthony Edkins for his help with *Il Trovatore* and Prof. Keith Bate with *Rigoletto*. With *Lucia*, I received much help from the Scottish Record Office, from Mr Donald White and the Rev. John Murrie both of Kirkliston, while in Galloway, I was guided by the Rev. Graham Dickson of Glenluce, Mr John Harvey of New Luce and Mrs Donna Brewster of Stranraer. I also consulted Mrs Isobel Rutherford of Hunthill.

Regarding illustrations, I wish particularly to thank Miss Ann

Grönhammar of the Livrustkammaren in Stockholm, Mlle Madeleine de Terris of the Bibliothèque Nationale in Paris and Padre Victor Diez Marina of the Franciscan Monastery in Pastrana. I have received enthusiastic help from all the picture agencies I have used, but would single out for special thanks Señorita Enriqueta of Archivo Mas and Señorita Nuria of AISA, both in Barcelona, and Mme Anne Salaün of Roger-Viollet and Mme Veronique Martingay of Giraudon, both in Paris.

Most of all, I would like to thank several friends who have patiently ploughed through early drafts of the book, and have helped me to make it more readable. Foremost of these I must mention Prof. Peter Veen and Mr and Mrs David Taggart, but the same applies to several members of my family. Finally, I wish especially to thank Mme Anne-Marie Lemaire for her guidance and hospitality in Paris.

FOR

ANN

SIMON BOCCANEGRA

Giuseppe Verdi

Libretto by Francesco Maria Piave
from a play by Gutiérrez

Dramatis Personae

Simon Boccanegra, *Doge of Genoa*
Jacopo Fiesco [alias Andrea], *A Guelph aristocrat*
Gabriele Adorno, *Genoese gentleman*
Paolo Albiani, *A goldsmith*
Pietro, *An agitator*
Captain of the Guard

Amelia Grimaldi, *Simon's daughter, found and adopted by Grimaldis*
Amelia's maid,

Conspirators, councillors, Guelph and Ghibelline rioters, guards

Synopsis

BACKGROUND

Simon Boccanegra is a Genoese corsair whose exploits have made him a popular hero. Some years previously, he fell in love with a young Guelph noblewoman, Maria Fiesco, but her father Jacopo did not let her marry him, even when she had his baby daughter. Instead, he locked her up in his palace, but Simon somehow managed to recover his child. He kept her hidden with a foster mother near Pisa, until one terrible day he found the woman dead and the child missing. He searched, but in vain because she had been found by the Grimaldis, and adopted by them in place of their own daughter who had recently died. They called her Amelia. Although allies of the Fieschi, the Grimaldis knew nothing of her origin, and all she could remember was that the old woman gave her the miniature of her natural mother.

PROLOGUE

It is September 1339. The Genoese are discontented with their aristocratic rulers. A mass meeting is to be held to elect an Abbot to defend the people's interests, and the likely choice is Lorenzino the usurer.

In the pre-dawn darkness outside the Fieschi palace, Paolo is suggesting to Pietro that Simon Boccanegra would be a better choice. Simon himself enters and rejects the idea. He is not interested in politics, but when they suggest that he might be elected not Abbot but Doge, he consents. As Doge, he could demand Maria's hand. He leaves while Pietro briefs his followers to shout for Simon. They depart to attend the meeting.

Fiesco emerges from his palace. His mind is not on politics because Maria has just died, and once again he curses her seducer, who now returns. Simon pleads for reconciliation and for Maria's hand. Fiesco does not tell him that she is dead, and says that he will agree if Simon returns his granddaughter, but Simon confesses that he has lost her. Spitefully, Fiesco directs Simon into the palace. Re-emerging stricken with grief, Simon is met by Paolo and Pietro who acclaim him Doge. Fiesco, to one side, swears vengeance.

ACT ONE

SCENE ONE: The scene is the Grimaldis' garden in the country. Twenty-five years have passed, Simon is still Doge, and the Grimaldi and Fieschi men have been banished. Jacopo Fiesco has remained, disguised as Andrea, to act as guardian for the supposed Amelia Grimaldi. He knows she is a foundling but no more than that. He is still plotting vengeance against Simon. Amelia has fallen in love with another of Simon's enemies, Gabriele Adorno, who blames Simon for his father's death.

It is early morning and Amelia is in the garden awaiting Gabriele, who soon arrives. She is pleading with him not to get involved in Andrea's plots when a messenger arrives to tell them that Simon is approaching. She warns Gabriele that Simon has plans for her, and that, if he wants her, they had better be married soon. As she leaves, Andrea arrives and gives Gabriele his consent. Both men now leave rather than meet Simon.

Simon, Paolo and others now arrive, and Simon asks to see Amelia alone. He tries to buy her favour by pardoning her brothers, but when he proposes that she marry Paolo, she rejects it violently. She protests she is not worthy, being but a foundling. Simon at once starts to wonder, they compare their miniatures of Maria, and are rapturously reunited as father and daughter. When Paolo returns, he is brusquely dismissed without an explanation.

The scene ends with Paolo and Pietro plotting to kidnap Amelia and hide her with Lorenzino. Paolo curses Simon's ingratitude.

SCENE TWO: Simon is sitting with his Council of twelve patricians and twelve commoners, amongst whom are Paolo and Pietro.

They deal with business items – a trading treaty with the King of Tartary and a proposal from the poet Petrarch for Italian unity. Simon passionately supports this but the councillors reject it. At this point sounds of riot are heard. Fearing it may be related to Amelia's abduction, Paolo and Pietro try to leave, but Simon stops them. A herald is sent out to calm the mob who are then allowed in. They bring Andrea and Gabriele captive, caught in the act of killing Lorenzino, who only had time to protest that he was detaining Amelia on the orders of a "man of power". Gabriele assumes this is Simon, intending her for a concubine, and wild with jealousy, tries to attack him, but Amelia herself rushes in to separate them, which merely strengthens Gabriele's suspicions.

In the meanwhile, Simon has guessed that it is Paolo's work. Sending Andrea and Gabriele into protective custody, he orders Paolo to unravel the crime. He also solemnly curses the culprit and orders a horrified Paolo to do likewise.

ACT TWO

Night has fallen. Paolo and Pietro are in Simon's room plotting once again, this time to kill him.

Paolo sends Pietro to fetch the two prisoners. He knows that he himself will soon be exposed, and is resolved to kill Simon first. He pours poison into Simon's water jug, and, when they arrive, proposes to Andrea and Gabriele that they murder him in his sleep. Andrea is outraged and sent away, but Gabriele is so mad with jealousy that he agrees, is given a dagger, and told to wait. Paolo leaves. Instead of Simon, Amelia arrives. She cannot adequately explain her presence in Simon's room, but, hearing him approach, she persuades Gabriele to hide. She then asks her father's permission to marry Gabriele. Simon complains that he has no sooner found her than she wants to leave him again, and for a bitter enemy, but he consents. Unluckily, Gabriele does not hear this conversation.

When Amelia leaves, Simon drinks some water and falls asleep.

Gabriele creeps out with his dagger raised, but Amelia rushes back. Simon awakes and demands to know who let Gabriele in, but he will not say. In anguish, Amelia tries to intercede, and lets slip that Simon is her father. Gabriele is stunned, and is pleading for punishment and reconciliation when more rioting is heard outside. This time it is a mob of Guelphs intent on killing Simon and rescuing Gabriele. Simon tells him that if he can pacify them, Amelia will be his.

ACT THREE

It is later in the same evening. Gabriele succeeded and is shortly to be married to Amelia. Paolo has been unmasked.

The captain of the guard is chatting with Andrea, and feels he can safely give him back his sword. This is not wise, for Andrea is still thirsting for vengeance. Paolo is brought through on his way to execution, and tells Andrea about the poison. Andrea reflects that he will have to move fast if he is going to obtain his own vengeance.

Sounds of the wedding are heard. Simon approaches. Andrea first hides but then confronts him, and reveals his identity and intention. To his astonishment, Simon reacts with joy. At last, after all these years, he can restore to Fiesco Maria's daughter, and claim his forgiveness. Simon's joy is soon overtaken by pain, and he is not surprised to learn its cause.

The bridal couple enter, followed by the Council, to receive Simon's blessing, but first Amelia must be told about Fiesco. With the pain now too great to hide, Simon blesses them. Making one last effort, he requests the Council to elect his son-in-law, Gabriele, to succeed him and falls dead.

The Mould Breaker

Even the most exciting moments in history, rich in personal drama, often lack a love interest. The story of Simon Boccanegra is an example. If one is to believe the opera, nothing happens except as the result of some passion, some jealousy or some misunderstanding involving a woman – either Maria Fiesco or her daughter, Amelia Grimaldi. It is only for love of Maria that Simon agrees to become the Doge. Years later, it is jealousy over Amelia that causes his death. Genoa was not short of chroniclers but they rarely mention women. They do record that in 1360, when he was fifty-nine, Simon was married to Costanza d'Elce, a Sienese noblewoman. As in the opera, he may have been still single when he first became Doge but it is hard to believe that he remained celibate for most of his life. That there is no historical record of an earlier wife or mistress does not mean that none existed. In fact Simon did have a daughter, Maddalena, whom he married to Luchinetto Visconti, son of the ruler of Milan. Although children were often betrothed very young in the fourteenth century, Maddalena must have been too old to be Costanza's child, which implies that Simon had an earlier involvement[1], but Maddalena was certainly not the original of the Amelia of the opera. Amelia is pure fiction, invented by the play's author, Gutiérrez, to give Simon a much-needed romantic interest.

In other respects, much of the opera is history. On 23rd September, 1339, Simon Boccanegra was elected by popular acclamation to be the first and perpetual Doge of Genoa. He was thirty-eight. On the 14th March, 1363 he died as the result of poisoning. In the meanwhile he had not, as the opera implies, enjoyed twenty-five continuous years of power. In 1344 he resigned and went into exile, where he remained until just before his re-election in 1356. If it was not love and Maria Fiesco that lay behind these events, what did? The answer involves a little bit of historical background.

Genoa was a republic and the chief city of Liguria, a rather infertile strip of coast between Monaco and the Gulf of Spezia. It has been suggested that the origins of Liguria's name relate to its inability to grow legumes. The Ligurians had long had a bad reputation as a fractious race, even in classical times. Virgil, in the *Aeneid* dismisses them in a contemptuous couplet:

> Like a true Ligurian born to cheat,
> At least when fortune favoured his deceit.

Their character had not much changed by Simon Boccanegra's day in the fourteenth century, but in the meanwhile they had become extremely rich. Lacking fertile lands, they had become traders and, above all, sailors. The swell of the sea pervaded their lives and their history just as it does Verdi's score. They were the most fearless and the most feared sailors in the Mediterranean. Richard Coeur de Lion adopted Genoa's patron St George and his cross at least partly because he knew what respect it commanded at sea. The Genoese made a great deal of money out of Richard and the other crusaders, transporting them to the Holy Land, supporting them there and, for a stiff fee, bringing them back again. In the meanwhile, they were developing contacts throughout the Levant, which in due course they converted into a trading empire with a string of colonies stretching to the furthest corners of the Black Sea. Through these, they imported the exotic wares of the East and sold them, often improved by Genoa's artisans, throughout Europe. Another of their trades was in mercenaries. Genoa's fleets and her renowned archers were for hire to whichever foreign monarch had the money to pay for them. Occasionally their hired flotillas might find themselves on opposing sides of a sea-battle, but the Genoese rarely had much compunction about killing each other, whether as mercenaries or in civil strife.

All these activities brought Genoa immense wealth. As a boy in about 1300 Petrarch saw the city from the sea, and was so impressed by its grandeur, its marble palaces and lofty towers as to write ruefully in old age to his companion on that voyage:

> Dost thou remember that time when the Genoese were the happiest people on earth, their country appeared a celestial residence even as the Elysian fields are painted?

One of the noblest of Genoese palaces was the Vialata, perched on a prominence near the harbour, and surrounded with fountains, terraces and hanging gardens. It was built of the black and white marble permitted only to the municipality, the Church and the top four Genoese families. It contained its own mint, which was useful, as were, in times of trouble, the tunnels which led down to the family's harbour and galleys, and which facilitated the family's escape to its country fortress at Montobbe. Vialata belonged to the Fieschi and was presumably the palace we see in the Prologue of the opera. No trace of it exists today for it was eventually destroyed by the Dorias so that not one stone remained upon another[2].

Like Venice, Genoa's trade inclined it to a republican form of government. Its trading expeditions were financed either privately or by syndicates, so that economic power was widely spread, militating against too much concentration of political power. Nevertheless, it was a stratified society with rigid class distinctions. There were four basic classes – aristocrats, merchants, artisans and the common people. The source of the city's wealth depended on the merchant class and, to a lesser extent, the artisans. The aristocratic class came about partly because of the city's need to have a territory around it, a protective buffer between it and jealous neighbours such as Pisa. A symbiosis had developed between the city and a number of feudal statelets strung out along the Ligurian riviera between Monaco in the west and Livorno in the east. The lords of these domains agreed to acknowledge the city's rule in exchange for access to its civic offices. They soon came to dominate the chief of these to the exclusion of all other classes, so that high office and nobility became synonymous. They also played their full part in the city's commerce, and supplied a series of outstanding military and especially naval leaders. While there were many families who claimed noble status, four stood out above the rest.

Two of these, the Grimaldi and the Fieschi, might be called the old nobility. As far back as 932 the Grimaldis had ejected the Saracens from Monaco, while the Fieschi were said to descend from a twelfth-century tax collector whose achievements earned him the nickname "Fisco". The Grimaldis on their rock became pirates, but the Fieschi had broad lands around Levanto and became politicians and strong churchmen. Down the years, they supplied two popes, seventy-two cardinals and over three hundred bishops. One of their political strengths was the ability sometimes to persuade the Pope to excommunicate Genoa, an effective ploy because it was bad for business. Disparate as they were, these two families were allies. They were Guelphs[3], looking to the French and the Pope for support.

Fiercely opposed to them were the Ghibelline families, the Dorias and the Spinolas, who looked to the Holy Roman Emperor for support. Their star had been rising throughout the thirteenth century partly due to the general trend in northern Italy. Every Italian statelet had its Guelph-Ghibelline rivalry, and a political shift in one could cause reactions in its neighbours, rather as positive and negative particles influence each other. This did not distract the Genoese Guelphs and Ghibellines from their almost constant internecine warfare, but it could influence the outcome. When one side was dominant, the other would usually have to withdraw to its castles outside the city, but sometimes its leading members might be entirely banished from Liguria. Exiles would often enter mercenary service[4]. It was at these times that it was so important to have a woman, like Amelia, who could stay behind to guard the family's possessions. While the titles Guelph and Ghibelline were not meaningless, they were largely a cover for a more elemental struggle for power. The old nobility and the *nouveaux riches* were at war.

Not surprisingly, the interests of the citizens of Genoa were often damaged by these family feuds, and their resentment sometimes boiled over. Down the years, the aristocrats had tried various expedients to keep the people quiet. One, quite common in northern Italy, was the appointment as chief magistrate of a *podestá*, a distinguished foreign nobleman who would be contracted for several years and given a salary and a staff. The hope was that, being foreign, he would be impartial, but this did not always prove to be the case. All too often, a *podestá* proved tyrannical and partial at any rate to his own interests. In 1257, the Genoese tried an experiment. Caught unprepared by some serious riots, the patricians agreed to the creation of a new office to be called the "Captain of the People". While all other main offices would remain in aristocratic hands, the Captain of the People would be a plebeian. He would be appointed for ten years, salaried and provided with a staff including a judge, two recorders, twelve serjeants and fifty men-at-arms. The *podestà* would be retained but would be subordinate to the Captain. As first Captain, they selected Guglielmo Boccanegra, a member of one of the leading merchant families.

The name Boccanegra is first mentioned in the Genoese annals as far back as the First Crusade in 1096, but it was quite a common name[5] and there is no knowing whether all those mentioned were related. There is no doubt, however, that in 1249, Guglielmo and his family made a lot of money out of Louis IX's crusade. Normally the Boccanegras' activities lay in the western Mediterranean and they were specialists in the meat trade and textiles but, like all Genoese, they were opportunists. By 1257, they had become one of the leading merchant families, with Ghibelline inclinations and requiring only a nudge upwards, such as an important office or a good marriage, to cross the line and become nobles themselves.

Guglielmo's appointment as Captain might have achieved that transformation had it run its full course, but it did not. The aristocrats had only accepted it in a moment of weakness, and were by no means reconciled to it. Guglielmo was inexperienced in government, and surrounded by aristocratic officials who did not all want him to succeed. He was soon in difficulties at home, and it was not long before conspiracies to remove him started to be exposed and punished ever more harshly. He did have some notable successes in the field of diplomacy, but ironically it was these that led to his downfall. The Venetians were so alarmed by the trading agreements he was achieving in the Levant that, aided by the Fieschi, they persuaded the Pope to excommunicate Genoa.

As his position weakened, Guglielmo sought to exploit it to his own benefit while he still had time. This did not improve his popularity, and, in 1262, he was forced out of office. He had not achieved nobility, but henceforth the Boccanegra family was singled out from all others in its class. It had been touched with greatness and several of Guglielmo's children married aristocrats. Guglielmo was Simon's great-uncle.

THE BOCCANEGRA FAMILY

Oberto Boccanegra
m. Villana

Guglielmo [Captain of the People] m. Iacopa   Lanfranco m. Contessa   5 Others

Sibilla m. Inghelto Spinola | Simona m. Simon de Negro | Nicolo m. Moisetta Avvocati | Ottobuono m. Aiguinetta Spinola | Ranieri m. Alterisia   Iacopo m. Ginevra Redenasco

Egidio m. Ricetta Ricio | Simon [Doge] m. Costanza d'Elce | Bartolomeo m. Eliana Adorno | Nicolo | Giovanni m. Fresca Doria | Lodisio m. Lino Spinola | Anfreone m. Bianchina Spinola

Maddalena m. Luchinetto Visconti   Battista m. Bianchina Guarca

Source: Professor Giovanna Petti Balbi

With Guglielmo's departure, the feuds started again, but the Ghibellines soon got the upper hand. For the rest of the thirteenth century, a Doria/Spinola duumvirate provided a stable government under which trade could prosper. It was towards the end of this period that Petrarch so admired the happiness and wealth of the

Genoese. It did not last. Not long after Petrarch's voyage, the Ghibelline coalition began to break up. The two branches of the Spinolas fell out, and drove the Dorias to make common cause with the Guelphs. For a time, a shaky Guelph government achieved power in the city, but mostly under conditions of siege. The interests of the citizens and even of the merchants, on whom all depended, went by the board. The trade guilds of the city were forced to set up their own system of justice for want of any other. A sinister new development was the recruitment by both sides of mercenaries, the Guelphs from Calabria and the Ghibellines from Germany. Since these Germans spoke no Italian, they could not tell friend from foe, and were apt to kill first and ask who it was afterwards. Altogether it was a terrible time in Genoa, which accounts for the note of regret in Petrarch's letter. Eventually, the Genoese came to their senses, but only to be confronted by troubles from a new direction.

In 1339, there was a mutiny in a Genoese squadron on mercenary duty with the French fleet in the Channel. The admiral, Antonio Doria, had apparently misappropriated the seamen's wages, and then made things worse by seeking French aid to quell the mutiny. They seized and imprisoned the ring-leader, Pietro Capurro from Voltri, but several galleys escaped, and set off home. Most of their crews came from Savona where they were welcomed home as heroes by the people, who rallied behind their demands for justice. Another Doria, Edoardo, was trying to calm things down when a false rumour started to spread that Capurro had been executed. Remonstrance turned to rioting which rapidly spread along the coast, and a large body of sailors and angry proletarians began to march on Genoa.

The Prologue of the opera is set just at this moment. In something of a panic, the ruling aristocrats decided it was time for a gesture. Since they had themselves adopted the title Captain of the People, they proposed to revive another office, that of "Abbot of the People", which had from time to time existed. It was normally filled by a plebeian whose role, like that of the Tribunes of classical Rome, was to represent the people and defend their interests. The Abbot had no formal power, but, acting as a lightning conductor, he might moderate the people's wrath. The citizens were invited to send twenty electors to the former palace of the

Abbots to select a man of their own choice.[6] These electors met on the 23rd September 1339, and, while they deliberated, a multitude of all classes of the population gathered in the square outside to await their decision. And they waited and they waited. It is never easy for twenty people to agree even when no-one is trying to manipulate them, but their deliberations were so prolonged that events outside overtook them.

Towards the afternoon, the crowd in the square began to get fidgety – a muttering began which was swelling angrily in volume when, quite spontaneously or so it seemed, a humble artificer, a goldsmith, climbed onto a wall and shouted: "Fellow citizens! Will you patiently listen to the advice of such an insignificant creature as I am?"

We do not know this man's name but the Paolo of the opera is also a goldsmith. The man's temerity inspired a confused reaction. Some hooted and threatened to silence such insolence with stones and blows, but others encouraged him, and soon he resumed with, so runs the report, all the aplomb of a senator.

"Whatever reception my advice may meet with," he said, "or whatever I may suffer for so offering it, I am determined to give vent to my thoughts. What need of these incertitudes, debates and delays in the election of an Abbot of the People? Here, in our midst, is Simon Boccanegra, a man of unexceptionable character. Choose him without more ado."

His words at once made a remarkable impression. The air rang with Simon's name which was soon being shouted from all parts of the square, seeming to be their unanimous choice for Abbot. The two reigning Captains, thoroughly alarmed, called Simon forth to sit between them while the electors, hearing the noise, rushed out of the palace to discover what was to do. Seeing what it was, they at once signified their assent, and sought to deliver to Simon the sword which was the symbol of the Abbot's office. Simon, however, turned it aside, signalling his rejection of the idea. Eventually the tumult was sufficiently calmed for him to speak.

"Citizens!" he said, "I cannot return to you too many thanks for such a mark of your goodwill but as none of my ancestors was ever an Abbot of the People, I am not inclined to introduce this office into my family. Confer it on some more suitable person."

No-one mistook his meaning. He would be Captain, like his forebear, or nothing. The reigning Captains were horrified, and pressed him to reconsider his position while a loud and confused buzz filled the square. Then someone shouted: "Make him our Lord, then! Our Doge!"

At once the cry was taken up on all sides. The crowd seemed so well drilled that it is hard to believe that it was not being manipulated, as in the opera, by some Pietro. Confident of the mounting support of the crowd, Simon was able to continue to act with great diffidence and humility.

"Well," he said as soon as he could make himself heard, "it seems I must consent – and I do – to be either Abbot or Doge as you think best."

"Doge! Doge!" roared the crowd "Not Abbot!"

"It is then your pleasure that I be Doge," said Simon artfully, "but no doubt what you intend is that I should be but an associate with the Captains in the Government."

"No! No!" they cried, "Govern alone as our Doge!"

In no time, this cry spread beyond the square, running like a brush-fire through the streets to ignite ever widening explosions of revolutionary enthusiasm, so that the patricians were only able with great difficulty and some danger to escape to their palaces. Indeed, several were manhandled and buffeted and some noble houses were looted. Simon himself had to intervene to rescue a near neighbour, Ramella Grimaldi, from a threatening mob while elsewhere the carnival was turning really nasty. There were people running armed through the city, behaving as though they thought that a People's Doge was a licence for anarchy. When Simon was informed of these excesses, he hastened to where the tumult was at its worst, and ordered some of the rioters to be seized and their heads struck off on the spot. According to the annals, "this timely punishment caused the new Doge to be greatly respected and restored a profound tranquility throughout the whole city." Even so, the deposed Captains felt it wise to leave.

Next day, in a popular assembly in the square opposite the Church of San Lorenzo, Simon was solemnly confirmed as perpetual Doge, transformed to everyone's astonishment into as absolute a ruler as Genoa had yet known. To assist him, a council of fifteen, known as the Ancients, was elected by the public while a foreign *podestá* was retained to administer justice. And three abbots were appointed each to safeguard the interests of one of the three main valleys of Liguria. The leading nobles on both sides were banished to their country seats, and all Guelphs barred from holding any office. The new office of Doge was never to be held by a patrician. Finally, the Doge should wear red, including a red cap.

In the opera Simon Boccanegra is a simple, bluff sea-dog, renowned for his exploits against the Barbary pirates. Alas, this was not so in reality. Of course, no-one in Genoa was entirely a stranger to the sea and the Boccanegra family had produced its share of sea captains. His elder brother Egidio was perhaps the greatest of them but Simon was a landlubber, a trader like Antonio in *The Merchant of Venice*. The brothers worked in close collaboration. Egidio commanded their galleys while Simon handled the business. Simon was neither simple nor bluff but a shrewd manipulator. There is little doubt that the events in the square on 23rd September were, at least to some extent, stage-managed by Simon with the help of Egidio, who was more than likely the Pietro of the opera. Some historians go so far as to suspect that the whole affair was planned by the Ghibelline nobles to get themselves out of a nasty situation, but, if so, their plan misfired when Simon refused to become Abbot. His diffidence was the tactic of an ambitious man.

Once elected as Doge, he proved a much more capable ruler than his great-uncle. Coming after the ruthless self-interest of the feuding families, it was easy to do better. Simon soon consolidated his reputation with tough but fair policies, treating commoners and the few nobles who remained in the city without prejudice. He placed great emphasis on unity and order, but was never able entirely to gain control over the dissident nobles in their fastnesses outside the city. His main concern, however, was to establish conditions in which the city's merchants and sailors could flourish and prosper, and win for Genoa the full fruits of their enterprise. Faced at the outset with a bankrupt exchequer, with the city's trade routes preyed on by corsairs [including the Grimaldis in Monaco], with the land outside the city still in his enemies' hands, and with famine threatening, his prospects did not look good. He was as energetic as he was firm. Building an effective fleet and attacking one by one the obstacles to the city's welfare, he soon wrought astonishing changes in its fortunes. These achievements were indeed crowned, as in the opera's council scene, by a trading treaty in which Genoa was offered preferential freedom by the King of Tartary to trade throughout the Black Sea.

One of the secrets of Simon's success was his concern to maintain good relations with other Italian states. In this he was ahead of his time, since for most Italians in the fourteenth century, the greatest enemy was not the distant Turk nor even the French, but the city next door. Even so, his energetic policies were not achieved without cost. A strong fleet was not cheap, and he had perpetually to raise taxes, while the freer trade for which his successes opened the way did not yield an immediate dividend.

Much more visible to the people were his own personal extravagances; he maintained two palaces at public expense.[7] In addition, he charged for his hunting falcons, a leopard and other animals which, though not perhaps very costly in themselves, were seen to be so in public perception. A much more serious expense was his personal body-guard of five hundred mercenaries. Furthermore, having able brothers whom he could entirely trust, he used them in positions of responsibility, engendering the inevitable allegations of nepotism. The Genoese were not free from envy.

None of this might have mattered had he not had so many implacable enemies outside the city gates. Having come to regard Genoa as their private property, the displaced patricians could in no way forgive this common little man who had usurped their birthright. For them, his every success was gall and wormwood. The greater the benefits he brought his city, the more they hated him who brought them none. The more popular he became, the more urgent became their plotting. They could not have hated him more thoroughly had he really ravished one of their daughters.

It was not long before the first would-be assassins began to infiltrate the city, and several were unmasked and executed, but soon the conspiracies began to involve townspeople who had allowed themselves to be suborned. Examples had to be made of them, too, which made Simon new enemies. Events were thus developing into a vicious spiral when one of Genoa's feudal neighbours, the Marquis del Finale concluded that, with no accredited nobility to fight for it, Genoa must now be virtually defenceless. He invaded, but Simon reacted so vigorously that the Marquis had to beat a hasty retreat, sending a messenger with his apologies. This was not good enough for Simon, who insisted that he come in person to be humiliated. After ceding some of his territory, Finale was displayed to the public in a wooden cage, and then sent home in ignominy. This somewhat restored Simon's popularity and, as a result, Genoa's control of Liguria became more effective, although the Grimaldis still held out in Monaco, and the lands of the Spinolas, north of the mountains that encircled the city, were never fully subdued. It was from these bases that the aristocrats eventually developed their counter-attack.

Although these successes did strengthen Simon's position, the Genoese were cantankerous and notoriously ungrateful people, and the aristocrats were indefatigable. The round of plot and punishment resumed, and Simon was soon losing friends again. His position depended on friends as it had no constitutional basis. How could so unruly a city have a constitution? Nor was the office of Doge sanctioned by custom or precedent. It was based on the acclaim of the mob which many suspected Simon had manipulated himself. Popularity with the mob is a sandy foundation for power, and the fickleness of the Genoese mob is well demonstrated by the opera, almost to the point of absurdity, as first one riot, then another, surges through the streets under the Doge's windows. The dissident lords were soon finding ever more fertile ground for their schemes with more and more malcontents gathering under their banners. It is a measure of Simon's achievements that he managed to unite the four patrician families, even if only in hatred for him. Eventually, in 1344, his enemies managed to collect sufficient armed followers to threaten the city itself.

It is an indication of the decline in his support that Simon seems to have been caught unawares at this point. Before he had time to react, his enemies' forces were already in the city's suburbs though not yet within the walls. Hastily closing the gates, Simon managed to rally support, but he wanted to avoid a bloody struggle; he offered to negotiate with the aristocrats, and to cancel their banishment. The word came back that he must first disband his mercenary bodyguard, the core of his security. The meaning of such a condition was inescapable. Rather than plunge the city into war, Simon summoned the Council of Ancients, explained the situation and said he would never remain as an impediment to the reconciliation of his fellow citizens. Having accepted power at their request, he would now be happy to lay it down for their welfare. His rule had lasted five years. Helping himself to 100,000 gold florins from the Treasury, he embarked for exile in Pisa where one of his brothers was *podestá*. Egidio took his squadron off to serve in the fleet of Genoa's ally, the King of Castile. It is something of a mystery why Simon gave up power without more of a fight, and it has been suggested that he may have quarrelled with Egidio, who had been so strong a support. On the other hand, Egidio's departure may have been the result rather than the cause of Simon's resignation. The annals do not speculate on such questions, but subsequent events indicated that Simon's departure might have been premature.

Left to deal with the rebellious aristocrats, the Ancients soon found that Simon's self-sacrifice had been in vain. They sent an embassy to negotiate with Spinola, the rebel leader, who told them that he would only re-enter Genoa sword in hand. This concentrated their minds wonderfully. They kept the gates closed and elected a new Doge – one Giovanni de Murta, a patrician but an unassuming and popular man. Helped by their apprehension of imminent retribution, Murta was able to create such fervour in the people, both in Genoa and in Savona, that Spinola and his malcontents abandoned their attempt without putting it to the test. Eventually, a reconciliation was negotiated and many exiled nobles were allowed to return, enabling Genoa to enjoy a period of welcome peace, but it was cut short in 1348 by a terrible visitation of the plague. In 1350, this carried off Murta himself. He was much mourned.

The choice of the next Doge was a disorderly affair. The Spinola faction saw a chance to put their own man in the job, and organised a so-called popular meeting to acclaim their candidate. This did not take long, and the crowd at once set off to install him in the ducal palace. In the meanwhile, the merchant faction had gathered in the Cathedral of San Lorenzo, which is just by the palace, and they managed to get their man, Giovanni de Valenti, into the palace first. The Spinolas' crowd was already on its way, but, hearing the great bell in the palace tower ring out, they lost heart and dispersed. Next day, Valenti's election was solemnised. His reign was a disaster. Rivalry in the Bosphorous led to war with Venice which started well, but then went so wrong that Genoa had to seek protection from Milan. Valenti resigned, and Genoa came under the rule of a Milanese governor, Pallavicini. It is possible that Simon had a hand in all this. Apparently living quietly in exile in Pisa, he had busily cultivated ties with the Milanese and especially with Giovannolo Mondella, Treasurer to Milan's cruel ruler, Luchino Visconti. He betrothed his daughter, Maddelena, to Visconti's son, Luchinetto, although this may not have seemed so clever when Luchino was murdered.[8] Despite this, Simon was still able to maintain his links with Milan.

Having saved the Genoese from Venice and made peace between the two republics, the Milanese did not withdraw from Genoa but continued to rule it through a governor. Naturally, with the danger passed, the Genoese soon found this irksome, and started to make trouble as only they knew how. Alarmed, the Viscontis turned to their Genoese friend, Boccanegra, and asked him to return to the city to give their man some support. He did not hesitate, but no sooner was he back in Genoa than he changed sides. While the Milanese governor was out quelling a riot, Simon sneaked into his palace with two hundred followers and shut him out.[9] The news that Simon was once again in control, though somewhat premature, spread rapidly through the city, the fighting died down and everyone went home, except of course the Governor whose home was closed to him. Much discouraged, he sheathed his sword and quit. Next day, in the absence of any further opposition, Simon was elected Doge for the second time.

This time, his rule was on quite a different basis. If Simon was able to return to Genoa because the Milanese trusted him, he was able to betray that trust because he knew he had other powerful backers, including the Emperor himself, who felt the Viscontis were becoming too ambitious. This time, Simon's rule was not derived from popular support but from a concert of states which did not want to see Genoa absorbed by Milan. This made him feel

more secure. He did not need to pander so much to popular sentiment, and could act more ruthlessly. He had soon pacified the rest
of Liguria, except, as usual, the rock of Monaco. He set up a much
grander court, introducing some of the pomp and luxury he had
seen in Milan. He seemed to anticipate his elevation to the nobility
and took great pleasure in various honours bestowed on him. The
Emperor, for instance nominated him *miles* or knight of the Holy
Roman Empire, but no-one actually conferred nobility on him.
Despite these vanities, he ruled well and, once again, Genoa
enjoyed a period of relative peace and prosperity. During its
course, Genoa acquired Corsica, which had long been fought over
by Pisa and Aragon. The oppressed Corsicans rebelled and
appealed to Genoa for help. Simon sent a brother with some
troops and an extremely liberal policy, who had little difficulty in
establishing a form of Genoese protectorate. On the whole, however, Simon's foreign policy was conciliatory. He did not want
expensive wars if they could be avoided. It is not true, as the opera
implies, that he dreamed of Italian unity. That was wishful thinking on Verdi's part. On the contrary, when the Pope tried to form a
league of Christian states to oppose the Turks, Simon refused to
take part. The Genoese did too much trade with the Turks.

Naturally, the fact that he ruled well did nothing to mollify the
dispossessed patricians. In the opera, the implacable hatred of
Jacopo Fiesco for the seducer of his daughter may seem overdone,
but in truth the hatred of the aristocrats for this usurper was no
less bitter. The plotting for his downfall and his death recom-
menced and continued unabated. If Simon became suspicious and
untrusting, it is hard to blame him, but the consequence was that
he became steadily more ruthless and unpopular. Towards the
end of 1362, he fell out with his closest and thus far most trusted
lieutenant, not the Paolo Albiani of the opera but one Leonardo
Montaldo. In Montaldo's place, he promoted Gabriele Adorno,
but by this time Simon was becoming isolated.

On the 13th March, 1363, he was a guest at a banquet in the
house of a rich Genoese, Pietro Marocello, in honour of the visiting King of Cyprus. Simon was taken violently ill, and foul play
was suspected, but it was never discovered by whom. If it was
poison, it was very slow acting for, although immediately struck

down at the banquet, Simon survived for several painful days. Some historians suggest that it was not poison, but a crisis in an illness which Simon and his closest collaborators had long anticipated and planned for. On the whole the subsequent course of events is more consistent with the poison theory, for his supposed friends and supporters were in a great hurry to replace him. They did not wait for him to die, but on the very next day, with rumours disturbing the peace of the city, they arrested Simon's brothers and elected his deputy, Gabriele Adorno, to succeed him. Simon was left abandoned, alone and in agony, to die. He was buried in a grand marble tomb that he had prepared for himself in the Church of San Francesco in Castelletto. He was taken there without a cortège and buried without honour. The Church and the monument have since disappeared. Only his effigy remains, lying in his ducal robes like a crusader. It can be seen in the Museo di San Agostino. It is the haughty effigy of someone who expected more from posterity than he received. It took Gutiérrez and then Verdi to bring him back from oblivion.

Gabriele Adorno was a merchant and very popular, but not at all like the ardent young lover in the opera. Born in 1320, he had married Violante di Giustiniani Garibaldi in 1347 and, as far as is known, he did not marry again. He certainly never married any daughter of Simon. He first reached some prominence in 1349, during the interval between Simon's two reigns, when Giovanni de Murta sent him to keep an eye on the dissident nobles around Monaco. He returned to Genoa just before Murta's death in 1350, but seems to have made himself scarce during the period of Visconti pre-eminence. He re-emerged when Simon regained power, became an Ancient, and eventually Simon's most intimate friend and aid. He was an excellent diplomat, and Simon used him for any delicate negotiations. His election as Doge was extremely popular for everyone liked him, but he was too weak. He continued Simon's anti-aristocratic policy but he did not have the same strength. The aristocrats were joined by Adorno's old rival Montaldo, and much of Liguria was soon in insurrection, supported by the Milanese. Adorno tried to buy off the latter by promising to pay tribute, but he was eventually forced by Montaldo to accept a humiliating treaty, rescinding all his anti-aristocratic policies. With all these distractions, Corsica was lost. Although he pulled off some diplomatic coups in the Levant, Adorno was never really able to regain the initiative. After seven declining years, he was displaced, tried to escape, was caught and imprisoned. He was soon released, however, and spent his last years peacefully with his family.

During Adorno's reign, the Boccanegra family went into exile, but some years later Simon's son Battista returned, and was able to play a positive role in Genoa's affairs, although he never managed to restore the family to what it had been. It never did attain nobility, and, by the end of the century, the Boccanegras had disappeared from Genoa. Egidio, on the other hand, was ennobled by the King of Castile, and, as the Count of Palma, he founded a dynasty in Seville. The Boccanegras' contribution to Genoa was over, but it had been a significant one. Guglielmo had first weakened the political mould, and then Simon had broken it. The patricians continued to dominate much of the city's life, especially its finances and its navy. They supplied a series of brilliant commanders and admirals, but they never regained the chief magistracy. Giovanni di Murta was the only nobleman ever elected Doge.

Unfortunately, it is not possible to record that this breaking of the mould brought the Genoese a liberal and orderly constitution. They soon found that plebeian families could be every bit as quarrelsome as patricians. They had merely exchanged the Spinolas, the Dorias, the Grimaldis and the Fieschi for Adorni, Fregosi and Guarchi. In some ways these were even worse except that, their own background being mercantile, they were at pains to develop the city's trade. On the other hand, the city's politics remained as turbulent as ever with the result that it gradually yielded its independence to its more powerful neighbours. Although throughout its two hundred years of existence, the office of Doge was always filled by an elected commoner, it was in due course reduced to impotence and pageantry. If Simon Boccanegra had a political vision, it was surely better than this, but it is difficult really to break a mould.

_____

1 The date of Simon's marriage to Costanza d'Elce is put by some historians as 10th March, 1360, when he was fifty nine years old, and there is no certainty that it was earlier. Costanza was much younger

than Simon and survived until 1402. She bore him a son, Battista, but there is no record of a daughter. This would imply that Maddalena was the daughter of some other woman, a theory which is reinforced by the fact that Luchino Visconti died in 1349 and his son Luchinetto was exiled. It is most unlikely that Maddalena would have been betrothed to him after this misfortune. We are forced to conclude that she was of betrothable age by 1349. There is no knowing whether she was legitimate or not.

2 The description of the Vialata is based on J.Th. Bent's book, *Genoa – How the Republic Rose and Fell*, whence came also the quotations from Virgil and Petrarch. The modern authority on medieval Genoa, Professor Giovanna Petti Balbi, does not think the Vialata had been finished in Simon Boccanegra's time, when the Fieschi palace was less splendid. She believes that most of the main events in his story took place in and around what is now known as the Ducal Palace. Much of this dates from the late eighteenth century but, hidden behind the Cathedral of San Lorenzo, there is a medieval wing and tower which dates from 1274.

The Vialata and Montobbe were both utterly destroyed in 1547 by Andrea Doria in revenge for the Fieschi uprising. Some say that the doorway to No.23 Via di Cannetto Lungo is a remnant of the Vialata. It is in about the right place. Montobbe is thought to be the same place as the modern Montoggio.

3 Like Whigs (Scottish waggoners) and Tories (Irish outlaws living by hunting) the origins of the words Guelph and Ghibelline were soon forgotten. They were the battle cries used by the opposing armies at the battle of Weinsburg in 1140. At this battle, the Dukes of Franconia [family name – Welf] and Bavaria [main stronghold - Waiblingen] contested the succession to the Holy Roman Empire. Shouted by Italians, Welf and Waiblingen became corrupted but their significance was never lost. The French to whom the Guelphs looked for support were the Angevin kings of Naples and Sicily rather than the de Valois branch in metropolitan France.

4 In 1345, the English victory at the battle of Crécy caused almost as much jubilation amongst the Ghibellines of Genoa as amongst the English themselves because of the number of Genoese Guelphs who fell in the service of the French.

5 The earliest spelling of the name is Bucanigra. Boccanegra therefore almost certainly derives from *Buca Nigra*, meaning a black ship. In 1199, the Genoese captured a Pisan galley called *il Bucanigra*. In a Genoese context, a naval origin is much more likely than a reference to a black mouth.

6 The description of the events in the square which led to the election of Simon Boccanegra as Doge for the first time is taken, almost word for word, from an eighteenth-century translation by R. Griffiths of *L'Histoire des Revolutions Génovèses* by Oudart Feudrix de Bréguigny.

The story's origins go further back to the history of Umberto Foglietta and eventually to the contemporary Annals of Giorgio Stella.

7 Apart from the oldest wing of the Ducal Palace, there are several buildings in Genoa associated with the Boccanegras. No. 26 Via della Maddalena is said to be the house where Simon was born and, amongst the buildings of the Ospedale Civile, in the eastern outskirts, there is the country villa which he is said to have built for himself. No doubt this is where he kept his leopard and his hawks. It is now used as a conference centre.

The older part of the Banco di San Giorgio, beside the harbour, was built by his great uncle Guglielmo when he was Captain of the People.

8 Luchino Visconti became Duke of Milan in 1339. He had thus far had a military life of extraordinary hardship, suffering a series of wounds which had left him disfigured, in pain and of a sombre disposition. His first wife had been a Spinola. When she died, he married another Genoese, Isabella Fiesco, a beautiful but depraved woman. She had three sons and a daughter while married to Luchino. When she told him that they were not his but by his nephew, Galeaz, he banished the latter. Isabella then asked his permission to undertake a pilgrimage to Venice which he granted, assuming that her request arose from some sense of contrition. It did not. She fitted out a luxurious flotilla of barges, on which she embarked with the most lively women of the court. They all sailed down the Po entertaining the riparian gentlemen as they went, and most particularly Ugolin de Gonzaga, Isabella's latest lover. When they got back to Milan, something in Luchino's greeting warned Isabella that this time she had gone too far. She decided to act first and poisoned him. He died on 24th January, 1349.

9 There is an alternative story about Simon's seizure of the Palace which has the governor at home but with hardly any guards when Simon arrives with his followers. When Simon threatens to fire the building if he does not yield it, the governor prefers discretion to valour.

IL TROVATORE

Giuseppe Verdi

Libretto by Salvatore Cammarano
from a play by Gutiérrez

Dramatis Personae

Count di Luna, *Officer of the King*
Manrico, the Troubadour, *Officer of the rebel Count de Urgel*
Ferrando, *Captain in di Luna's forces*
Ruiz, *Captain in Manrico's forces*
An old Gypsy
A messenger

Leonora, *Lady-in-Waiting to the Queen*
Azucena, *A gipsy, Manrico's foster-mother*
Inez, *Friend of Leonora*

Soldiers of di Luna and Manrico, nuns, gipsies

ACT ONE

The Duel

SCENE ONE: The night guard are lounging outside the guard-room of the Aljafería Palace in Zaragoza. They are nervous of being caught asleep by the irritable castle governor, the Count di Luna. He often prowls at night, especially since a mysterious Troubadour has started serenading his love, Leonora, one of the Queen's ladies-in-waiting. The soldiers ask their captain, Ferrando, to entertain them with the old story about di Luna's brother, Garzia. When Garzia was still a baby, an old gipsy woman was caught one night standing over his cradle and, suspected of sorcery, was burnt at the stake in Bizcaya. In revenge, her daughter Azucena kidnapped Garzia, and apparently burned him too, for a charred little body was subsequently found in the same place. The boys' father never believed Garzia to be dead, and, on his own deathbed, made his other son swear to keep up the search. Neither Garzia nor the gipsy have been seen since, but Ferrando swears he could recognise her still.

SCENE TWO: It is nearly midnight, and Leonora and Inez are in the palace garden, hoping to hear the Troubadour. Leonora does not know who he is, but loves him, believing him to be the mysterious knight who triumphed at the last tournament before the Count of Urgel started his rebellion. Summoned by the Queen, she eventually allows Inez to lead her indoors.

Di Luna now enters and, seeing her lighted window, resolves to visit her at once, and declare his love. Just as he is mounting the first stair, he hears the Troubadour's lute. Leonora has heard it too and, rushing out into the dark, mistakes di Luna for her lover. Seeing them embracing, the Troubadour breaks cover. While Leonora explains, di Luna demands to know his name. He is Manrico, the famous Urgellista rebel. As the two men rush off to fight a duel, Leonora swoons.

ACT TWO

The Gipsy

SCENE ONE: Months have passed. Manrico defeated di Luna in the duel, but spared his life. Since then, di Luna has defeated him in battle, and left him for dead on the field, but Azucena, his supposed mother, found him there, still breathing, and has been nursing him back to strength. They are in a gipsy camp in Bizcaya, on the very spot where her mother was burned. While Azucena sits brooding and Manrico dreams of glory, the gipsies sing a cheerful song, and then depart.

In her reverie, Azucena recounts her version of Ferrando's story, and we learn that, in her frenzy, she threw her own baby instead of Garzia onto the fire. Manrico, who has never felt like a gipsy, is immediately interested. If it was her own son that she burned, he asks, who then is he? Roused from her daydream, Azucena backtracks. Of course Manrico is her son. If not, why should she have rescued him, and nursed his wounds. Honourable wounds, he boasts, but she chides him. Why did he not kill di Luna when he had the chance? He cannot explain. He thought he heard a voice, bidding him stay his hand.

A messenger now arrives from Urgel, who has captured Castellor, and wants Manrico to come at once to take command of its garrison. Furthermore, he warns that Leonora, in despair over Manrico's supposed death, is about to take the veil in the convent nearby. Ignoring his unhealed wounds and Azucena's pleas, Manrico rushes off to intervene.

SCENE TWO: It is night outside the convent near Castellor and di Luna waits with his followers, intending to abduct Leonora before she takes her vow. Ferrando chides him for his rashness, but di Luna exults that she will soon be his. Chanting is heard, and di Luna and his men hide. When the nuns arrive with Leonora and Inez, di Luna emerges, but has barely explained his plan, when Manrico also enters. While di Luna and Leonora react to this apparition, he tells them he is flesh and blood, as are Ruiz and his men, who now enter, armed and shouting "Viva Urgel." Hopelessly outnumbered, di Luna is disarmed but allowed to escape, while the lovers withdraw to Castellor.

ACT THREE

The Gipsy's Son

SCENE ONE: Di Luna has rallied, and is besieging Castellor. His troops are sitting about when Ferrando arrives, and announces that they are to attack the castle at dawn. Exulting at the prospect of action, they disperse. Di Luna enters, seething with jealousy. He is gazing up at the castle when Ferrando rushes in. A gipsy spy has been caught. Azucena is brought in in chains, protesting that she comes from Bizcaya, and has nothing to do with the war. Both di Luna and Ferrando are suspicious, connecting Bizcaya with Garzia. Questioned about him, her shifty answers convince Ferrando, and he unmasks her. When in her panic, she blurts out that Manrico is her son, di Luna realises that he now has the means both to blackmail his enemy and avenge Garzia. She is dragged away to be burnt.

SCENE TWO: Inside Castellor, Manrico is briefing Ruiz about the expected attack. Leonora's fears are banished by the prospect of marriage. The organ starts to play, but as she and Manrico turn towards the chapel, a fiery glow lights the scene. Ruiz hurries in to say that di Luna is about to burn a gipsy, and, looking out, Manrico sees that it is his mother. All other thoughts fly away – he must make a sally to save her. Leonora is left alone.

ACT FOUR

The Torture

SCENE ONE: It is night on the roof of the Aljafería, outside the Tower of the Troubadour. Manrico's sortie failed, and Castellor has fallen. He and Azucena are now prisoners in the Tower, but Leonora and Ruiz escaped, and stealthily they now enter. Ruiz leaves her alone to carry out a desperate plan. She intends to save Manrico, by selling herself to di Luna, and then to take poison. While unseen monks begin to chant a miserere, Manrico's voice from the tower soars in a passionate farewell. Leonora hides when di Luna enters with some retainers, whom he dismisses with orders to execute the prisoners in the morning. He is soliloquising about how his love for Leonora is driving him to this abuse of power, when she appears before him. She begs him to release Manrico, and when he will not, she offers him her deal, with the proviso that she must be the one to tell Manrico that he is free. Ecstatically di Luna agrees, but, behind his back, she takes poison.

SCENE TWO: Manrico and Azucena, in their cell, are trying to console each other. Azucena is terrified, but eventually he is able to sing her to sleep. Leonora enters to tell him he is free to leave, but that she cannot leave with him. At once, a terrible suspicion fills his mind. What has she sacrificed to obtain his release? Furiously, he reproaches her, and refuses to leave despite her entreaties, but when the poison begins to work he understands, and is devastated. But still he will not leave. As she expires, the Count enters, and orders Manrico's immediate execution. Azucena awakes as Manrico is led out, and, too late, tells di Luna that he has killed his own brother. Her mother has at last been avenged.

Jaime the Hapless

People who make fun of opera often cite the story of *Il Trovatore* as an example of its absurdities. They have good reason. The bonfires and the babies, the mysterious Troubadour, his gipsy foster mother and even Leonora his love, are all products of the playwright's highly romantic imagination. Whereas most librettists start with a historical episode and embellish it for their purposes, Gutiérrez seems to have done the opposite. Having worked out a plot of extreme improbability, he dressed it up with a little history to make it both more stirring and more plausible. He wisely chose incidents and people from the romantic fringes of Spanish history which his public would know about, but rather vaguely. A British equivalent might be the massacre of Glencoe, heavy with emotion but obscure in its factual details. He was so successful that his audiences apparently believed *El Trovador* to be true, and began to make pilgrimages to some of its locations. Opera audiences, even less sure about Spanish history, cannot share his full intention. While they are more than compensated by the music, a little historical background might yet enhance their appreciation of *Il Trovatore*.

Gutiérrez actually weaves together three quite distinct historical episodes, well separated in time and place. The background to the play is the uprising of Count Jaime de Urgel, which places the story firmly in the kingdom of Aragon, between 1410 and 1413.[1] Jaime *el Desdichado* or James the Hapless, as he is known, was a Catalan equivalent of Bonny Prince Charlie, robbed, according to many, of his right to the crown of Aragon by cleverer men. Catalans still lament his fall as a milestone on the road to their subjugation by Castile. Jaime himself does not appear in the play which is about a fictional lieutenant, Manrico, but the two men have so much in common that, if *El Trovadór* is not an allegory of Jaime's tragedy, it is certainly meant to share its pathos.

Jaime never had a lieutenant called Manrico or Manrique, which is the Spanish form of the name. In fact, Jaime's main supporter was called don Anton de Luna, but since de Luna is a name of bad repute, Gutiérrez wished to use it for his villain, not his hero. There was a popular saying, "May you meet with de Luna", a more elegant version of "go to hell".[2] He therefore turned to another episode in Spanish history, a generation later and in Castile, where for some twenty years, several members of the Manrique family wrote poetry, and fought the good fight against their King and his wicked chancellor, don Alvaro de Luna, a distant relative of don Anton.

Having thus already mixed two different bits of history, Gutiérrez introduced yet a third with his locations. Much of the play takes place in the Aljafería palace in Zaragoza, and the nearby castle of Castellár, which somehow became transformed into Castellor in the opera. Both are in Aragon. Several centuries earlier, the Aljafería had been the stronghold of the Moorish kings of Zaragoza, and it is still extant today. Castellár, on the other hand, was already a ruin in Jaime's day. The two fortresses had confronted each other across the Ebro during the wars to liberate Zaragoza from the Moors. In fact, Castellár was built as a base for the Christian forces attacking Zaragoza and the Aljafería. It therefore stood for everything good in Spanish history, while the Aljafería was a natural habitat for villains. A visitor to the Aljafería can still see the guard room where Ferrando entertains the sentries, the colonnaded garden with its orange trees and fountains, and above all the great Tower of the Troubadour, from which Manrico is supposed to sing his farewell. A visit to Castellár requires more dedication. El Castellár is in fact the name of a range of hills rising along the north bank of the Ebro, resembling the curtain wall of some vast fortress. A visitor to the ruins of the castle needs to cross the bridge at Alagón, some miles upstream, and then take the first track to the right along the crest of the hills.

Castellár is about five miles down this track. The ruins sit on top of a hill, dominating a river crossing and the plain beyond. Zaragoza is not much more than a smudge in the distance. Castellár is so ruined that it is hard to tell, but it does not seem to have been a very large fortress. Not far away, there is a ruined convent.

One of the features Manrico shares with Jaime the Hapless is a perfectly disastrous mother. Jaime's mother, doña Margarita, was no gipsy. On the contrary, she was very conscious of her descent from the Palaeologus Emperors of Byzantium, and she was consumed by a raging ambition for her son that would have made Lady Macbeth quail. When the elderly King Martin's only son died in 1409 leaving no legitimate heir, she was sure that her ambition was to be fulfilled. Her son Jaime had the strongest claim to become King of Aragon and an empire greater even than Byzantium. Admittedly, he was not King Martin's closest male relative. There was a French boy and also a Castilian who were closer, but both were related through women, and disbarred by the custom of Aragon. Jaime was the first of pure male and legitimate descent. In addition, he was married to the King's sister, Isabel. It was generally assumed in all three provinces of the realm that he would succeed. All it needed was the old King's confirmation, but that was withheld.

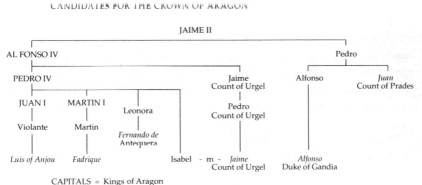

CANDIDATES FOR THE CROWN OF ARAGON

CAPITALS = Kings of Aragon
Italics = candidates for the throne

One reason was that Martin cherished a wish for an illegitimate grandson, Fadrique, to succeed. A second reason was that Martin simply could not stand doña Margarita. She was so domineering that he had to send her a copy of his orders if he wanted Jaime to obey them. He seriously doubted if Jaime was fit to reign, and so, to test him, he appointed him as *Lochtinent*, or viceroy, to the province of Aragon. Such an appointment was usually given only to the King's heir, and it meant also that Jaime could maintain an army, which would be useful if the succession was disputed. Doña Margarita was overjoyed, but she underestimated the old King's cunning. He was banking on Jaime making a mess of things, but just in case he did not do so of his own accord, he sent messages to one of the leading families in Aragon, the Urreas, to make trouble.

In the meanwhile, Martin remarried and set about trying to have a new son, subjecting himself to a regime of rich meals designed to stimulate his flagging libido.[3] In case this should fail, he also put in hand a study of the legal precedents concerning the succession. Was there a legal way to avoid nominating Jaime? He finally asked Benedict XXIII, one of the three rival popes who were disputing the papal throne at that time, to legitimise Fadrique, the bastard grandson. Benedict XXIII was an Aragonese, in fact another de Luna, and agreed, but he took his time. He liked Fadrique to whom he was related, but he was more concerned with his own claim to the Papacy, which he thought the French might support if he helped their candidate, Luis of Anjou, to the throne of Aragon.

Surpassing even Martin's hopes, Jaime made a spectacularly bad start as *Lochtinent*, when an outraged Aragonese noblewoman accused him of having abducted her daughter and given her to one of his retinue. This was but the overture. Jaime's mission was to pacify a feud which was raging between the Urrea family and the de Lunas. Feuding was something that medieval nobles regarded as their right. A knight was useless for anything but fighting, and if the king did not arrange a war to absorb the energies of the upper classes, they soon started to work them off on each other. Provided the rules of chivalry were observed, such feuds were perfectly legal, and could lead to pitched battles with hundreds of knights on each side. Jaime's mission of pacification did not really have a chance, but he would have done better to try to remain neutral between the two factions. Instead, deliberately goaded by the Urreas, he threw in his lot with the de Lunas. He made a bad decision, for don Anton, the head of the de Luna faction, was an atrocious man, stupid and violent; while the Urreas were led by a shrewd politician, the Archbishop of Zaragoza, who was a great friend of Benedict XXIII. It did not take Jaime long to make mortal enemies of the Urreas, whose one objective thenceforth was to keep him from the throne.

Martin, meanwhile, was not doing very well regarding a new heir, and his other two ideas were not making much progress either. Benedict repeatedly told him that it took at least two years to legitimise a bastard decently, and the group of wise men the King had summoned to study the succession problem had not yet even met. Feeling himself ailing and not wanting to leave Jaime so powerfully placed, Martin revoked his appointment, but before Jaime could comply, an especially potent meal precipitated Martin into a crisis. He declined rapidly, and his courtiers were summoned to hear his last will and, in particular, his nominee as successor. Hour after hour they stood silently round the bed, straining to catch the feeblest whisper. Suddenly, into their midst burst doña Margarita dragging doña Isabel by the hand. Before anyone could intervene, she was shaking the moribund King by the shoulders, and hissing, "Confirm the kingdom to my son! You deny him against all right!" Hatred is as invigorating as any other emotion, perhaps more. The apparently half-dead King sat up, and said in a firm voice, "I do not know that that is right. I deny that it is so." He then collapsed again. Defeated, doña Margarita was led away. She had proved only one thing: Martin's failure to nominate her son was no oversight. She now had to leave it to courtiers, whom she knew were no friends of Jaime's. Sure enough, when they emerged next day from their vigil, the King had not named Jaime, but had asked that they should choose whomsoever "justice indicated".

Martin's death introduced the two troubled years which are the background to the opera. Just as Manrico starts with di Luna helpless at the point of his sword, so did Jaime start with the throne his for the taking. Although formally relieved of his command, he still had his forces intact. He was Catalonia's favourite son; the two leading families in Valencia, the Centellas and the Vilareguts, though disagreeing with each other in every other way, both accepted him as the rightful heir; the de Luna faction of Aragon were his partisans; only the Urreas opposed him and he could have dealt with them. He had but to stretch out his hand and the crown was his. He did not do so. When the messengers came from Barcelona conveying the dead King's testament, and asking him to disband his forces "lest their existence should unduly influence our deliberations", Jaime meekly complied. He merely requested, in return, that the Catalans should support his claim to the throne.

. Why did he hold back? Unlike Manrico, he surely heard no voice from heaven saying, "Do not strike!" It may have been over-confidence. Like Manrico, he was obsessed with lineage to the exclusion of any other argument, and was no doubt sure that he would be the one whom "justice indicated". He may rightly have thought that the crown would sit the more securely on his head if obtained legally, and was prepared to wait. More probably, it was timidity. Without his mother by his side, he lacked the nerve to take such a momentous decision. Whatever the reason, he disbanded his forces, resigned his office and joined his mother and his wife in his fortress at Balaguér to await the outcome of the legal process.

Things at once started to go wrong in Aragon. Hardly believing their luck, the Urreas began to organise an opposition. Guided by Benedict, they chose the French candidate, the infant Luis of Anjou. Naturally, they were opposed by the de Luna faction, but in the series of debates that followed, poor don Anton was no match for the Archbishop of Zaragoza. He did not just lose every argument. Time and again he was utterly humiliated. Eventually, after a particularly bruising experience at a meeting in the south of the province, he decided to try to seek a private discussion with the Archbishop. He knew that, on his way home, the Archbishop would stop for the night at La Almunia de doña Godina, some thirty miles south-west of Zaragoza. He invited him to an unarmed meeting at night outside the town. It was this meeting which inspired the confrontation scene outside the monastery with which opera-goers are familiar. It also was this meeting which gave rise to that proverb – "May you meet with de Luna!"

Whether de Luna intended mischief or feared it, he deceitfully concealed a strong force in the vicinity of the meeting place. The Archbishop arrived, seated on a mule, and with only a handful of followers. If de Luna hoped to reach a better understanding in private, he was mistaken. Monfar describes what happened. Although the discussion began civilly enough, the Archbishop's mastery of debate and acid tongue were soon fraying de Luna's patience, and the angrier he got, the less coherent became his own arguments. He was eventually reduced to shouting: "Once and for all, will Urgel be King?"

Perhaps for once not choosing his words very wisely, the priest replied: "Not while I'm alive."

De Luna: "Then say he will be if you are dead – or in prison."

Archbishop: "Perhaps if I am dead, but if merely in prison – never!"

So saying, the priest turned his mule to leave, but too late. De Luna, beside himself, struck him to the ground. This was the signal for his followers to intervene, and in no time the Archbishop was dead and his handful of followers either dead or overpowered.

Just as Manrico for a second time has di Luna outnumbered and at his mercy after the ambush in Act II, so did Jaime now have a second chance to take the throne. Demoralised and with their leader dead, the Urreas were in no fit state to resist, had Jaime followed up this murder with resolution. That he did not indicates that it was probably not a premeditated crime. Quick thinking was not de Luna's strongest suit, and, far from taking the offensive, he withdrew making preposterous excuses for the murder. He had had to defend himself from these aggressive clerics, he said, and greatly regretted their death. With authentic de Luna subtlety, he challenged anyone doubting the truth of this to meet him in single combat. No-one did so, but Benedict XXIII excommunicated him and his followers. This wiped out Jaime's faction in Aragon at a stroke, since excommunication debarred the de Lunas from further participation in the debate. From this moment on, Jaime's fortunes relentlessly decline, as do Manrico's from the moment when, after the ambush, he withdraws into Castellor.

Once more, the Urreas could breathe again, but with such violent enemies so close at hand, they immediately decided to abandon

Don Carlos and Company

their distant and under-age French candidate for someone better able to protect them. The Regent of Castile, don Fernando de Antequera, had almost as good a claim and was a proven leader and soldier, fresh from a famous triumph over the Moorish King of Granada. His first step was to offer the Urreas the services of a thousand Castilian lancers; not, of course, in order to influence the selection of a new King, but to allow the question to be settled in an atmosphere of law and order.

Even Jaime could see that Aragon was slipping from his grasp, and so he redoubled his efforts to secure Valencia. He had learned nothing. Instead of trying to pacify the feud between the Centellas and Vilareguts, at least for long enough to secure their support, he entered the conflict, managing, once again, to choose the wrong side, and then failing to give them the promised support in good time. Before Jaime could raise a force, he had to obtain the permission of the Catalan Corts, who dearly loved to debate and took their time. In the meanwhile, substantial numbers of Castilian lancers were somehow finding their way from Aragon into Valencia. Jaime's partisans were defeated, and, when his reinforcements finally got there, they were annihilated. Valencia was henceforth as anti-Urgel as Aragon. Jaime was reduced to ineffective guerrilla tactics in order to influence the outcome of the debate on the succession, which was now about to take place.

This was the celebrated Compromise of Caspe, reached in a small town near to where the three provincial boundaries meet. In its monastery, three delegates from each province came together and studied, over the course of nine months, the credentials of all six candidates for the throne. Even at this late stage, Jaime appears to have believed that his case, based purely on heredity, was unassailable. At any rate, it was sloppily presented, while Fernando put forward a finely argued and subtle submission. In fact, it did not make much difference for the conclusion was foregone. The delegations were rigged in favour of Fernando who even had a saint, St Vicente Ferrer, supporting him. Fernando won on the first vote. There was then some debate as to how best to break the news to Jaime.

The Catalan delegation was given the task. Fernando offered Jaime a dukedom and a large sum of money. Left to himself, Jaime would probably have accepted. Since he had not expected rejection, he was ill prepared for insurrection, especially against a prince who was a proven general, and who could summon the whole might of Castile to his aid. But he was not left to himself. His mother was convinced that Caspe was nothing more than a conspiracy of contemptible small men and that, if the flag of rebellion was raised, the people, at least in Catalonia, would rise to a man to defend their beloved and rightful prince. *"O re o nada!"* she told him, "Either king or nothing!" However, even she realised that the people might hesitate to risk their lives for a prince who had neglected to make any preparations for such an emergency.

Pressed by Fernando to declare his loyalty, Jaime twisted and turned to gain time, while he tried to recruit the English, the Gascons and even the Moors to his cause. He entrusted his chief negotiator, the calamitous de Luna, with everything; all the family's money and more, his mother's and his wife's jewels, even large chunks of his future empire, to be traded for the support he so desperately needed. Fernando in the meanwhile, knew exactly what was happening. He intercepted Jaime's letter to the Moorish king and published it, making it difficult for any true Christian to support such a renegade, however well bred. In the meanwhile, Jaime and his women remained locked up in their fortress capital, not Castellár but Balaguér. They had no idea how rapidly their support outside was ebbing away. When de Luna returned from Gascony, without the money or the jewels but with plenty of English promises, they decided the time had come to declare their rebellion.

They were immediately outlawed, but, even so, their strength was not so contemptible that their rebellion could thus be ended by a pen stroke. Balaguér was one of the strongest defended cities in Spain – much more formidable than Castellar – but, unfortunately, it was not yet provisioned for more than a three month siege. Still, doña Margarita was sure that the English would arrive before long, and that the Catalans would then join the cause. De Luna was less sure about it, and declined to join his leader in Balaguér, preferring to hold out in his rather better-provisioned castle at Loarre.

Jaime understood the weakness of his situation. While his mother pleaded with him to stay with her, safe inside Balaguér, he knew that he must sally forth to rally any remaining supporters. For once, he disobeyed her and marched on the nearby city of Lerida, which was said to be wavering. He found its gates firmly closed. Easily discouraged, he went home to mother to await the English, but the army that arrived outside the walls was Fernando's. To add to Jaime's misery, it consisted at least half of Catalans, eager to distance themselves from a lost cause.

Even so, Jaime defended his castle better than Manrico. Fierce battles were fought for various outposts and between the artillery of each side. Jaime got rather the better of the latter, immensely annoying Fernando by taking pot shots at him as he rode amongst his troops, conspicuous on his white horse and in a red cloak. Such behaviour was against all the rules of chivalry, and proved that Jaime was no gentleman, especially as Fernando had done a secret deal with doña Margarita not to bombard the women's quarters. Jaime's cause was hopeless, however. There was no help on the way, his forces were steadily driven back and, after three months, his supplies were running short. It was becoming widely known amongst the garrison that Fernando treated deserters well. It is remarkable how loyal Jaime's soldiers remained, but not so his mother. When she realised there was no hope for him, she secretly sent Isabel out to sue for such terms as she could get for the women. As an afterthought, she asked also that her son be imprisoned, not executed. This was all one to Fernando. The next night, Jaime was pushed out through a sally port, called La Puerta del Torrente, to go to kneel before his conqueror. It was not quite the same as Manrico's reckless sortie from Castellor but its purpose, to save his mother's skin, was no different. La Puerta del Torrente is still there today and in use. Rather symbolically, it leads to the town's rubbish tip.

The opera does small justice to Urgel's rival Fernando, the unseen enemy against whom Manrico battles in vain. In fact he was a splendid man. When still in his teens, he became Regent of Castile and protector of his infant nephew, King Juan II. He not only united a turbulent country, and won a famous campaign against the Moors at Antequera, but he proved a conciliatory King of Aragon. Although a brilliant soldier, he knew that a bribe, however great, was always cheaper than war. He was ahead of his time and only fought when he had to. He never bothered to go after de Luna in Loarre.

Naturally, his trust was sometimes misplaced. Doña Margarita was no sooner freed and forgiven by him than she tried to poison him. Her greatest venom was reserved for Fernando's wife Leonora, who might be rich but was a parvenu with not a drop of royal blood in her veins. Margarita was a vicious and heartless woman, worse by far than Azucena, with whose obsessions we can sympathise if only because she is such an underdog. Fernando was as good as his word with Jaime, who lived his natural span in prison, dying in 1431 in Jativa, where a splendid tomb has recently been erected to him. He is making a comeback as a Catalan hero, a status he no more deserves than does Bonny Prince Charlie in Scotland.

Fernando survived Margarita's plot but not for long. Never strong, he succumbed to the doctors in 1416, leaving behind him a situation in Castile almost as confusing as that which Martin had left in Aragon. A large part of the trouble was the fault of Fernando's own sons. As Regent, he had placed them in positions of great power in Castile and Navarre, but they had none of his loyalty to his nephew, the King. King Juan turned out to be a weakling, but he found an improbable protector. This was don Alvaro de Luna, the great enemy of the Manriques.

Don Alvaro was held in great loathing by most of the Castilian nobility. His father had been an obscure knight descended from the same Aragonese family as don Anton, but he had married beneath him, if, that is, he had married. No-one knew much about don Alvaro's mother. Perhaps she was a gipsy! Don Alvaro's lack of breeding was one of the reasons for the nobles' hatred of him. They could not accept it, that so common, grasping and altogether vile a wretch should have such wealth and power showered upon him by a King who was little better than his captive. Nevertheless, for most of twenty years don Alvaro was the King's Chancellor and Constable of Castile. Fernan Perez de Guzman describes him as small but well built and strong, a good horseman and skilled at arms and games. He was cunning and not to be trusted, being avaricious and a dissimulator, but he was brave and daring enough to seize opportunities. Perez lists those who were at one time or another seized and imprisoned by de Luna. These include Perez himself and several Manriques. It was, in fact, the seizure of the head of the Manrique family, don Pedro, that started the series of events that led to de Luna's final downfall in 1451. Once in the nobles' hands, de Luna was subjected to dreadful humiliations, being dragged through Castile in a cage until he was finally executed. Jorge Manrique wrote him an epitaph of a sort in his *Stanzas on the Death of his Father*:

> And then the mighty Constable,
> The Master whom we knew
> Highly favoured,
> It does not help to speak of him
> Except to say we saw he was
> Beheaded
> His infinite treasures,
> His towns and hamlets
> And his writ,
> What became of them, but tears?
> What were they but regrets
> When he quit?[4]

The Manrique family was ancient, noble and numerous. They were all either churchmen or warriors, but that could have been said of most noble medieval families. But at a time when a knight who could read and write was still considered rather suspect, the Manriques were remarkably cultivated. Several of them have found their way to a place in the pantheon of Spanish literature, but the greatest was Jorge, who is widely regarded as the father of Spanish poetry. His uncle Gomez Manrique was also a poet, and one of the earliest Castilian dramatists. He wrote a nativity play for his sister's convent. Jorge's brother Pedro also wrote poetry of a light-hearted, rather satirical kind. Far the most celebrated were Jorge and his father Rodrigo. It is certain that Gutiérrez had one of them in mind when he wrote his play, but it is hard to say which. Historically, it should have been Rodrigo, who was more nearly a contemporary with Anton de Luna, but Gutiérrez probably did not care. He merely wanted the family name.

Contemporary opinion would certainly have seen Rodrigo as the greatest of them all. At the age of twelve he had joined the knightly order of Santiago, and had spent his life fighting for it, and for what he thought was right. This meant he was generally against his feeble king, and for one or the other of the sons of don Fernando de Antequera. He felt they were men he could respect. He became Master of the Order and never gave up the struggle until, in his old age, the two branches of the royal family were united by the marriage of the cousins, Ferdinand of Aragon and Isabella of Castile. He took part in no less than fifty battles, and was given the nick-name *Secundo Cid y Vigilantisimo*. He married three times, and it was when he was wooing his second wife, doña Beatriz de Guzman, that he wrote the serenade:

> *The good news that I long to hear*
> *Do not deny, beloved heart*
> *Tis that th'art come to that point where*
> *Whatever fortune we may share*
> *Shall bind us tighter, not to part.*[5]

Not very many of his works have survived – only four serenades, two carols and a ballad. He died of cancer, mourned by his son Jorge.

Jorge left behind much more poetry, but his most celebrated work is the *Stanzas on the Death of his Father*, already quoted. Ostensibly written in his father's honour, some suspect that the poem was partly inspired by a premonition of his own death, which did occur soon after. Although he never rose to the heights of military command achieved by Rodrigo, Jorge was as doughty a fighter, and was killed in action fighting for Ferdinand and Isabella. It was during the siege of Garci-Munóz, the stronghold of the dissident Marques de Villena. Fernando de Pulgar describes his end in his chronicles:

> And the King and Queen, receiving this news, sent cavalry, under the command of Jorge Manrique, to the lands of the Marques de Villena, to guard the region and resist any aggression that the Marques might attempt . . . Jorge Manrique and Pero Ruiz de Alarcon were on most days engaged in battle against the Marques and his men, and there were a number of skirmishes. In one of these, Captain Jorge Manrique daringly made his way so far into the midst of the enemy that his men could not see where he was so as to rescue him. The enemy wounded him with many blows and he died fighting near the gates of the Castle of Garci–Munóz.[6]

NOTES

1 The Crown of Aragon, as the combined kingdom was known, was a federation of Catalonia, Aragon and Valencia. These three provinces had originally been carved out by their ruling families during the reconquest of Spain from the Moors. During the subsequent 500 years, the Catalan Counts of Barcelona had absorbed the other two families, but the original counties had retained their own constitutions and customs. The Count-Kings of Barcelona had to deal separately with each of their provinces. They were, by the fourteenth century, the longest reigning royal family in Europe.

 The three provinces differed greatly in character, the Catalans in particular being a strongly commercial and sea-faring people. They were the fiercest competitors of the Genoese and the Venetians, and they had won themselves an island-based empire stretching all the way to Athens. They had strong democratic tendencies and their Corts or parliament, in Barcelona, was powerful and by no means subservient to the King. Aragon and Valencia, on the other hand, were more agricultural and feudal.

2 "Con de Luna te topes" or sometimes "Con don Anton te topes"

3 Martin was only fifty-one but suffered from quartain fever, an unpleasant, recurrent form of malaria. He believed himself to be impotent, to cure which he underwent some medieval treatments of a nature, according to Victor Balaguér, that no reputable historian would describe. Martin's own theory was that his trouble was obesity and we are left to wonder why those around him thought rich food would help. His final crisis was brought on by eating a roast duck, which had been specially fed to make its flesh more nutritious and stimulating.

4 Pues aquel gran condestable,
maestre que conoscimos
    tan priuado
no cumple que del se hable
sino solo que lo vimos
    degollado.
Sus infinitos tesoros,
sus villas y sus lugares,
    su mandar,
que le fueron sino llores?
fueronle sino pesares
    al dexar
[Translation by Anthony Edkins]

5 Grandes albricias te pidó
No las niegues, corazón
Qu'eres al lugar venido
Do lo ganado y perdido
Acaban nueva prisión

6 Extract from Fernando de Pulgar, translated by Professor Alan Deyermond.

RIGOLETTO

Giuseppe Verdi

Libretto by Francesco Maria Piave
after Victor Hugo's Le Roi s'amuse

Dramatis Personae

The Duke of Mantua
Rigoletto, *his fool*
Count di Monterone)
Count di Ceprano) *courtiers*
Borsa   )
Marullo   )
an usher
a page
Sparafucile, *a murderer*

Gilda, *Rigoletto's daughter*
Maddalena, *Sparafucile's sister*
Giovanna, *Gilda's duenna*
Countess di Ceprano

Courtiers, soldiers, servants

ACT ONE

SCENE ONE: The Duke of Mantua's palace is crowded with fashionable guests. In their midst, the Duke is telling Borsa about his plans to seduce an unknown young beauty whom he first saw in church three months earlier. He has attended the same church regularly and has discovered where she lives. Meanwhile there are plenty of more accessible ladies all around them, the charming Countess di Ceprano, for example. The Duke explains his philosophy concerning women, which is to chase them all, be constant to none, and ridicule their husbands. The Count di Ceprano, who has been listening, must now watch impotently while the Duke accosts the Countess, and leads her offstage. Before following his master, Rigoletto so taunts the Count that he draws his sword, but the jester can rely on the Duke's protection.

Marullo now enters with sensational news. He has discovered that, hidden in a backstreet, the hated Rigoletto keeps a young mistress. What a chance for them to get their own back on him by abducting her! Their laughter is interrupted when an angry Monterone arrives, demanding to see the Duke, who has seduced his daughter. The Duke and Rigoletto re-enter, and the latter mockingly confronts Monterone, asking him what right he, a pardoned traitor, thinks he has to complain about his daughter. Monterone ignores him, and so upbraids the Duke that he is arrested, whereupon, in a voice of thunder, he places his Curse upon the Duke and jester alike. The Duke just laughs, but Rigoletto is horrified.

SCENE TWO: In a dark backstreet, Rigoletto's house stands opposite the Ceprano mansion. A high wall surrounds its modest courtyard which contains a single tree and a bench under a balcony. Still muttering about the Curse, Rigoletto is about to enter when he is accosted by Sparafucile who explains his business. A professional assassin, he uses his pretty sister, Maddalena, as a decoy, but Rigoletto has no immediate need of them. As he enters his courtyard, Gilda comes to greet him, and it is revealed that she is his daughter, that her mother is dead, and that she has recently returned from her convent school. Although he keeps her mewed up and in ignorance even of his own name, she is beginning to love this strange, deformed father who is so possessive of her. Shuddering at the thought of the dangers outside, Rigoletto bids Giovanna take good care of his only treasure in this world of tribulation.

The Duke, dressed as a student, arrives outside and, hearing a noise, Rigoletto emerges to investigate. While he is peering into the darkness, the Duke slips in behind him, throws Giovanna a purse and hides behind the tree, undetected by father and daughter. He overhears that Gilda is Rigoletto's daughter and, when her father leaves, that she is sighing for the young man who has been following her back from church. Encouraged, he emerges to declare his love. He pretends that he is a poor student, Gualtier Maldé, but alarmed by more noise in the street he leaves by the back door. Gilda slowly climbs to her room, singing dreamily of his dear name, Gualtier Maldé.

The noise was Marullo's raiding party assembling outside but, before they are ready, they are disturbed by Rigoletto. The quick-witted Marullo tells him that they have gathered to abduct Countess di Ceprano, and Rigoletto is only too pleased to join in the fun. Given a blind mask and easily disoriented, he is made to hold the ladder, while the abductors enter, not the Ceprano House, but his own, and carry off his daughter. Too late, he tears off the mask and discovers what has happened. The Curse is at work.

ACT TWO

Next morning, the Duke is alone and anxious in his ante-chamber, having found Gilda's house open and deserted, but his worries turn to joy when his courtiers enter and tell him of their escapade. Rigoletto's woman is waiting for him in his room, and the Duke rushes to join her.

Rigoletto now arrives, and tries to find out what has gone on, but no-one will talk. He suspects what is going on, however, when a page from the Duchess demands to see the Duke. The courtiers' confusion confirms the truth. His truculence dissolves into abject pleading, especially addressed to Marullo, and then to fury, when a distraught Gilda rushes into his arms.

Rigoletto demands that they be left alone. When the courtiers leave, she confesses her love for the Duke, and is alarmed by the violence of his reaction. He forgives her, but not him. They will leave the court, but first he has some accounts to settle. At this moment, Monterone passes through the room under guard. Pausing before the Duke's portrait, he reflects bitterly that his Curse has had little effect, but Rigoletto calls after him that he will yet be avenged. Gilda is determined not to let this happen.

ACT THREE

A month has passed. The scene is the waterfront outside Sparafucile's wretched inn with its dingy bar and bedroom above. In the dark outside, Gilda is still protesting her love which her father has brought her here to cure. He bids her watch through a crack in the wall as the carefree Duke, dressed as a soldier and singing about women's inconstancy, starts to flirt with Maddalena. Sparafucile comes out to check with Rigoletto that he has got the right man. Meanwhile, Gilda is mortified by what she sees and all express their emotions in a famous quartet. Gilda promises to obey her father, who tells her to go home, disguise herself as a man, and ride to Verona, where he will join her. She asks him to come with her, but he has something to do first. Full of foreboding, she departs.

Sparafucile comes out again, and they strike a deal; Rigoletto may return for the body at midnight. A storm is gathering, and the Duke, deciding to stay until it is past, goes upstairs to bed. Maddalena starts to plead for his life. He is so handsome and so charming. Why not kill the old hunchback instead? Sparafucile is too professional for that, but agrees that, should a traveller seek shelter before midnight, he will kill him instead. Gilda overhears. Now dressed as a man, her anxiety has brought her back to the inn. In despair, she resolves to die in the Duke's place. As the storm reaches its climax, she knocks, enters, and is stabbed.

Rigoletto returns, savouring his revenge while he waits for midnight. The hour strikes, he knocks, and Sparafucile drags out a heavy sack. He offers to help dump it in the river, but Rigoletto wants no help and asks instead for a torch. Sparafucile refuses this, and bidding him beware the nightwatch, withdraws. As the storm recedes, Rigoletto is left alone to gloat over his victim.

It is at this moment that the Duke decides to go home, happily singing his favourite song. Rigoletto at first cannot believe his senses, but there it is again! Who, then, is in the sack? Feverishly, he tears it open and discovers his own daughter. She is not quite dead. She asks his foregiveness, while he pleads with her not to leave him alone. It is too late, and she dies in his arms. Monterone's Curse has been fulfilled.

One Carat Short

Near the ducal palace in Mantua, in a backstreet there is a little house with a walled garden in front. It is called Rigoletto's house, implying that this is where he tried to hide his daughter Gilda from the prying world. Local opinion has it that Rigoletto was probably a jester at the court of the fourth Duke of Mantua, Vincenzo I. Vincenzo's particular claim to fame is the virility test, which he was obliged to take by his second wife's relatives, but, having passed it, his subsequent career would have made him a colourful hero for this story.[1] Alas, he must be set aside. *Rigoletto* is an adaptation of Victor Hugo's play, *Le Roi s'amuse*, which had to be withdrawn after its first night in Paris. Even the easy-going Louis-Philippe could not tolerate a play that showed a king behaving so scandalously. In choosing this play for an opera, Verdi knew he would have to demote his tenor from a king to a duke or even further. He must have been relieved that Vincenzo's descendants did not object.

Before considering the opera's historical roots, it must be repatriated to France. It is set in 1523. The Duke is the King, François I, and Rigoletto is Triboulet, his celebrated jester. Monterone, utterer of the Curse, is the Count de Saint-Vallier, mainly remembered as the father of Diane de Poitiers. Like Monterone's daughter, Diane never appears on stage, but it is her supposed seduction by François that is the subject of the Curse. Marullo is the poet Clément Marot. In the play, some of the other courtiers are based on real originals, but, in the opera, only Ceprano emerges from the chorus, and he could be based on any one of several discomfited husbands. The other characters are fictional. Triboulet never had a daughter, nor did he hire an assassin to kill his friend the King, but François did have one or two youthful escapades, which may have sown the seeds of Gilda, Maddelena and even Sparafucile in Victor Hugo's mind. These anecdotes are not enough to provide a recognisable historical parallel for the story of *Rigoletto*, but it is still of some interest to compare the opera's chief characters with their originals. Even this limited objective proposes a problem. Verdi was mainly interested in Rigoletto, the jester, and his duke is a two-dimensional figure of secondary importance. For historians the reverse is true. They are more interested in even minor kings, than in the most celebrated of jesters. Few of the history books even mention Triboulet, but there is almost a surfeit of material about François. He was certainly not a minor king, and even Verdi had little hope of doing him justice in the course of one opera.

François's life divides tidily into three parts. His first twenty years culminated in 1515 when he came to the throne. Then followed an exuberant and joyous decade in which the Rigoletto story is set. This phase ended in the disastrous battle of Pavia, François's capture and his two humiliating years as the prisoner of the Emperor Charles V. Released in 1527, he spent his last, longest and saddest phase trying to restore his wounded vanity and recapture his zest for life. He died in 1547.

François has always been a controversial figure. Many of his biographers have been hard on him. Within fifty years of his death, the de Valois dynasty had been replaced by the Bourbons, who had every reason to denigrate him, and his reputation declined, reaching a nadir in the nineteenth century at about the time Hugo was writing. Since then, the trend has been to rehabilitate him. The safest course is to rely, as far as possible, on the evidence of his contemporaries, focusing on that happy second phase, when he was young, triumphant and, against all the odds, a king.

It was against the odds because his father, Charles d'Angoulême, was only a distant cousin of the King, and relatively poor, rebellion and exile having ruined the family's fortune. Charles had hoped to marry money, but had been forced to take the twelve-year-old Louise de Savoie, politically useful but penniless. Disappointed, he reverted to his two great interests, pretty women and the Renaissance, which was in full flood in Italy. Louise did not have a fortune, but she was a remarkable girl, tough, intelligent and precocious. She determined to make life in their château at Cognac as comfortable for Charles and his mistresses as their moderate circumstances allowed. In return, she learned from them to appreciate art and literature, to delight more in gallantry than morality, and to value money. She became a thoroughly Renaissance princess.

SUCCESSION TO THE THRONE

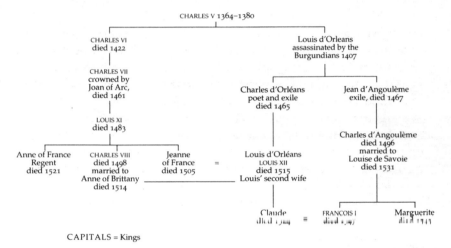

CAPITALS = Kings

When she was sixteen, Louise had a daughter, Marguerite, and two years later, François. Two years later still, Charles died leaving her in control of her little family. They lived in happy isolation in Cognac, but the great hope that sustained her was that by some miracle her son, her Caesar as she called him, would one day come to the throne. She resolved that if he did, he would be a different kind of prince, bringing light, beauty, culture and, above all, women into the austere court of France. She set about to train her children for this possibility, steeping them in languages, literature and all the fine arts, but stressing too the importance of the physical side of life, of athleticism and courage in a man, and seductiveness in a woman. They were both apt pupils. Her diary indicates approvingly that François had his first sexual adventure aged ten.

It was not long before the distant throne began to come closer. Her Caesar had a splendid physique and rude health, in stark contrast to his cousins who obligingly began to die off.[2] By 1498, only his uncle Louis XII, childless and in indifferent health, stood in the way. Louis was a much-loved king of the old school. One of his favourite sayings was "Mean king – good king"; his court was austere, and women were rarely seen in it. Appalled at the way Louise was bringing up François, Louis resolved to do everything he could to prevent him reaching the throne. He set aside his barren wife to marry his predecessor's widow, Anne of Brittany, who bore him two children, but both were girls, Claude and Renée, who could inherit Anne's duchy, but not the throne of France.[3] In 1504, a serious illness warned Louis that time might be running out. Lest he should fail to prevent François's succession, he decided to take the boy in hand. He summoned him to the court at Blois, and sent Louise to live under supervision at Amboise, deprived not only of her son, but also of her lover. She never forgave those involved but, much as he loved his mother, François was delighted to escape from the idolatry of his womenfolk, and to mix more with young men. He soon collected round him a band of the most high-spirited, with whom he proceeded to get into all sorts of trouble.

It is to this period that we owe the story of Jeanne le Cocq, lovingly recorded by François's sister Marguerite in her *Heptameron*. It is Jeanne's story which finds some echoes in Gilda's. Jeanne was the wife of a well-known lawyer, much older than herself, named Disomme. François first saw her in church at a wedding. She was clearly not averse to his admiring gaze, but the problem was how to meet. She rarely left her home and never on her own, but, one evening, a message reached François that Disomme would be out, and the door unlocked if he cared to call.

Dismissing his companions, François went at once but, on letting himself in, came face to face with Disomme. Some young men might have found themselves at a loss, but François launched into an explanation that he needed confidential legal advice, and had presumed to come secretly to consult the wisest lawyer in Paris, etc. The wisest lawyer was not wise enough to see through this, and, much flattered, he led François into his study, summoning his wife to bring refreshments. Jeanne, kneeling to serve François, managed to whisper, "The cupboard by the front door," which was all he needed. His legal problems solved, he said he preferred to depart in secret as he had come, and would see himself to the door. He did not have to wait long in the cupboard for Jeanne to join him. Their affair lasted some time, and they found a more convenient way to meet. Disomme's house adjoined a monastery, and the intervening wall was no obstacle for the athletic François. It offered a safer alternative to the front door, and the good monks were much gratified that the young prince should have chosen their humble chapel for such regular devotions. They even gave him a key, so that he should never be frustrated if the urge to pray should come upon him at an inconvenient hour.

Louis recovered from his illness, but Queen Anne had no more children and, in 1514, left him a widower. The miracle Louise had prayed for was nearly complete, which Louis acknowledged by making François marry his plain little daughter, Claude, the new Duchess of Brittany. Claude inherited all Anne's careful savings, which François now set about spending with gusto. "We work in vain," sighed Louis. "This oaf will ruin everything." Not everyone shared his opinion. The Italian Castiglione visited France at about this time, and recorded his admiration of François in *The Courtier*:

> *Castiglione*: "The French recognise only nobility of arms and esteem all else as naught. Thus they not only fail to prize but they abhor letters."
> *Magnifico Giuliv*: "You say truly that this fault has long been prevalent among the French but if kind fate decrees that M. d'Angoulême shall succeed to the crown as is hoped, I think that just as the glory of arms flourishes in France so too ought that of letters to flourish in the highest state for it is not long since I, being at court, saw this prince and it seemed to me that besides the grace of his person and the beauty of his face, he had in his aspect such loftiness, joined however with such gracious humanity, that the realm of France must seem too small for him."[4]

But Louis was not yet beaten. He at once announced his own intention to remarry, and chose Henry VIII's young sister Mary Tudor. Louise was in an agony of apprehension, fearing not so much that the decrepit King would get Mary with child, but that her own Caesar might do so, and, on its very threshold, cheat himself of the throne. The one thing she had not taught him was self-restraint, and Mary was said to be very pretty and lively. To make matters worse, Louis sent François to Calais to welcome Mary, and lead her by leisurely stages to her wedding at Abbeville. The two young people did get on well, but Mary did not conceive.[5]

Although Louis was delighted with Mary, it soon became common knowledge in the Court that, if she had a baby, it was most unlikely to be his. Furthermore, the strain of keeping up with so young a bride soon began to tell on Louis. In particular, her refusal to change her English eating habits tried him sorely. After only three months, the poor old man gave up. Muttering that his life would be his New Year gift to her, he died punctually on 1st January, 1515. All that now stood in François's way was the possibility that Mary was already pregnant. Louise had to watch in anguish with what alacrity he rushed to comfort the pretty widow, but she need not have worried. Mary had other plans, and was writing to her brother in England of her "extreme pain and annoyance . . . by reason of such suit as the French King made unto me not according with mine honour." To cool his ardour, she confided to François that she loved the Duke of Suffolk, whom Henry had promised she could marry, once she had done her duty with Louis. François was not used to coming second in such matters, but he took it in good spirit. Mary was not pregnant, and François became King.

His contemporaries all agree that he was a magnificent looking man. For his sister Marguerite he was quite simply "the perfection of grace and beauty," while his secretary, de Vielleville, describes him as "the handsomest and tallest man in the court with a splendid seat on a horse." The Venetian envoy, Cavalli, reported; "His aspect is altogether royal so that without ever having seen his face or portrait a stranger has but to look at him to say, 'That is the King.' All his movements are so noble and majestic that no prince could be his equal." The Welshman, Ellis Griffith, more down to earth, wrote of his long nose and hazel eyes, his agreeable voice, his animated expression and his muscular buttocks and thighs, but added that he had bandy legs and flat feet. There are of course a great many portraits which confirm these descriptions. One of the most delightful is Clouet's sketch of him with a twinkle to his eye and a curl to his lip, as though on the brink of some mischievous proposition. There is no doubt that he had charm too, more perhaps than was good for him. Cavalli was "tempted to say that his wisdom is more on his lips than in his mind." Sir Thomas Cheyney, an English diplomat, hinted that he might be a little shy. "If a man speak not to him first, he will not likely speak to him, but when he is once entered, he is as good a man to speak as ever I saw." Perhaps a little diffidence added to his charm. Is that not why Gilda so loves Gualtier Maldé? It may have been rather superficial, but François's charm was fresh rather than patronising.

He fulfilled all Louise's hopes as regards the court. "A Court without women is like a spring without flowers," he once said. Chivalry was replaced by gallantry, courtiers with pretty wives were expected not to leave them at home, and François never attempted to be faithful to Claude. If the Count di Ceprano in the opera has an original, it could well have been the unfortunate Count de Chateaubriant, whose wife Françoise was much admired by the King. The Count devised a strategem to keep her at home, while appearing to summon her to court. He had two identical rings made, and told Françoise on no account to come, no matter what instructions he might send her, unless he sent her his ring. For a while it worked well. The King was mystified by all Françoise's excuses, because he had felt that she was not indifferent to him, but eventually he bribed Chateaubriant's valet to betray the secret, and had an identical ring inserted into the Count's next letter. The Count's amazement and fury when his wife arrived were enjoyed by all. Françoise duly became the King's first official *maîtresse-en-titre*, and for the next few years stayed permanently at court, while the Count sulked at home in Normandy.

As in the opera, the high spirits of the King and his courtiers were not confined to the court. There exists a private journal which was being kept at this time by an anonymous gentleman, now referred to as *"le Bourgeois de Paris:"*. The diarist seems to have been well informed about everything from the latest Parisian scandal to the Turkish invasion of Egypt. He records it all with a total lack of emotion and never expresses a personal view although he sometimes attributes to others feelings that he may have been entertaining himself.[6] In an entry in 1517, he wrote: "Practically every day, the King and some of his young favourites ride around the town in fancy dress and with masks before their faces, going to various houses to play and make merry, which the people take very badly." It was probably on one such foray that François first saw *La Belle Ferronière*, who may have been the inspiration for Maddalena.[7] She was standing chatting in the doorway of her husband's armourer's shop [whence her name], when François and a companion, disguised as simple soldiers, rode by. They rode on, but the King told his companion to go back later to procure her for him. François's reputation was already so bad that the companion decided to tell the lady that it was the Queen, universally loved and pitied, who wished to see her, having heard such reports of her beauty. At first suspicious, the woman was lured by promises of all the good fortune that lay ahead, should the Queen add her to her household. Hiding herself in a voluminous cloak, she allowed him to carry her off on his pillion, and did not notice, until too late, that they were heading in the wrong direction, and already passing out of the city gate. Her cries for help brought the watch running, but her captor spurred his horse, and soon delivered her to her royal admirer, who seems to have overcome her resistance. In one version of the story, she was simply returned to her husband after three months, ruined but a great deal richer. There is, however, an alternative, more operatic version, which is that the two men shared her for a period during which the husband deliberately contracted syphilis, in order to pass it on through her to the King. Unsurprisingly, there is some evidence that François contracted a venereal disease but not necessarily from *La Belle Ferronière*. There is a Leonardo portrait in the Louvre entitled *La Belle Ferronière*, but many believe it depicts an Italian noblewoman.

There is no doubt that François's reputation as a womaniser is well deserved. The opera does not exaggerate in this, but by concentrating on only one characteristic, it is grossly misleading. It was not for nothing that he was called François the Great. As Castiglione forecast, he transformed France and not only in the field of letters, although it was there that he and his sister made a direct contribution. He was a genuine connoisseur with a real feel for quality, taste and originality. He brought architects, painters and sculptors to France. Several of the Loire chateaux are part of his legacy. Leonardo da Vinci died in his service, and his patronage of Benvenuto Cellini could fill a chapter in a biography.

He was a splendid athlete, and almost caused an international incident at the Field of the Cloth of Gold by throwing Henry VIII with too much nonchalance. It was meant as a bit of fun between brother monarchs, but it was just as well that at the critical moment lunch was announced and attention diverted. Few could match his skill at arms and horsemanship. He loved hunting and tournaments, and in particular, the staging of mock battles with wooden castles, artillery firing bladders, and armies of several hundred on each side going hammer and tongs at each other, with the King in the foreground of the action where the ladies could admire him. Although meant to be fun, there were often several dead and many wounded at the end of the day. François himself was once knocked unconscious for two days, when a defender of a high tower dropped a burning log on his head. When he came to, Louise was for punishing the man, but François just laughed and said, "I must take what comes if I want to play the fool!" He was brave, and once proved it conclusively. A new entertainment had been devised for the court. A huge wild boar had been released in an arena to savage a number of dummies disposed for this purpose. The gasps of the ladies turned to shrieks when the boar broke through a barrier, and came pounding up the steps leading to their loggia. As others engaged in a general *sauve-qui-peut*, François calmly drew his sword, confronted the charging beast and slew it with a single thrust.

His attitude to war was much the same. It was a chance to show off but, sadly, without the ladies present. His main idea of tactics was to charge at the head of his knights at the first opportunity. At Pavia, in 1525, this brought him to disaster and captivity, while half his knights lost their lives trying to rescue him. Even then, disarmed and surrounded, he seemed to enjoy the way the Hapsburg soldiers gazed in wonder at his armour; but defeat and imprisonment, and the shameful way he obtained his release, did not leave his vanity intact.[8] He spent much of the last phase of his life trying to repair it. During these twenty years, he cut an increasingly melancholy figure, seeking but not finding escape in the old pleasures that once had worked so well. Of course, he went on womanising, but the gentle Françoise had been replaced by the grasping Anne de Pisseleu and her *petite bande de dames*. Anne, selected for him by Louise, was neither fond of him nor faithful. One day, his sister Marguerite found him sitting disconsolate and alone in a room at Chambord. Asked what ailed him, he did not reply, but took a diamond ring and scratched on a window pane *"Souvent femme varie – Bien fol qui s'y fie."* In his play, Hugo quotes this couplet unchanged, but in the opera it becomes the aria *"La donna e mobile . . . chi lei confide mal cauto il cor"* – "Woman is fickle . . . poor fool who trusts her." The aria is cheerful in the opera. It has been transplanted to a more cheerful period of François's life.

There was another way in which François's vanity brought him to disaster at Pavia. It was at the root of his quarrel with his leading subject and best general, the great Constable of France, the Duc de Bourbon. François was jealous of Bourbon's wealth, his reputation as a soldier and the devotion he inspired in his followers. Not only was he more admired than his King, but Bourbon was strait-laced, and would have nothing to do with the revels at court. Bourbon's ultimate crime came when, having lost his wife, he was invited to marry François's mother, Louise, and refused with contempt. François and Louise, whose venom can be imagined, now set about, by every means fair or foul, to ruin and humiliate him, with such good effect that Bourbon was driven to plan treason, but it miscarried. He was lucky to escape to join the Emperor Charles V, leaving his followers to the mercy of François. Chief of these was the Count de Saint-Vallier, the father of Diane de Poitiers. She was well away from it all, having been married to the Grand Sénéchal of Normandy, who had no connections with Bourbon.[9] Saint-Vallier had also had no knowledge of the plot until the last moment, when he refused to join, and did his utmost to dissuade Bourbon, but, having failed, he neglected to warn the King. By a curious coincidence, it was Diane's husband who stumbled on the plot by chance, and who did warn François.

The Sénéchal's loyalty did not save his father-in-law from François's fury. On the contrary, Saint-Vallier was singled out for such rigorous treatment that the story was soon abroad in Paris that there was more to it than his connection with Bourbon, and that Diane's honour was involved. *Le Bourgeois de Paris* was much intrigued by the affair and records the rumour that Saint-Vallier had earned this harsh treatment by threatening the King for having violated his daughter. The diarist evidently was a witness when, on a freezing day in January 1524, Saint-Vallier was brought out, propped up on a horse by a soldier, for public execution. Stripped to his shirtsleeves, he was administered the last rites and made to kneel on the block, but the executioner was in no hurry. He and the other officials stood around him chatting for a long time, until a messenger eventually arrived with a commutation of the sentence to solitary confinement for life. Saint-Vallier made no attempt to hide his relief. Shaking with cold and fear, he crossed himself and kissed the block several times. The diarist does not record, as some historians have claimed, Saint-Vallier's notorious comment" *"Dieu sauve le bon con de ma belle fille qui m'a si bien sauvé."*[10] This is probably an embellishment of the truth, propagated by the likes of Brantôme, who repeats it with great relish.

Diane's admirers do not believe a word of this story and maintain that, although she became one of the great courtesans of history, she was faithful to the old Sénéchal while he lived. What could be more natural than for the King to reward her husband's loyalty by sparing her father's life? On the other hand, François and Diane cannot have been unaware of each other's attractions. On one of the many portraits of her, he wrote in his own hand: *"Belle à la voir, honneste à la hanter."* "Beautiful to look at, charming to be with." And then there is a verse scratched on a chimney piece in the Château de Loury.

> *In this retreat, the great François Premier*
> *Could always find some new delight.*
> *Oh, happy place which hid from sight*
> *Flower of Beauty, Diane de Poitiers.*[11]

While it remains controversial, it is easy to believe their intimacy. One needs but to compare their portraits, his by Clouet and hers by Flandrin, to feel it almost inevitable. And then there are some unsigned letters, undoubtedly addressed to the King and suppos-

edly in Diane's hand, pleading for a favour and citing their intimacy in support.[12] There is no proof however, and her many supporters accuse Victor Hugo of doing her a great injustice. Whether
or not Saint-Vallier cursed the King, he was not the venerable old
man of the opera but barely forty when condemned. His experience is said to have turned his hair white and given him the especially severe fever which afterwards bore his name. He did not
serve his full sentence, but was released and restored to all his
possessions under the treaty by which François secured his own
release from captivity. It was not until much later that Diane
became the mistress of François's shy second son who reigned as
Henri II.

Verdi wisely does not try to portray François in the round. He
concentrates on his womanising and not unjustly. Gilda would
certainly have had good reason both to love him, and to rue it.
François defies any summing up, but perhaps, if anyone had the
right to try, it was his sister. She wrote: "This prince was a man
somewhat enslaved to pleasure, having great delight in hunting,
games and women, as his youth led him, but having a wife of a
peevish disposition, to whom none of her husband's content-
ments were pleasing . . . but he would always have a sister with
him, for she was of a joyous nature, and a good and honourable
woman withal."[13]

Another whose treatment in the opera falls short of justice is
Clément Marot, although Marullo is probably the most attractive
of its characters. His father was Jean Marot, a milliner and versi-
fier, who came to the notice of Anne of Brittany, and was brought
into her court as a secretary. His best known poem is probably his
epic, celebrating Louis XII's campaign in Italy. The father's influence obtained an excellent education for the son, but Clément
Marot was too wild to make much use of it, which probably saved
a natural talent from becoming inhibited by the sterile forms into
which medieval poetry had got itself imprisoned. His verses are
as fresh today as ever. Many are short *estrennes* – graceful and
witty offerings to court ladies, mostly in their praise but never
sycophantic. He also wrote longer poems such as *Le temple de
Cupido* dedicated to the King, and, like his father, wrote many
poems celebrating current events, in the manner of a laureate. He

translated the psalms into French, which delighted religious reformers, but offended the conservatives. He became increasingly suspected of heresy, but for many years was protected by Marguerite who was also attracted by the Reformation. Even she could not protect him once her brother opted definitely for the counter-reformation, and started burning heretics. Marot fled into exile and, after various vicissitudes, during which he was gaoled both by the Catholics for heresy and the Calvinists for frivolity, he died in Turin in 1544, a chastened but still a cheerful man. All through these travails, he kept on bombarding the court with poems, hoping vainly to win his way back. No hint of self-pity mars his style, always light, elegant and graceful. An appropriate epitaph might be this quatrain, probably addressed to his beloved Marguerite:

> *In the springtime of my mischief making*
> *I flew just like a swallow on the wing*
> *First here, then there; now in old age I'm brought*
> *Sans fear nor care, to what my heart has sought.*[14]

The part of Marullo is small, but it nevertheless captures the essentials. Marullo stands out from the boorish young courtiers. He is wittier, thinks quicker and is also more sympathetic. When Rigoletto finds them all outside his house, it is Marullo who handles the situation. When Gilda emerges distraught from the Duke's room, it is Marullo who shepherds the courtiers tactfully away. It is to him that Rigoletto turns for sympathy. It is true that Marullo is cruel to Rigoletto, but Rigoletto deserves it. It is hard to believe that Clémont Marot would have been unkind to Triboulet, who did not.

Triboulet was born in Blois towards the end of the fifteenth century. His family name was Le Feurial, and his nickname was formed from a play on the archaic verb *tribouler* which meant to pester, to cause trouble. Presumably Rigoletto was invented in the same way from *rigoler,* to laugh and have fun. In justice, their nicknames should be reversed for the real Triboulet was much more amiable than the stage Rigoletto. It is not provable but almost inconceivable that Triboulet should have had a daughter. In his day, jesters had a very lowly status, not much above that of household pets. Indeed, the records show that Triboulet had a sort of minder, a man called Bournier who was paid *quarante livres tournois* per year to look after him. In fact, lowly status was probably essential if jesters were to perform their function, and poke fun at their betters. Before François, the court was male dominated, its humour broad and its fools crude rather than clever. Jesters were often forced to undergo gross indignities cheerfully. One, for instance, had to entertain the court of Mantua by being buffeted and tossed by a tuskless wild boar. In Triboulet's day, they were not so much wits as tumblers, buffoons and freaks. As time, women and the Renaissance brought sophistication to the court, jesters had to refine their act. As their status rose, so did the risks they ran. Chicot, the official jester to Henry IV, was of gentle birth, and bore arms in time of war. At the seige of Rouen in 1592, he captured the Count de Chaligny and, as a graceful gesture, offered his prisoner to the King. The Count was so outraged to discover that he had yielded to a jester that he struck Chicot a blow on the head, from which the poor man died two weeks later. In 1509, Triboulet also went to war, in the suite of Louis XII on the Italian campaign, celebrated by Jean Marot's long poem. In it, Marot describes Triboulet's behaviour at the siege of Peschiera, where the little man was so terrified by the noise of the French bombardment that he was found hiding under a camp bed. No gentleman could admit to being upset by the chattering of such a poltroon.

All the same, Triboulet must have been quite a character for there are a lot of contemporary references to him. He was enough of a personality at the court to be portrayed by the artist Clouet, who never did a portrait of Marot. Nor was his celebrity confined to the Court. Rabelais, needing a fool to advise Panurge about marriage, naturally introduces Triboulet.[15]

In trying to discern the real Triboulet through the mists of time, his celebrity brings its own problems. An incrustation of incidents and stories has formed around him which cannot all be attributable to him. There is a nice story, for instance, about the Emperor Charles's visit to France. The Emperor distrusted the English Channel, and sought François's permission to travel from Spain to Flanders through France. François agreed, hoping to regain some face by making a show of French magnificence, which was foolish, for Charles V had little time for that sort of thing. If he had money to spare, he spent it on lances not luxury. Triboulet, according to the story, had more common sense than his King. He said he intended to present the Emperor with his fool's cap, since presumably François would immediately imprison his old enemy. "Why – no!" cried François, "By my faith as a gentleman, he shall have free passage." "Then, Sire, I shall present my cap to you!" The fool was right. No good came of Charles's visit, but the story must belong to some other jester because Triboulet had died several years earlier. More probable is a similar story in which Triboulet is sitting in a corner, listening to François and his advisers discussing by which route to march to Italy [and to the disaster at Pavia]. "What I would like to know," said Triboulet, "is how you propose to come back." "Ah," said the King, "we will march back with the drums beating." "Or more likely beaten!" growled the fool.

In the early nineteenth century, there was a spate of books about Triboulet and his fellow jesters, like Caillette who is also an historical figure but hazy, and much less celebrated. The main source was a book called *Deux Fous* by Bibliophil Jaques who liked to leaven his fantasies with a little history. Many other books, such as J. Doran's *History of Court Fools* leaned heavily on this suspect source. So too did Victor Hugo. Triboulet's reputation for bitterness originates from these fictions, for his contemporaries found him congenial. The earliest and fullest description of him is by Jean Marot: "Deformed head, no wiser at thirty than when he was born, low forehead and bulging eyes, big nose, hollow chest, long flat stomach, high humped back, he mimicked everybody, sang, danced and sermonised, all in so jolly a way that no-one could take offence."[16]

There exist two pictures of him. Clouet's drawing shows us a rather coarse face with quite a twinkle in his eye but no malice. The other picture, *La Vierge de la Balance*,[17] in which he is a grotesque detail in an otherwise serious painting, makes him look a bit dotty but no less good-humoured.

Triboulet probably gained his place at court through the kind heart of Louis XII, and a prank that he once played on one of the court pages. Apparently Triboulet used to scratch a living, begging on the streets of Blois, playing his bagpipes, and trying to attract attention by mimicking and chaffing the citizens as they went about their business. As a consequence, he had to put up with a good deal of abuse himself, especially from the young pages running errands from the court. One day, he tried to get his own back on one of them, snipping off the backside of his doublet. The boy, unaware of what had happened, was much teased on his return to court. Gathering a group of colleagues, he set forth to teach Triboulet a lesson. Seizing him, they dragged him to the gibbet, but instead of hanging him, left him there nailed to it by the ear. It has been suggested that it was this incident which persuaded King Louis to take him into his service and protection.

Unlike Rigoletto, Triboulet was clearly popular with the courtiers and in no way seen as a threat. There is only one story which hints otherwise. In it, Triboulet has gone too far and enraged a courtier called Bonnivet, who is out for his blood. The King assures his clown that if Bonnivet attacks him, he'll have him hanged within the quarter of an hour. "Ah, Sire," cries Triboulet, "Could you not hang him a quarter of an hour *before* he attacks?" The story is improved by the fact that Bonnivet was a particularly conceited man, a womaniser, far too handsome for his own good and not much respected.

Triboulet seems to have been quite vain. He apparently affected the tightest fitting clothes, which had the effect of accentuating his deformity. He liked bright colours and usually adopted those of the reigning mistress of the day. Notwithstanding his deformities, he lived a long time, apparently dying in 1536 – at least, that is when the payments for his upkeep came to an end. If this is right and if, as Jean Marot implies, he was thirty at the time of Peschiera, he died aged fifty-seven, quite old for the time. Confusingly, his only epitaph had been written in Latin some years earlier by Jean Voulte: "I lived my life a jester, finding favour with the King by this title alone: I now go to see if I shall be buffoon to Jove, the supreme King."[18]

For his epitaph to appear several years too soon is, of course, just the sort of joke a jester had to put up with. A better timed and more appropriate summing up was that by the writer, Bonaventure Despériers. He described Triboulet as a twenty-five carat fool with only twenty-four carats, a delightful fellow but not quite all there.

NOTES

1 Vincenzo was first married to Margharita Farnese of Parma, but, after two years, there had been no consummation. It seems likely that some genuine physical problem on her part prevented this and he determined to set her aside. Her brother took this as an insult to the family, and accused Vincenzo of impotence, with the consequence that no other bride could be found for him, until he had submitted himself to a virility test. A humiliating set of rules was drawn up. Having been searched for hidden implements, he was to perform before neutral witnesses. An attractive virgin called Giulia was found, offered generous terms to try her best, and the couple were prepared like prize fighters for their encounter. Not surprisingly, the first two attempts failed, but the third produced masses of blood, and Vincenzo claimed that his penetration must have been witnessed. Giulia herself was not convinced of it. She appeared to have been deflowered but how? At this point, some uncharitable observer suggested that it might have been wiser to base her pay on productivity rather than time spent on the job, and she immediately changed her tune. Vincenzo received his diploma, which his subsequent life proved to be no more than just.

2 Louise's arch-enemy, the Duc de Bourbon, was wont to muse about how unlike a de Valois François looked, and how exceedingly like a certain handsome miller in Cognac.

3 The Salic Law, which excluded females from the succession to the throne, was of vague origin. The Salians seem to have been a Frankish tribe in the days before the Merovingian kings began to achieve some political order. There is some doubt as to where their lands were. Some place them in modern Holland, in the area of Drenthe and Gelderland, but according to Shakespeare: "Which Salique, as I said, 'twixt Elbe and Sala, Is at this day in Germany called Meisen." [*Henry V*] Sala is near Dudislava in southern Moravia. The Salic Law had long decided succession to the French throne, but never that of the Duchy of Brittany.

4 Translation by L.S. Singleton [abridged] Doubleday, N.Y., 1959.

5 There is a story that Anne Boleyn was a member of Mary Tudor's train, and that, inevitably, François "knew" her long before Henry. This is most unlikely since Anne was only seven years old at this time. He might have had her elder sister, Mary Boleyn, who did accompany the princess to France, but the story is probably just an early example of French chauvinism.

6 His policy may have been born of caution. In an entry in 1515, he records the fate of one Cluché, a street comedian who used to entertain the crowd with political satires. One of these, called *La Mère Sotte* gave a scurrilous version of François's affair with Jeanne le Cocq and Maître Disomme. One day a group of burly young men arrived and asked to see it, but half way through they broke it up, and thrashed Cluché to within an inch of his life. They then put him in a sack, and were carrying him towards the river when his cries for help brought rescue.

7 Ferronier, now archaic, meant someone who fashioned objects of iron, such as an armourer.

8 The Emperor would not release François except on humiliating terms. He was to renounce all his claims in Italy; he must restore the hated Bourbon to all his former state and grant him the hand of the Princess Renée; he must supply substantial land and naval forces and even serve himself should the Emperor call upon him to do so; he must marry the Emperor's sister Eléonore; he must return the province of Burgundy which the French had won from the Emperor's grandfather, Charles the Bold; finally, he must submit his two eldest sons to the Emperor as hostages or, alternatively, twelve French gentlemen.

François and his mother tried everything to mitigate these terms, even offering the Emperor the hand of Marguerite, an offer which was contemptuously ignored. Their sticking point was the cession of Burgundy, but the Emperor insisted. In the end, François made a secret vow in the presence of the French ambassadors that he would accept these terms but not fulfil them. The Emperor accepted but was prudent enough to demand the simultaneous exchange of the hostages. A vessel was moored for the purpose half-way across the River Bidassoa which defined the frontier. Here, François encountered the hostages travelling in the other direction. These had to be his two young sons, the twelve gentlemen having prudently failed to materialise. François sent his weeping children on their way to exile and imprisonment, knowing full well that he had no intention of fulfilling the treaty and redeeming them.

On reaching the French bank, he did not look back but sprang on a horse, shouted, *"Me voici Roi derechef!"* – "I'm King again!" – and galloped off. He was supposed to ratify the Treaty as soon as he reached the first frontier town, but, instead, he sent a message that he would have to consult the citizens of Burgundy first. The Emperor knew what that meant.

9 The post of Sénéchal was akin to that of Lord Lieutenant but, of course, in those days it had real military significance. Diane's husband's name was Louis de Brézé, but they were both usually referred to by the title. The Sénéchal had been told of Bourbon's plan by a priest, who had learned of it in the confessional.

10 Even today it is hard to translate Saint-Vallier's comment with felicity. If he did make it and if he had earlier cursed the King, he had greatly revised his priorities in between.

11 *Dans ce pourpris, le grand François Premier*
   Trouva toujours jouissance nouvelle
   Qu'il est heureux ce lieu qui seul recèle
   Fleur de Beauté, Diane de Poitiers.

Rigoletto

12 One of these letters reads: *"Je crains tant que unne petite ocasion soyt cause
d'une pour moy grande trystesse que je suys contrainte de m'adresser à vous,
non comme roy, non seulement comme seigneur et maystre, mays comme au
plus seur et veritable amy . . ."*
[I am so afraid that a small matter may be the cause of such a
great sorrow for me, that I am forced to address myself to you, not
as King, nor as my lord and master, but as my most sure and true
friend . . .]
Other letters indicate that it was not such a small matter. One
mentions *"des liens de dure pryson"*. This and the writer's intent to
"aller apres mon mary en Picardie" add circumstantial support to the
theory that she was indeed Diane.

13 Translation by Francis Hackett, Heinemann, 1934.

14 *Sur le printemps de ma jeunesse folle*
Je ressemblais l'hirondelle qui vole
Puis ça, puis là; l'age me conduisait
Sans peur ni soins, où le coeur me disait.

15 In Book III, Panurge is having difficulty making up his mind about
marriage and can get no useful advice from all the wise men he
consults. Pantagruel therefore suggests that he consult a wise fool and
they naturally send to Blois for Triboulet. He turns out to be more fool
than wise. In fact, he is a half-wit. Panurge is only half-way through
explaining his problem when Triboulet's attention begins to wander.
He interrupts, thumping Panurge on the back, hitting him on the nose
with his bladder and saying; "By God, God, mad fool, beware the
monk, Buzançay hornpipe." He then wanders off to play and will pay
them no more attention. Panurge and Pantagruel spend some time
trying to read a delphic meaning into this, but it is sheer nonsense.

16 *". . . de la tête écorné.*
Aussi saige à trente ans que le jour qui fut né,
Petit front et gros yeux, nes grant, taille à bosse,
Estomac plat et long, hault dos à porter hote
Chacun contrefaisait, chanta, damsa, précha,
Et de tout si plaisant qu'onc homme ne facha."

17 *La Vierge de la Balance* can be seen in the Museum of Picardie.

18 *Vixi morio, regibusque gratus*
Solo hoc nomine: viso num futurus
Regum morio sim, Jovi supremo
[Translation by Professor Keith Bate]

DON CARLOS

Giuseppe Verdi

*Libretto by G. Méry and C. Du Locle
(in French) after Schiller*

Dramatis Personae

Philip II, *King of Spain*
don Carlos, *Infante of Spain*
Rodrigo, Marquis of Posa, *friend of don Carlos*
The Grand Inquisitor
Tebaldo, *Elizabeth's page*
Count Lerma, *Spanish Ambassador to France*
A herald
A monk, *suspected of being Charles V*

Elizabeth de Valois, *Princess of France*
Princess Eboli, *a leading lady of the Spanish court*
Countess d'Aremburg, *Elizabeth's companion*
A heavenly voice

Courtiers, soldiers, monks, priests, peasants, Flemish burghers

ACT ONE

It is 1558. The scene is a clearing in the forest near Fontainebleau, where the peace negotiations between France and Spain are nearing their conclusion. Under their terms, Elizabeth and Carlos are to be married.

Elizabeth and her page Tebaldo are taking part in a hunt, and pass through the clearing, distributing alms to some foresters, who follow them away. The Infante Carlos emerges from behind the trees. He has come incognito from Spain, hoping to glimpse his intended bride. Enchanted by his first sight of her, he does not have long to wait for a second. In the gathering mist, Tebaldo and Elizabeth have lost their way, and return to the glade. Elizabeth is exhausted, and Carlos offers to protect her while Tebaldo fetches a litter from the Château, whose lights are now visible through the gloom.

Carlos builds a fire, and when Elizabeth questions him about the Infante he gives her a locket with his miniature, and she recognises him. Both are declaring their love when, to complete their happiness, a distant cannon signals the signing of the treaty.

Tebaldo returns and, to their consternation, salutes Elizabeth as Queen of Spain. There has been a last-minute change, and she is to marry not Carlos but his father, King Philip. The Spanish ambassador, Lerma, arrives to confirm this news, followed by many courtiers and foresters. They are joyful at the prospect of peace, and beg their princess to seal it by accepting. Dutifully but sorrowfully, she consents. While the crowd rejoices, Carlos and Elizabeth lament.

ACT TWO

SCENE ONE: Some time has passed. Elizabeth and Philip have been married, and Carlos has come to grieve in the solitude of the monastery of St Yuste. Here, his grandfather, the Emperor Charles V, has recently ended his days, though some say his tomb is empty, and that he has become a monk. One of them does seem familiar to Carlos. His friend Rodrigo, Marquis of Posa, arrives. Posa wants to talk about the troubles of Flanders, but Carlos is too lovesick to care. Posa is shocked but urges him to forget his love by going to Flanders, and, once there, declaring himself King and champion of the Flemish. Carlos agrees, and the two are pledging everlasting comradeship, when the King and Queen arrive for their devotions.

SCENE TWO: The libretto places the next scene in a "delightful spot" by a fountain outside the St Yuste monastery gates, but it is often set in its equally delightful cloister.

The ladies of the court are enjoying these surroundings when Tebaldo arrives with the Princess Eboli. The two sing a romantic Moorish song. A melancholy Elizabeth enters and is introduced to Posa, who has brought a letter from her mother in France. With it, he slips her a note from Carlos urging her to trust Posa as his friend. Posa requests her to grant Carlos an audience. Posa says that Carlos is cast down by Philip's disapproval but Eboli, who is listening, fancies that Carlos is really pining for her love. Elizabeth grants the request, and Posa leads Eboli and the other ladies away. Carlos arrives and formally asks the Queen to support his petition to go to Flanders. Although she at once agrees to do so, he does not leave, but begins to rave about his love for her, and when she tries to calm him, he swoons at her feet. As she bends over him, he half-wakes and tries to embrace her. Thoroughly alarmed, she fends him off, and he rushes away, only just in time, since the court now returns, followed by the King. The King asks why the Queen has been left alone by her French lady-in-waiting, whom he punishes with banishment. Aghast at this insult to the Queen, all depart except the King and Posa.

Philip asks him why it is, when he wishes to reward his good service, that Posa seems to avoid him. Posa makes an impassioned plea for Flanders. Although Philip is immovable, he is grateful to Posa for speaking his mind honestly, but he warns him to beware the Inquisition. He then confides his suspicions about Carlos's relations with the Queen, and asks Posa to discover the truth.

ACT THREE

SCENE ONE: It is night. Carlos is waiting in the palace gardens in Madrid. He is reading a note of assignation which he believes is from the Queen, but which is actually from Eboli, who soon arrives masked. Carlos, still deceived, begins to talk of love, and when she removes her mask, he draws back, stunned. Eboli realises he has mistaken her for the Queen, and is furious. Posa, who now enters, tries first to mollify, and then to threaten Eboli, but to no avail. She leaves, swearing vengeance, and Posa persuades Carlos to hand over to him any incriminating documents.

SCENE TWO: The next scene is the great *auto da fé* that was held in Valladolid on 8th October, 1559. It is set in the square outside the cathedral, already filled with a festive crowd, hailing the power of their King.

A procession of the clergy arrives with their victims, followed by the resplendent court, including Posa and the Queen. Finally the King appears, and all are kneeling in homage when Carlos brings forward a group of Flemish burghers. Elizabeth and Posa are horrified and the King icy, as Carlos pleads their cause. Blundering on, he demands to be made governor of Flanders, and, when rejected, he draws his sword. While the guards hesitate, Posa steps forward and disarms him. Carlos is escorted away, and the King rewards Posa with a dukedom. The festivities now proceed. As bonfires light the sky, a heavenly voice is heard offering comfort to those about to die.

ACT FOUR

SCENE ONE: Philip is in his study brooding over Elizabeth's indifference. He recalls her shock on first seeing his white hair. A King can command everything except love. The Grand Inquisitor arrives, venerable and blind. Philip seeks his advice about Carlos's behaviour. If he condemns his son to death, would the Church give its support? The Church would, but wants the dissenter Posa in return. Philip refuses to abandon his one honest friend, and the Inquisitor leaves, having threatened in vain.

Elizabeth enters in great agitation, believing that her jewel case has been stolen. It is sitting on Philip's table. Taking from it the locket which Carlos gave her in Act I, he accuses her of unfaithfulness, and she faints. His calls for help bring Posa with Eboli, who is stricken with guilt for, in her jealousy, it was she who stole the jewel case. Seeing that time is running out for Carlos who alone can redeem Flanders, Posa decides to sacrifice himself to save him. When the Queen revives, the men leave her to deal with Eboli, who is given the choice of exile or a nunnery. Alone, Eboli bewails her own fatal gift of beauty which has led her into these ruinous intrigues. In her remorse, she too resolves to save Carlos.

SCENE TWO: In his prison cell, Carlos awaits his father's judgement. Posa arrives, saying that he has diverted the King's anger onto himself so that Carlos may live and save Flanders. A shot is fired and Posa falls. As he dies, he tells Carlos that the Queen will await him at St Yuste, to say a last farewell before he leaves Spain. Philip now arrives to release his son, but Carlos rejects him. In the meanwhile, an angry mob outside is clamouring for Carlos's release. Philip orders the gates to be opened, and the crowd surges in, Eboli amongst them. Furtively she urges Carlos to fly. The Grand Inquisitor arrives, and while he quells the multitude, Carlos slips away.

ACT FIVE

At St Yuste, while Elizabeth awaits Carlos, she longs for France and yearns for death. When Carlos comes, she bids him be strong and follow his destiny. Their lingering farewell is interrupted by the King who has followed with the Grand Inquisitor and guards. While Philip himself apprehends Elizabeth, the pikemen make to seize Carlos but, with drawn sword, he backs towards the tomb of Charles V, which opens. A monk emerges whom all recognise as the Emperor. He leads Carlos into the safety of his tomb.

A Great Scandal

On 8th July, 1545, don Carlos was born to be heir to an empire far greater than Charlemagne's. It was ruled over by his grandfather, the Hapsburg Emperor Charles V, and it stretched from Hungary to Peru. Although Spain was its greatest province, the heart of the empire still lay in the Duchy of Burgundy, a string of provinces running south from Friesland through Holland, Flanders and Luxembourg to the upper Rhone, separating the French from the Germans and inhabited mainly by staunch and hearty Dutch-speaking people with a reputation for good living. It was to these people that the Emperor felt closest. He was Burgundian by upbringing, nature and behaviour, and consequently had many problems with his Spanish subjects. He therefore sent Carlos's father, Philip, to grow up in Spain.

The Hapsburgs had come a long way from home. In the twelfth century they had started with the little Hapsburg tower perched on a hill near Zürich. The name is a shortening of Habichtsburg or Hawk's Castle. Looking down from its battlements to where three broad valleys meet, it is easy to see how the tower got its name, and how the family got its first fortune. Down the centuries since then, the Hapsburgs, and not least the Emperor himself, had done their share of fighting but their most useful talent had been for marriage. Charles V no longer owned that little tower, but he had inherited Austria from his grandfather and Burgundy from his grandmother. And then, greatest of all, Spain and its empire had been acquired through his mad mother, Juana. Juana *la Loca* was the only surviving child of Ferdinand and Isabella, who first united Spain and who sent Columbus to America. It was not just many lands that bore down on Carlos's rather narrow shoulders, but many august generations too.

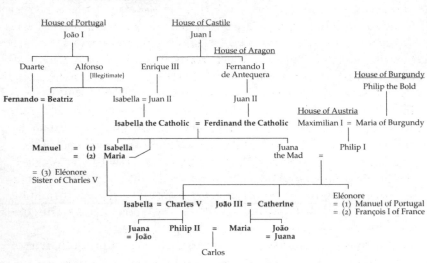

HAPSBURG INBREEDING

Bold = marriages of cousins

In a family prone to inbreeding, marrying a madwoman, whatever her inheritance, can have dire consequences. There were traces of instability in the Emperor, who sometimes had to struggle with extremes of elation and depression. By the age of fifty-five and feeling worn out, he abdicated and retired to the monastery of St Yuste, where much of the opera takes place. This instability was much worse in his grandson, Carlos, in whom quite small frustrations could produce spectacular rages, sometimes, as in the opera, leading to fainting fits. There can be no doubt that his upbringing exacerbated his faults. He was first over-cosseted by a doting aunt and nervous courtiers, and then rejected and humiliated by an unsympathetic father. Philip was quite different from both Charles and Carlos. Nicknamed *el Prudente*, the Cautious, he was very conscientious and filled with an unbending sense of duty and of destiny, but he was not a forgiving man. He was better fitted to be a son than a father. Had Carlos been brought up by his grandfather, things might have turned out differently.

Whatever his faults, Charles was a great man who could value and work with all sorts of people quite different from himself. Charles admired Philip and saw that he was reliable, so he entrusted him at a very young age with the regency of Spain. Some years later, when Philip was 22, Charles decided it was time that he met his other future subjects, and summoned him to Flanders. On the way, Philip made a triumphal journey through the Hapsburg dominions in Italy and Germany. At every stage, he was fêted with banquets, tournaments, and all the boisterous entertainments which his father was known to enjoy. He cut a miserable figure. His every instinct was ascetic and solitary. He hated the parties. He was so hopeless at tournaments that one observer commented that "no-one did so badly as the Prince – quite unable to break a lance!" He could not unbend, and refused even to try to speak anything but Spanish, expecting his future subjects to adapt to him. Perhaps he saw his father's affability as unkingly.

Philip's journey was not just a disaster in itself, but the beginning of a huge tragedy. Instead of warming to him, the Flemish simply could not understand him, and wondered how the Spanish could have so transformed the son of their beloved Charles. The dislike was mutual. Charles must have realised all this, but there was not much he could do about it. He knew that no man could be everything to everyone, and he still admired Philip, perhaps all the more for retaining his dignity and regality under such trying circumstances. Philip shortly gave further proof of his dedication by agreeing to marry sour old Mary Tudor, simply in order to bring the English back to the true faith, and yet another country into the Hapsburg hegemony. Philip might not get on with the Flemish, but Charles, in his youth, had far worse problems establishing himself in Spain. Perhaps he envied Philip his austerity. Charles knew only too well how much he himself had abused his own body, and how he was now paying for it. The last years had not gone well, and perhaps a complete change was what the empire needed. When he abdicated, Charles divided his empire between his brother Ferdinand, who inherited central Europe and the Holy Roman Empire, and his son Philip, who got Spain with its empire in Italy and the New World, and Burgundy. This last was a mistake. Ferdinand would have made a much better ruler for Flanders, but Charles could not bring himself to alienate his own homeland from his own seed.

Philip's reign started gloriously. Within a year, his soldiers had routed the French at St Quentin. With France at his mercy, Charles would have followed up energetically, but Philip hesitated, enabling the French to scramble together some sort of defence. It was not the last chance he missed through procrastination, but the French were glad when peace talks started at Cateau Cambrésis. The proposed marriage of Princess Elizabeth with don Carlos was central to the treaty from the start, but within a month the negotiations had to be suspended because of the death of Philip's wife, Mary Tudor.

Dutifully married, Mary had been Philips' second wife. Much older than he was and embittered by family troubles, she had fallen deeply in love with him. While not reciprocating such love, Philip had been kind and sympathetic. He had spent some time with her in England, keeping tactfully in the background. He tried to moderate her enthusiasm for bonfires, not so much because he disapproved of them as such, but because he feared they might give Spain a bad name amongst the English. He was right about that. When she died, the hoped-for link with England died too. Philip did propose rather half-heartedly to Mary's half-sister Elizabeth, but, probably to his own relief, he was rejected. There was a range of other dynastic opportunities for him to consider, but when he returned to Cateau Cambrésis his mind was made up. He would himself take the French princess. She was less than half his age and he had never seen her, but her beauty and character were everywhere praised, and it was important to establish a lasting peace with her country as quickly as possible.

Philip was no stranger to love. One thing he shared with Charles was a lusty libido. Although only sixteen when he first married, he had already fathered some bastards, having seduced their mother, doña Isabel de Osorio, with promises of marriage, which she must have been very foolish to believe. She was the sister of a powerful nobleman, and the affair caused quite a scandal; many considered Carlos's inadequacies to be divine retribution for Philip's mistreatment of doña Isabel. Philip's first marriage in 1543 was also a love affair. His cousin, Maria of Portugal, was his own choice. Boyishly excited, he had gone incognito, like Carlos in the opera, to get a glimpse of Maria as she was welcomed into her future country. He was delighted by what he saw, but alas, it was over all too soon. She died two days after the birth of Carlos. The doctors blamed a lemon, incautiously eaten too soon after the event, but the Emperor suspected his lustful son of over-taxing her. This was one aspect of Philip's temperament he felt he understood and he once wrote to him: "When you are with your wife, be careful not to overstrain yourself . . . And because this is somewhat difficult, the remedy is to keep away from her as much as you can." Philip had not heeded him.

Carlos therefore never knew his mother, and during his formative years, between 1550 and 1559, his father was away in Flanders and England. Philip was a distant stranger who, although he barely knew his son, constantly interfered with the efforts of those who did. Initially, Carlos was placed in the care of Philip's sister and regent, Juana. Philip's letters frequently accuse her of spoiling him, and probably she did. The boy was weak and suffered from quartain fever (a form of malaria). He needed some cossetting and she needed someone to cosset. Juana had briefly been Queen of Portugal, but when her husband died she had been driven out by her mother-in-law, and forced to leave her own infant son behind. Perhaps she loved Carlos in his place. She did not hide from Philip that Carlos was backward, but that was typical of the family. Forgetting that he himself had not learned to read until he was seven, Philip fretted about his son's childishness. Convinced that Juana was not strong enough, he put Carlos into the care of two men: don Garcia de Toledo would be governor while Honorate Juan would be tutor.

The latter was an excellent choice. He was kind and won the boy's confidence and love. A part of the tragedy of Carlos was that, later on, when he really needed someone he could trust,

Honorate Juan was gone. In the meantime, Juan was not much more successful than Juana had been at developing the boy. Carlos's daily regime was far from demanding, but he would react badly to pressure to work harder. Carlos knew full well what power he would one day wield, and could not understand why he should be denied his slightest whim. His tutors were in an awkward position. They had authority now, but who could tell how soon the tables would be turned on them?

When Carlos was eleven, his grandfather visited him on his way to St Yuste. Charles's impressions were not entirely negative. His stories of the wars thrilled the boy, though Carlos was shocked to learn that the Emperor had not always won, and, indeed, had sometimes run away. This amused the old soldier who liked the boy's military ambition, so lacking in Philip, but he, too, worried about his arrogance and lack of respect for his elders. Mindful of the family failing, or perhaps because he could think of nothing else, Charles bade them keep the boy away from women, and went on his way. Carlos liked his grandfather, but his own behaviour did not improve for long. Not long afterwards and in desperation, his governor and Juana wrote to the Emperor, asking him to take the boy into his care, and to teach him some discipline, but by this time Charles was dying, and he refused. Carlos was fourteen when Philip returned to Spain, already apprehensive as to what he had sired.

If Carlos was a difficult son, Philip proved a disastrous father. Unlike Charles, he made no allowances for people's differentness. Two stories illustrate the contrast. Philip, as a boy, had a great friend, Ruy Gomez, the son of one of his mother's Portuguese ladies. One day, Ruy Gomez got into a fight with a page, and, when Philip tried to intervene, Gomez accidentally felled him with his fist. Although it was a childish affair, Charles was furious, and sentenced Ruy Gomez to death. No-one could strike the Infante unpunished. Philip, however, reacted so hysterically that the Emperor first commuted the sentence, and then granted a full pardon. When, soon after Philip's return to Spain, Carlos had a quarrel with a page and insisted that the boy be hanged, his father did not even bother to investigate the case. Icy with rage, he assumed that Carlos was in the wrong, publicly boxed his ears, and told him not to be so stupid. To be so humiliated by his own father, and before all the court, was a turning point in Carlos's life. From now on, he concluded that if his own father was against him, so would be the court. He began to detect a mockery behind their deference, which incited him to still worse behaviour. If only Philip could have shown him some love. Philip *could* love, but for Carlos he soon felt nothing but shame and disgust. Why had God not granted him a son like his young half-brother, don John of Austria, so handsome and talented, or like his elder sister Marguerite's boy, Alexander Farnese? Still, it was God's will, and he must somehow prepare Carlos to rule half the world. Close supervision and firm handling were needed. If the boy behaved like a child, he must be treated like one until he learned better. Carlos merely learned to hate his father.

In Philip's defence, it must be said that Carlos had some very unattractive characteristics. For instance, he is said to have enjoyed roasting animals alive. Philip, as a keen naturalist, must have found this repulsive but he was once incandescent with rage, when Carlos, in a sulk, galloped one of his favourite horses literally to death. There was also the celebrated occasion when Carlos stunned the whole court by biting the head off a beautiful pet lizard which had nipped the royal finger. Young boys are often cruel to animals, but Carlos did not stop there. His household accounts contain several entries apparently compensating young girls for maltreatment. Still, these were harsh times, and Carlos would not have been the first or the last psychopath to sit on a throne. Much of his worst behaviour may have reflected a need for attention, which his better behaviour failed to attract. This could also explain the gluttony which his ascetic father found so distasteful.

On his return to Spain in 1559, Philip was fêted as a conquering hero. One of the first events held in his honour was the great *auto da fé* in Valladolid, (featured in Act III of the opera). The phrase means 'protestation of faith'. It was applied by the Inquisition to people suspected of non-conformity. They would be made to wear conical hats and yellow robes and were required publicly to renounce all faiths other than the true faith as defined by their inquisitors. Should they refuse, they were liable to a series of barbaric punishments, including being burned alive. Even if they repented, they still did not always escape death, though it would then take a less painful form. The *auto da fé* had been invented as a method of repressing the Moors and the Jews, but once the Reformation started, it was increasingly used against heretics. Four months earlier, a batch had been dealt with in the presence of Juana, Carlos, most of the grandees of Spain, the diplomatic corps and other notables. It had been such a success that the Holy Office had postponed its sequel until the King could be there. It was felt that he would be sure to enjoy it, and he did. Although he does not seem to have attended very many such events himself, he certainly recommended them to friends as a highly enjoyable experience.

According to Llorente, who analysed the Inquisition's records long afterwards, the chief victim of this great occasion was an illustrious nobleman called don Carlos de Seso. As he was led past the King, he shouted, "So this is how you have me burnt!" "Aye," replied the King cheerfully, "and if my son were a heretic like you, I would carry the wood to burn him myself!" Throughout the proceedings, Carlos sat dutifully in the stand beside his aunt, Juana. Altogether, thirteen persons, one corpse and one effigy were burnt. None of them were Flemish, but one, a dominican priest named Dominic de Roxas, had been caught with documents revealing his plan to flee to Flanders. Llorente says that this man was a son of the Marquis de Poza, several members of whose family had been punished at the previous *auto da fé*. The Marquis himself apparently escaped the attention of the Inquisition.

Poza is a shadowy figure, scarcely discernible in the pageant of history. He seems to have been a courtier of some seniority but little weight, but he is undoubtedly the original of the operatic Posa, even though they do not resemble each other. Elizabeth's biographer, Martha Freer, suggests that he would have been totally forgotten but for a scandal. One night, Poza was caught climbing out of the window of one of Elizabeth's maids-of-honour. According to Freer, he paid with his life, not on the scaffold, but meanly in an arranged assassination in the street, though this is contradicted by a report that he was a pall-bearer at Elizabeth's funeral. Later, Philip's enemies, seeking evidence of his hand in Elizabeth's death, suggested that there was more to Poza's story than met the eye. Vischard de Saint-Réal, writing in the seventeenth century, created the myth that Poza was a secret boyhood friend of Carlos, and was caught acting as his go-between to Elizabeth. Schiller, who used Vischard as an important source, then endowed Poza with the political ideals which make him a key character in the drama, which he certainly was not in real life.[1] The real Poza would surely be amazed by his operatic alter ego. He was not at the *auto da fé* to see his wretched son burnt. Nor was Elizabeth, who had not yet reached Spain.

While historians have disagreed about almost everything to do with Philip, so respected in Spain, so hated elsewhere, his third queen, Elizabeth, is a rarity. All are unanimous that she was beautiful, sweet-natured, conscientious, intelligent and queenly. No wonder even Verdi had to struggle to bring such a paragon to life. To become queen of a great country was the highest destiny a princess could hope for, and Elizabeth accepted it unquestioningly, but not without apprehension. Her marriage ceremony to Philip's proxy, the gloomy Duke of Alba, and Philip's own austere reputation, must have added to her misgivings at leaving a French court, so full of sunshine and pleasure. Spain had for so long been France's chief enemy, and its court was said to be a formal, gloomy and bigoted place, where intrigue meant something other than flirtation. Furthermore, Spain had a very bad record for mal-treating its queens.

But Elizabeth was a girl of high courage, and she knew her duty. Barely sixteen when she left home, she was determined to play her role well, both as the wife of Philip and step-mother of his difficult son, and as the loyal daughter of her own mother, Catherine de Medici. She would be worthy of her Spanish subjects' love, and yet use her influence to the benefit of France. It is witness to her gifts how well she could combine such potentially conflicting roles, while retaining the trust of all concerned. Her method was simple. She did everything quite openly, so that no-one burdened her with secrets or involved her in intrigue. In the court of Spain this was refreshing, and all the more remarkable in that Philip himself set such a contrary example. He regarded dissimulation as the essence of kingship. He once told Elizabeth that "when great princes openly assert their resolve to do such and such things, their secret resolve is to do nothing; or the very opposite." As a result, no-one trusted Philip, of whom they used to say, "His dagger follows close on his smile." One reason for Philip's contempt for Carlos was the latter's total inability to keep a secret. Ruy Gomez once said of him that "to think was to speak." Elizabeth also spoke her thoughts, but hers were intelligent and worth hearing, while Carlos's all too often were not.

At first, Philip does not seem to have realised what a pearl he had married. No boyish eagerness this time, he let Elizabeth progress slowly from the border at Irun, before meeting her for the first time at Guadalajara, not far from Madrid. There, when at her first sight of him she could find nothing apt to say, he said angrily, "What are you staring at? To see if I have grey hairs?" This celebrated moment is recalled in Philip's soliloquy in Act IV of the opera. *"Je la revois encore, regardant en silence mes cheveux blancs, le jour qu'elle arriva de France."* In fact, on that day, Philip was still only thirty-three and in the prime of life though, of course, that can seem old to a girl of sixteen. They were married in Guadalajara on 2nd February, 1560.

Elizabeth's first months in Spain were much bedevilled by the squabbling of her ladies. There was fierce rivalry between her French companions and the Spanish ladies appointed by Philip. Initially, the chief of these was an old battle-axe called the Countess of Uruena, for whom the French were no match. At first Elizabeth was at a loss to know how to resolve their hatreds without hurting anyone's feelings, but when she heard that the King was becoming irritated, she sent back all of her Frenchwomen but three, whose status at court was too low to threaten her Spanish ladies' pride. There is no mention in history, nor even in Schiller's play, of the Countess d'Aremburg of the opera. By the time of the main events in the opera, Uruena had been replaced by the equally formidable Duchess of Alba, who was assisted by Princess Eboli. As chief lady-in-waiting, Eboli was the keeper of the keys to all Elizabeth's locks, including her jewel case, an arrangement which may have caused some mischief in real life, as it does in the opera.

It was typical of Elizabeth to dispense with her French ladies. She had made up her mind to become a good Spaniard, and she could see that she must let go of her native land. She soon spoke fluent Spanish with an engaging accent, and refused to speak French, unless it was the only common language. She adopted the heavy Spanish fashions, and abandoned the frivolous blond wigs then in favour in France. She was soon as popular in Spain as she had been in France. Elizabeth de la Paix became Isabella de la Paz.

There is no doubt that Philip loved her and she him. His self-pity in the opera is not justified by the historical evidence. Most women seem to have found him easy to love, discovering, per-haps, that a little tenderness soon melted his austerity. Some of his letters give us a glimpse of this gentle Philip, especially those writ-ten, much later on, to the two daughters Elizabeth bore him, who were always his favourite children. Elizabeth must soon have found the key for she wrote joyfully to her mother: "Philip is so good a husband and renders me so happy by his attentions that it would make the dullest spot in the world agreeable to me."

After the wedding, Elizabeth's stamina was severely tested by a series of welcoming ceremonies, which became steadily more splendid and demanding as she approached the heart of the nation. Her entry into Toledo required her to remain in the saddle for nine hours. It was there that she first met Carlos, standing with his aunt Juana to greet her on the steps of the Alcazar. He had been too ill to attend her wedding. Philip, watching her entry from a window, did not appreciate the strain he was putting on her. As soon as the last ceremony was over, she fell desperately ill with smallpox. Philip was distraught and hardly left her bedside. It was the first of many such vigils. Throughout her short life in Spain she was dogged by illness, provoking fussy letters from her mother, full of nostrums, recipes for cordials and much old wives' lore. Catherine was forever urging her to send for French doctors, and Elizabeth would probably have done so, had she not known what offence it would cause. Spanish doctors at that time were particularly terrifying.

Contrary to the opera, Carlos was initially anything but wel-coming to her. He appreciated that his security as heir apparent would be undermined if the King had another, more engaging son. Indeed, he must have known his father well enough to realise that in such an event it might be more than his inheritance that he would lose. He saw his young step-mother, therefore, as a threat, and he warned her that if she ever had a son he would hate both of them. Not long after her arrival, he was sent off to the university of Alcalá, with don John and Alexander Farnese, to see if study in the company of manly young relatives would help him to develop. Problem children are seldom improved by the example of better behaved children, and it seems to have been a quarrelsome time. Carlos's only counter to their superior intelligence and athleticism was constantly to remind them that he would one day be their king, which must indeed have had a sobering effect on them.

A few months after his arrival at Alcalá, a great misfortune occurred, which ended Carlos's university career and changed his life. He was hurrying downstairs one evening, apparently to keep an assignation with the daughter of one of the gardeners, when he missed his footing, fell and knocked himself out. He was found unconscious. At first the damage seemed minor, but, after about ten days, his head began to swell to elephantine size. He became feverish, fell into a coma, and none of the bleedings and potions of the local doctors had any effect. The King rushed to Alcalá to be with his son, and sent for a celebrated French surgeon, Dr Vesale, who trepanned Carlos, but with no immediate benefit. It was decided, in desperation, to try Fra Diego de Alcalá. Fra Diego was a saintly Franciscan of the neighbourhood who, after a blameless life, had died some considerable time before.[2] His remains were exhumed, and laid beside the unconscious Prince, over whose face they draped the shroud. The fever began to abate. Those present, apart from Vesale, had no doubt that they were witnessing a miracle. The Prince himself was later convinced of it. But alas, it was only a partial miracle. The recovery was not complete. From this point on, his malarial attacks became more frequent and more serious. Worse still, his behaviour became even more eccentric and violent. The court was soon rife with gossip of the Prince rampaging through the streets at night with a few cronies, insulting the citizens and molesting their women. There were other more laughable stories.

There was a Genoese money lender, Grimaldo, who, having loaned the Prince 1500 ducats, sought to withdraw gracefully from his presence, saying that all he had was at the Prince's disposal. Carlos called him back at once, and said that, in that case, he would have it all, or at least 100,000 ducats. In vain did Grimaldo protest that it was but a figure of speech, a compliment. Eventually Philip's friend, Ruy Gomez, had to intervene and Grimaldo was dismissed with the advice "not to bandy compliments with princes". Less fortunate was Carlos's bootmaker. It was the fashion at that time for young bucks to wear huge boots, and Carlos had to have a pair bigger than anyone else's. The King heard about it, and privately modified the Prince's instructions, but when the diminished boots were delivered, Carlos flew into a rage, and forced the man to eat them. Other incidents were more worrying. He tried to kill several members of his household staff whose conduct had in some way irritated him, and on one occasion tried to stab Diego de Espinosa, the Grand Inquisitor, who had banned from court an actor called Cisnero, a particular favourite with Carlos. In vain, the kneeling prelate begged for mercy. Luckily, members of the Prince's own household heard the commotion and intervened. To be thus attacked by the Infante of Spain put the victim into a dilemma, since to defend oneself too well could be as fatal as not well enough.

Diego de Espinosa was the second of two Grand Inquisitors who held office during the period covered by the opera, but he was in office when the crisis came concerning Carlos. Theoretically he is the one that we see in the King's study in Act IV, but he was neither very old nor blind. Nor was he such an awe inspiring character. Inquisitors in Spain owed their appointment to the King, not to the Pope, who mistrusted an institution whose aims were more political than religious. It deserved its horrible reputation, but it was successful in a way, since Spain was spared the horrors of the Thirty Years War.

As Grand Inquisitor, Espinosa was a member of the Council of the State and an important adviser to the King, but he did not have the influence over him implied in the opera. Some time after the death of Carlos, Philip discovered that Espinosa had deliberately misled him about a matter of state. Quite out of character, he lost his temper so violently that Espinosa actually died during the night. Presumably his heart failed at the wrath of a King of whom they were wont to say, "God keep you from his too great kindness."

Although very devout, Philip does not seem to have been in awe of any of his Spanish clergy, but unlike Charles, whose army once sacked Rome, he did venerate the Pope, and value his good opinion. Carlos was also devout, and there is no reliable evidence that he regarded Protestantism with anything but enmity and fear.

Carlos did not return to Alcalá after his recovery. Resuming his life at court, he began to get to know Elizabeth better. He soon lost his distrust of her. Here at last was someone who offered him sympathy and friendship, someone who did not patronise him or sneer at him behind his back, who did not always assume him to be wrong. While totally loyal to Philip, she did not feed his dislike of Carlos with tittle-tattle, but sought rather to heal the rift between them, just as she does in the opera. Carlos soon found her apartment to be the most congenial place in the court, and spent much time there. Usually, his aunt Juana would be present as well, for she also became a close friend of the Queen, but sometimes he was with Elizabeth alone and in private, as far as a Queen is allowed privacy. The French ambassador reported that he often came upon them sitting together "engaged in earnest conversation". One of her ladies wrote to Catherine de Medici that "the Prince loves the Queen singularly well and – as I suspect – would have no objection to be more closely related to her."

Carlos certainly became devoted to Elizabeth, and allowed himself, out loud and in public, to regret that his father had robbed him of such a wife. He quite abandoned his fear that she would have children to rival him, declaring that if she had any, he would want to share his inheritance with them. He went further, writing her sonnets in French. His chosen form was the *dixaine*, containing ten lines each of ten feet. Carlos's poems are rather clumsy, but are not entirely devoid of wit or of genuine feeling. One is addressed to Elizabeth's parrot.

> *If only, happy parrot, you were able*
> *To tell her of my fondness and desire,*
> *To let her know through inoffensive babble*
> *How passion is consuming in its fire*
> *The dutifulness which she should inspire.*
> *She would vouchsafe more willingly her ear*
> *If it was you that told of my despair,*
> *Than if the truth depended on my word.*

Don Carlos

So listen, parrot, to my earnest prayer.
Speak on my behalf, for you are heard.[3]

He was also quite skilful in the way he reveals his own feelings without compromising her. He seems quite reckless in his disregard for his own safety. He scarcely bothers to disguise his hatred for his father.

> *Since talking, Madame, is itself an easement*
> *For my sharp pain, I mean to break the silence*
> *And tell you of my jealousy and torment,*
> *No way assuaged because I have shown patience.*
> *You, to whom a friendship's not pretence,*
> *I ask you only show me some compassion*
> *And listen to my tale of desperation*
> *Because a wretch is causing me distress,*
> *A man who so delights in defamation,*
> *That he is quite unworthy of our grace.*[4]

Not many people can write poems or even make jokes in foreign tongues. Philip certainly could not do so. Carlos's sonnets are quite an achievement. History's verdict that he was a nincompoop and unfit to reign was probably right, but there are details in his story which imply that he was not totally inadequate. His poetry is one of them.

It is striking that no contemporaries, least of all Philip, harboured any anxieties about Elizabeth's relations with Carlos, but there were probably many reasons why she was trusted, not least the openness of her character, and her obvious devotion to Philip. Some intimacy with Carlos was only to be expected in a rigid court, where royals could only be familiar with other royals. Elizabeth, while able to project a queenly gravity in public, was still quite a child. She delighted in childish games like knucklebones, loved to dance, and even to play with dolls when in private. She really needed a playmate, and who better than her rather backward stepson of the same age? Furthermore, both the King and the court must have been heartily thankful, that here, at last was someone who had succeeded where all others had failed. Elizabeth had an almost miraculous influence on Carlos, and, while she was near to advise and calm him, he behaved well. She herself, not without some pride, once told the French ambassador that "he cannot be more obedient and well disposed than he now is. Although it is true that he despises and ridicules the actions of the King, his father, and finds fault with all that Madame la Princesse [Juana] and the little princes of Hungary can say or do,[5] yet he approves of all my actions; and this without dissimulation or artifice on his part, for he knows not how to feign." Probably the real reason why no-one was suspicious was that it never occurred to anyone that Elizabeth could possibly feel attracted to or want to flirt with someone quite so unprepossessing.

Coello's portrait does not actually make Carlos look unprepossessing, but to do so might have been unwise. It shows us an immature person, uncertain, even timid in bearing and unable to carry his clothes, more likely to inspire motherly feelings in a woman than love. Even then it is a little flattering, if we are to believe contemporary writers. One vivid description will suffice. It was sent by the Austrian ambassador to his sovereign, Ferdinand, Philip's uncle, who was considering Carlos for his granddaughter Anne. The ambassador had every reason to weigh his words carefully.

> In many ways he is intelligent but in others shows less understanding than a child of seven. He asks questions continually but without discrimination as if from habit. He shows little ambition and his only enthusiasm seems to be eating where his excesses are said to be the cause of his sickly condition. Not entirely bad-looking, his head is nondescript, his brow low, his chin extremely long and his skin pallid. He is not broadshouldered and lacks height. One shoulder is a little higher than the other and his back a little humped. His chest is narrow and his legs weak, the left one being longer than the right. His voice is thin and wheedling. He stammers and has problems with his 'l's and 'r's. Still, he manages to make himself understood. He is violent, irritable to the point of fury and many people wonder what might happen if he was out of control. Still, he is extremely pious, fond of trustworthy, honest people and is very generous. In short, Don Carlos is a frail and feeble minded prince but, on the other hand, he is the son of a powerful monarch.

Nevertheless, Elizabeth was clearly fond of him, and was not alone in that. Juana too, though he distrusted her, never lost her affection for him. He did appeal to women, and to people who were close to him, like his personal staff. Perhaps they were touched by his very childishness and vulnerability. Many must have seen how afflicted he was by his father's contempt. Elizabeth certainly wanted desperately to reconcile them, which was unselfish of her, since only Carlos stood between her own children and the throne. And she obviously realised how important she had become to him. The trouble was that she could not always be near and then, without her to soothe him, the threshold of his impatience would fall rapidly, and he would react violently to the slightest check. It was when she was away that his follies were at their worst. If only Honorate Juan could have been there to supplement her efforts, but he, alas, was dead.

The King had given the main responsibility for Carlos to his childhood friend, Ruy Gomez. Their friendship had continued into adulthood, and Gomez was now the King's closest adviser and chief minister. Philip had given him a beautiful, rich and noble wife, Ana de Mendoza, and a Neapolitan title, Prince of Eboli. Gomez was a subtle, charming and infinitely talented courtier, but Carlos hated him as his father's spy, aided and abetted by his fiery little princess. Now that he was nearly twenty, Carlos found it extremely humiliating to have to have a mentor at all, and to have no responsibilities himself. At his age, Philip was already ruling Spain as regent.

When Carlos was nineteen, Philip did try to give him some responsibility, making him chairman of the Council of State. Alas, it did not work. Carlos seems to have tried hard, but could not cope with the complexity and diversity of the discussions, and began to suspect that, notwithstanding their deference, the other members were not taking him seriously. Their position was extremely tricky since Carlos always intemperately opposed whatever Philip wanted. By this time, he was no more able to be fair towards his father than his father was towards him. The council had no doubt on which side their own safety lay. Carlos's reaction was to give up trying, and to become childish and disruptive. His appointment had to be rescinded, which added to his humiliation and frustration. The King reconfirmed Eboli's stewardship, and forbade him to leave Madrid, telling him that "if you do not keep an eye on him at all times, he might not be where you left him when you get back." Eboli moved with his wife into apartments adjacent to those of the Prince. He told the French ambassador that this task would now continue until Carlos married, "after which his wife will take care of him". The selection of a suitable wife for Carlos now became one of the two main preoccupations of the King and his council. The other was the growing crisis in Flanders. These two issues also dominated Carlos's scattered thoughts. For him, they represented two possible escape routes from the hated court.

Despite his eccentricities, there was no shortage of candidates for Carlos's hand. His aunt and former guardian, Juana, pressed her own suit strongly. Being much older than the Prince, she presumably saw herself not so much as his wife but more as a fond queen mother, ruling Spain through him. The Castilian Cortes [parliament], fearful lest he should fall under the influence of a foreigner, strongly supported her. They passed a motion to this effect which enraged Carlos. For him, marriage to Juana meant continued tutelage. Uninvited, he burst into their chamber, and told them, in quite unprincely language, to mind their own business. The King had some difficulty calming them down again. There were several foreign candidates for Carlos's hand. An early favourite was Mary Queen of Scots, but the chance was lost through Philip's procrastination. Meanwhile, Elizabeth was promoting the cause of her younger sister Marguerite. Carlos himself set his heart on his cousin, the Archduchess Anne of Austria. It may seem strange that so many should want so unstable a prince for a consort, but much can be forgiven the heir to half the world. Indeed, an ambitious woman may see feeblemindedness as an asset in a rich husband.

The leading candidate was Anne. Her grandfather Ferdinand was strongly in favour, and so, in principle, was Philip. He hesitated, however. For one thing, Ferdinand would expect him to give the newlyweds a country to rule over, probably Flanders. It was an open secret that Ferdinand not only disagreed with Philip's bigoted approach to Flanders, but also suspected that Carlos was not as bad as Philip made out. Philip was unwilling to give any of his lands away, least of all to Carlos. Furthermore, he was beginning to wonder whether Carlos was fit for marriage. Once married, he would be less easy to control. Philip's own father had had problems enough with rebels exploiting his mad mother Juana. He did not intend to let anyone use Carlos in the same way. So he procrastinated, driving his son further into despair.

The young man's hopes began to turn therefore to the other possibility, a role in the struggle for Flanders. Things were going from bad to worse. Exasperated by Philip's interference, Marguerite of Parma, Philip's half-sister and regent in Flanders, had sent him a bitter letter of resignation: "You have shown no regard for my wishes or reputation. By your extraordinary restrictions, you have prevented my settling the country in the way I believe it should have been." Carlos was not alone in his frustrations, but at least Philip had not tried to regulate what size of boots Marguerite wore.

Faced with these dilemmas, the King formed a plan to go himself to Flanders. He announced that he would take his son with him, probably to avoid having to make him his regent in Spain, but Carlos did not mind why. The prospect enthralled him. He would get away from court, and start to see the world. Perhaps he might even get the chance to show what he could do in battle. Ponderous preparations for the expedition were put in hand, but no date was set, and soon Philip's ability to procrastinate began to show itself once again.

To be fair, there were real problems. One was the choice of a regent in his absence. Having discounted Carlos, his second choice should have been the Queen. She was very young however and after all, French. Furthermore she was pregnant again, and her health was anything but robust. On the other hand Elizabeth made it clear that, much as she liked Juana, she would feel slighted if made subject to her. Rather than choose, the King decided he would do nothing until after the Queen's confinement, which was still some months away. The knowing winked at each other and sniggered. They had never believed the King would go. It was not his style to lead from the front. He was only happy at the centre of his web, poring over the despatches, writing his notes in the margin, talking with his secretaries far into the night, and holding back his governors from doing what they wanted and ought to be doing. Not a detail, throughout his vast empire, was too small for his interference.

As the months went by, the French envoy, Chantennay, wrote to Catherine de Medici: "Everything goes on from tomorrow to tomorrow, the only resolution is to remain irresolute. The King will allow matters to become so entangled in the Low Countries that if he should ever visit them, he will find it easier to conform to the state of affairs than to mend it. The lords are more kings than the King himself. It seems impossible that Philip should ever conduct himself like a man." Meanwhile, Carlos was putting it more wittily. "My father deems," he said, "that the Emperor journeyed sufficiently for himself and his son. The King therefore reposes now both for the Emperor and his own pleasure."

When, in 1567, the forbidding Duke of Alba was appointed to Flanders, it was clear that Philip, whatever he might say, had no intention of going himself. Carlos exploded with anger. When Alba came to take his leave, Carlos flew at him with a dagger shouting, "Don't go to Flanders or I'll kill you." The old warrior fended him off without too much difficulty, but it was a sad relapse in the boy's behaviour. In his bitter disappointment, Carlos now wrote a satirical book called *The Great Journeys of King Philip II*. Each chapter dealt with one such journey:

Chapter One. Madrid to el Pardo.
Chapter Two. El Pardo to el Escorial.
Chapter Three. El Escorial to Aranjuez.

and so on, each chapter recounting a famous journey, crisscrossing Madrid from one palace to another, in the most boringly domestic manner. In it, the King does not even venture as far as St Yuste, where so much of the opera takes place. In this Carlos was unjust. The King quite often went to that part of Spain, where the hunting was good, and where he believed the climate would suit the Queen's health.

Martha Freer relates that Carlos produced this book on an impulse one day in the Queen's apartments having first embarrassed her and everyone present by the virulence of his comments about his father. One of those in attendance was the chief lady-in-waiting, Eboli. The Queen was in the act of reading Carlos's book, with some amusement, when a message was brought that the King was unwell. She at once dropped it, and went to him. Carlos followed, but first prudently locked the manuscript away in a cupboard. The Princess of Eboli did not follow, but taking her duplicate key, extracted the incriminating paper, and had a copy made, which she was able to lock in the cupboard before Elizabeth discovered the theft. It cannot have been a very long book. Eboli gave it to her husband, and he duly passed it to the King. The Queen, unaware that she had been compromised, burnt the copy at the first opportunity, without looking carefully at it. Not all historians repeat this story of Eboli's mischief-making, and Freer does not imply that it was due to jealousy, as is her theft of the jewel box in the opera. Nor was the outcome so disastrous. The King already knew how his son openly vilified him, and must have realised what a blow he had dealt him in sending Alba to Flanders.

Carlos's unconcealed rage naturally fuelled the subsequent rumours that he favoured the Flemish cause. While he automatically opposed his father on all matters great and small, there is no hard evidence that he had any sympathy for the Flemish, and certainly not that he had any contact with their emissaries, whose mission to Madrid was already delicate enough. Constantly under surveillance, they would have been mad to confide in so indiscreet a prince. Throughout the whole affair of his arrest and death, no-one accused Carlos of heresy, although, according to Llorente, the Holy Office did doubt his fitness for power, as did many people. All the evidence is that he was extremely pious, and believed that the Dutch heresy should be stamped out. The likely truth, given his taste for such things, is that he simply wanted to do a bit of stamping himself. Of course, had he ever been put in authority in Flanders with Anne of Austria at his side, he might well have proved putty in the rebels' hands, and turned to rebellion himself. That might have saved a deal of misery, but Philip never intended to let him go, except under his own supervision.

With both legitimate escape routes now blocked by his father, Carlos in desperation began to plan his own get-away. It is not clear exactly where he intended to go. It might have been Flanders, but more probably it was Vienna, to plight his troth to Anne. He knew that there was much sympathy felt for him in that court, and little for his father. His plans seem to have been extraordinarily inept, but one must remember that he had neither authority nor friends. Even so, to start by confiding his escape plan to his father's most intimate friend, the Prince of Eboli, seems a little extraordinary. He also wrote to a number of Spanish lords, requesting their financial support for "an enterprise he had in mind". He invited don John, recently appointed Grand Admiral, to flee with him, or, failing that, to put a flotilla at his disposal. He tried to organise horses for his escape through the Director of Postal Relays. If ever he needed a Posa or even an Honorate Juan, it was now. Aware of his desperation, however, even the Queen became cautious, insisting that the Duchess of Alba be present whenever he paid a visit. There is something heartrending in these naive plottings, all of which were naturally reported to the King, and quietly frustrated.

Sensing what was happening, Carlos became ever more pathologically suspicious. One day, after don John had been to see the King, Carlos suspected him of spying and flew at him with a knife, but don John was able to defend himself. Things came to a head when Carlos asked his confessor to absolve him from the sin of wanting to kill a man. The priest refused to absolve him, unless he said who it was. Carlos would not do so, which precipitated a crisis. Unabsolved, Carlos could not receive communion, but publicly not to do so would have triggered all manner of dangerous speculation, linking him perhaps with the Reformation. Carlos suggested that the problem could be solved by giving him an unconsecrated wafer, but this only put the Holy Office into an even greater state. Amazingly, it does not seem to have occurred to him simply to dissimulate. He was made to discuss his problem with ever more eminent divines, until one wormed out of him the fact that the object of his hatred was, indeed his own father. Philip decided it was time to act.

Even so, this wary man spent a fortnight wrestling with the problem by himself at el Escorial. Despite his abhorrence for Carlos, he clearly found it hard to act against his own blood, and to destabilise the clear succession to the throne. Furthermore, he was not absolutely sure how his subjects would accept the arrest and imprisonment of the Infante, who was not unpopular. Internationally too, he could expect much suspicion if not condemnation, since all the world knew how the two men hated each other, but not all felt that Carlos was to blame. Eventually, on 18th January, 1568, he returned to Madrid, and assembled the key members of his Council, including the Grand Inquisitor, Eboli and Lerma. He addressed them at some length concerning his anxieties regarding the Prince, and his decision that, like the Emperor's mother, Juana *la Loca*, he must be taken into custody for his own good and that of his peoples. They agreed.

Some reports say that while all this was going on the unsuspecting Carlos was playing cards with his stepmother, but this is unlikely. Carlos was not entirely stupid; he knew that he was in danger, and that his father had returned to Madrid, and called his Council. In various naive ways, he had tried to see to his own safety. He had arranged for his bedchamber to be protected by a most elaborate series of locks, and he had secreted in it quite an armoury of loaded weapons. Philip, whose tentacles reached everywhere, had procured from the locksmith a key which rendered the whole system inoperative, and he knew exactly where all the weapons were. Even so, Philip took no chances. He donned full armour, and collected a posse of pikemen before proceeding with his companions to the Prince's chambers. There, he sent the other lords in ahead to surround the sleeping Prince and seize his weapons. Philip then entered to confront him. Carlos woke.[6]

"Who is there?" he asked

Philip: "It is the Council of State."

Carlos: "What does your Majesty want of me?"

Philip: "You will soon learn."

He then instructed Lerma to remove everything from the apartment which Carlos could use to do himself a mischief, and "to guard him well, serving him with proper respect but executing none of his orders without first referring them to me."

"Your Majesty had better kill me than keep me prisoner," said Carlos. "It will be a great scandal. If you don't kill me, I will do away with myself."

"You will do no such thing," replied Philip. "That would be the act of a madman."

Carlos: "Your Majesty treats me so that I am forced to this extremity. I am not mad but you drive me to despair."

The King left without bandying any more words. He never spoke to his son again.

From this point on, Carlos disappears from view. He is guarded

constantly by a watch of lords, instructed to discuss only triviali-
ties with him. He is allowed no dangerous implement. His food is
cut up for him. He is allowed to read only religious works. He is
permitted no sight of the outside world, nor contact with those
living in it other than his gaolers. Eboli had one of the walls of
Carlos's room removed and replaced by a lattice, the better to
observe him. Juana and Elizabeth, distraught at this turn of
events, were told brusquely by the King that they were not
allowed to visit him. Don John, who had put on mourning, was
told to take it off. Philip was evidently at pains to consign all that
concerned his son to oblivion. Perhaps this was a cover for his
own hurt, but he also appears to have been nervous of an uprising
such as occurs in the opera, and wanted to stifle gossip. In real life,
no disorder took place.

Philip stopped all couriers leaving Spain until he had written
personally to all the crowned heads of Europe to explain what he
had done, but his letters were so elliptical and obscure, that they
merely increased the mystery. It is natural in any family with a history of madness, let alone a royal one, not to use the word if it can
be avoided, but Philip's lack of frankness simply increased suspicion, and made some of the recipients extremely angry. The Pope
insisted on a proper explanation, and Philip sent him one in code,
the contents of which have never come to light. All the letters made
it clear, however, that his son's detention was not a punishment
with a term, but an indefinite custody related to his unstable condition. The truth is that Europe was shocked, but not surprised.

Philip next proceeded to organise a secret trial of his son *in
absentia*. His aim was probably to prepare evidence to justify the
formal disinheritance of the heir. The papers relating to the trial do
not produce any evidence that Carlos supported the Flemish
rebellion, nor that he had had improper relations with the Queen.
Amongst the papers seized in Carlos's room there had been nothing more incriminating than a list of those he hated and wished to
kill, and of those he loved. The King, Alba and the Prince and
Princess of Eboli figured amongst the condemned. His Aunt Juana
and his stepmother, the Queen, were amongst those he loved.

All these legalities were overtaken six months later when Carlos
obliged by dying in prison. This aroused tremendous speculation.

The King was naturally suspected of murder. It would not have been his first nor his last. The murder hypothesis gained added weight, because Carlos died within days of achieving reconciliation with the Church, and being allowed, against Philip's wishes, to receive communion. Philip's weird logic might well have seen this as paving the way for a murder, which he would have hesitated over while his son lacked absolution.

The King was away from Madrid during Carlos's last days, which was why the young man was able to compose himself enough to take communion. Carlos's excitability rose and fell in relation to his father's proximity. The French ambassador reported that, "after this act [the taking of communion] the prince was gentle and tractable; very joyous was the news of this alteration to those who desire the prince's freedom; they deducing therefrom that the said prince has not a defective intellect and want of common discretion which the King his father and others assert." The ambassador goes on to speculate that the Prince's imprisonment had been directly the consequence of his failure to take communion, and necessary "to remove the impression on the minds of some persons, principally of the reformed party, who publish everywhere that the said prince appertains to their sect; which is false as he, on the contrary, bears them mortal hatred." Finally the ambassador discounts any likelihood that Carlos will be released. "In truth, there remains not the slightest hope that he will ever become wise or worthy to succeed to these realms, as his capacity becomes day by day more defective."

Self-neglect was a much more probable cause of Carlos's death than murder. His erratic eating habits, swinging from binge to fasting and back, seem to have grown more extravagant in prison. Whenever he felt feverish, which was often, he would send for quantities of ice in which to immerse himself. No-one sought to restrain these follies, and Carlos was almost certainly killed by reckless self-abuse.

Rumours of foul play redoubled when his stepmother, Elizabeth, also died three months later. Some said it was of a broken heart, and there is no doubt that she had been terribly upset by the final breakdown between Philip and Carlos, and by the latter's fate. She took no pleasure from the consequence that a child of hers seemed likely to succeed. "My esteem for him," she wrote to the French ambassador on the day after his arrest, "and the pain the King feels at having to distrain him have affected me so much that I fear I cannot express my feelings adequately. I could not feel for my stepson's misfortunes more, were he my own son. If I desired to see him, it was to do a service but God has willed that he should show himself as he is, to my great regret." The ambassador added "The Queen is in grief and tears for love of the two of them." The King had to order her to stop her weeping.

Stories that she had been murdered were inevitable, given Philips' reputation in such matters, but they were more prevalent abroad than at home. At the time, however, even Philip's greatest enemies did not connect her death with an illicit love for Carlos. William of Orange, among the first to accuse Philip of her murder, linked it to political expediency. He suggested that Philip needed her out of the way, so that he could strengthen his relations with Austria by marrying his niece, Anne. Most of the stories originated later from the poisoned pen of Antonio Perez, one of Philips' confidential secretaries, who became disaffected and one of his greatest traducers. After his exile, Perez promulgated a long, sensational and easily disproved story, that Elizabeth was forced to take poison in the King's presence. It is all quite unbelievable, but it was in due course promulgated further by writers such as Vischard de Saint-Réal.

The truth is surely much simpler. Still only twenty-two, Elizabeth was brought to her fourth childbirth in as many years in the autumn of 1568. Add to her depression over Carlos the ignorant attentions of the Spanish doctors, who bled every patient white whatever their ailment, and it is easy to conclude that the Queen died of a miscarriage, aggravated by debilitation and exhaustion. The French ambassador was in constant and anxious attendance throughout the Queen's last days, and his evidence rules out any question of foul play. This did not stop gossips like Brantôme from spreading their own version of affairs, but they loved to complicate simple solutions. Women died in childbirth all too often in the sixteenth century.

The King never left Elizabeth's bedside, and when she died, he, who never showed his emotions, wept copiously. He retired into a retreat for a month to mourn her, seeing no-one except the French ambassador, and him only once. Everything about his behaviour, then and subsequently, would lead us to believe that her death ended that part of his life which most nearly approximated to happiness. Her two daughters seem thereafter to have been his principle source of joy. If he contributed to Elizabeth's death, it was probably by ignoring his father's advice against overdoing marital sex.

While the Marquis de Poza is rather a vague figure, that other key manipulator in the opera, the Princess Eboli is not. Whether or not she did steal Carlos's book from Elizabeth's cupboard, it surely was not through frustrated love for him. When Carlos was still a backward fourteen, Eboli started a series of pregnancies that must have left her little time and energy for adultery. Between 1559 and her husband's death in 1573, she bore him nine children. What is more credible is the rumour, again vouched for by Perez, that the eldest of these was by the King, having fair hair and somewhat Hapsburg features. If true, it was probably with her husband's connivance. This most polished of courtiers knew when to yield. He admitted to losing deliberately to the King at cards. Why not at love too? After all, it was the King who had obtained this illustrious wife for him. It would have been consistent with her character to have welcomed the King as a lover, but not Carlos. With his unprepossessing looks, his low standing at court and his inability to keep his mouth shut, Carlos would have been the last person she would have chosen.

Born in 1540, Princess Eboli was an heiress of the rich Mendoza family. The King arranged her marriage in 1553 to his favourite, Ruy Gomez, to provide him with wealth and status. Although many years her senior, he was well able to keep her under control. As chief lady-in-waiting, she was close to the Queen, but never one of her especial confidantes. She may have gained her place on Carlos's list of enemies simply by association with her husband, but she had a natural talent as a busybody. He must have had plenty of opportunities to get to know her when the Ebolis were living in the apartment next to his. She was not at all a gentle or sympathetic character. After her husband died, she gave ample evidence that she was easy to hate.

Small and beautiful, though with a patch over one eye[7], the Princess had an ambitious and volatile temperament. She loved to be at the centre of things at court, married to the King's closest friend. His death threatened her with an obscure future as a widow, raising her nine children on her family estate at Pastrana, near Guadalajara. That, she decided, was not for her. One theatrical gesture followed another. First, she would be a nun, entering the convent she and her husband had founded; but she quarrelled violently with its abbess, St Teresa, and eventually the nuns could stand her no longer, and walked out. So she returned to court, and started a liaison with Antonio Perez, which led to the downfall of them both. Perez had been one of the King's three confidential secretaries, and a protégé of Prince Eboli. Having some of his subtlety and charm, he partly inherited Eboli's position of influence with the King, becoming his chief minister. However, he had none of Eboli's loyalty and steadiness. He was soon plunging into every sort of intrigue, with the discontented Princess as his accomplice. It was strongly asserted that they were lovers, but this was never proven. One witness said he had caught them in a compromising situation, but he was murdered soon afterwards, and it was this murder that was their eventual undoing. The victim's family implacably pursued the truth, until the King was forced to put his minister under house arrest. Perez eventually escaped, and after some hair-raising adventures reached foreign soil. In exile, he prospered for a while, peddling his anti-Philip *canards* in whatever court was disposed to listen, but their value declined as they lost their freshness, and so did his. The Princess fared no better. She was first banished from the court, and then, because of the extravagant existence she started leading in Pastrana, was imprisoned in a room of her own house, and forbidden sight of or access to the outside. *"Ah don fatale!"*

Some two years after Elizabeth's death and with fine irony, Philip took for a second time a bride originally destined for his son. He married the Archduchess Anne of Austria who bore him, at last, a male heir, sound in mind and body if a little degenerate in spirit, who eventually succeeded him as Philip III. Philip III's reign was inglorious, but he is not to be blamed for Spain's decline. The nation had first been bled white by the Emperor's perpetual wars, and then intellectually isolated by the bigotry of Philip II, who so feared the ideas of the Reformation that he caused Spain to turn its back on the cultural development of the rest of Europe. It was a long time before it emerged from this isolation.

Perhaps the tragedy did not belong to don Carlos alone, but to all of Spain. Might-have-beens are a sterile speculation, but, in this case, it is difficult not to wonder how things might have turned out if Mary Tudor had not died just when she did. It is hard to believe that Carlos, with so excellent a queen as Elizabeth "to look after him", could have made a bigger mess of things than his father. It would at any rate have been a different mess. What is certain is that his tragedy was not one of star-crossed love, nor of frustrated idealism, but mostly a catastrophic clash between a "frail and feebleminded prince" and an intolerant father. One day when they were boys, don John and don Carlos were quarrelling. As usual, don John was winning the argument, so, as usual, don Carlos was reduced to pulling rank. "I cannot argue with an inferior," he said. "Your mother was a harlot and you are a bastard." To which John was sufficiently heated to reply, "At any rate my father was a much greater man than yours." Carlos thought he saw a chance to make trouble for him and rushed off to sneak to his father, but to his dismay, Philip merely said, "But don John is right. His father – and mine – was a much greater man than yours."

_____

NOTES

1 Schiller's Posa seems partly based on don John of Austria, an illegitimate son of Charles V and a disreputable woman called Barbara Blomberg. Some time after Carlos's death, and loaded with honour after his victory at Lepanto, don John persuaded Philip to appoint him as Governor of Flanders. It is not certain whether he was cherishing ideas of seceding from Spain, but he was suspected of wanting a crown of his own. It could also well be that he regarded the Dutch heresy less severely than Philip. Whatever the truth, it is certain that he soon afterwards died, very suddenly, very mysteriously and quite young.

Don John was perhaps the person who most nearly could claim to be a boyhood friend of Carlos, although, of course, they did not much like each other. Initially, don John was liked and trusted by the King. His subsequent career, related above, could have inspired the suspicion that all along he had, like Posa, sympathised with the Flemish rebels. He has more in common with Posa than anyone else, but the details of his life were too well known to be adapted to Schiller's dramatic structure.

2 Fra Diego's first miracle had occurred one day when he was distributing bread to the poor. The bread changed itself miraculously into roses, to the astonishment of all and perhaps to the disappointment of the poor.

3 Si vous pouviez, o heureux perroquet
Ma volonté et mon affection
Bien déclarer par votre bon cacquet.
Si vous pouviez dire ma passion
Étant au lieu de ma devotion,
L'on prêteroit plus volontiers l'oreille
À vous disant ma douleur non pareille
Que si moi-même en disoit verité.
Perroquet donc, je vous pris et conseille
Parlez pour moi, puisque este écouté.

4 Puisque parler, Madame, est un allégement
À mon grief mal, je rompray le silence
En vous disant mon envy et tourment
Bien n'a servi ma longue patience,
Vous qui avez d'amitié cognaissance
Vueillez de moi prendre compassion
Et entendez ma déploration;
Car un ingrat cause est de mon souci,
Un homme plein de tant de fictions
Qu'il ne mérite avoir de lui merci!

5 The princes of Hungary were the two sons of Maximilian, King of Hungary, who was the son of Philip's uncle, Ferdinand of Austria. The two princes had been sent to be brought up in the Spanish court. By this time, their parents were trying to get them back, but meeting some resistance from Philip. He was always loath to give away a good card, however come by.

6 The record of this exchange is part of an eye-witness account of the events surrounding the Prince's arrest, written by one of his valets a few days after they occurred. Although widely quoted, not all historians trust this account which, in some other respects, seems to conflict with that of other witnesses. I have used his version of the dialogue because it is fuller and it does not so conflict in any material way.

7 Some historians suggest that Eboli's patch was a feature added later to her persona. Certainly her contemporaries, who often mention her beauty, do not refer to her patch, and it sits awkwardly in the portraits of her, as if it might be an afterthought. On the other hand, it is difficult to understand why it should have been introduced if it has no basis in reality. There is also a separate controversy as to why she wore it. Some say she suffered an eye injury out hunting as a girl, but others say it was merely to hide a disfiguring squint.

LUCIA DI LAMMERMOOR

Gaetano Donizetti

Libretto by Salvatore Cammarano
after Sir Walter Scott

Dramatis Personae

Enrico, *present owner of Ravenswood*
Edgardo, Master of Ravenswood, *son of the former owner of Ravenswood*
Arturo, *a rich laird*
Raimondo, *Chaplain of Ravenswood, Lucia's tutor*
Normanno, *Enrico's steward*
Lucia, *Enrico's sister*
Alisa, *Lucia's companion*

Ashton retainers, wedding guests

Synopsis

BACKGROUND

The drama is set in Scotland during the reign of William and Mary and takes place in the area of Ravenswood Castle, Edgardo's ancestral home in the Lammermoor Hills. Much impoverished as a consequence of the country's troubles, the Ravenswoods have lost most of their property to the Ashtons and are now reduced to Wolf's Crag, a dilapidated old tower on the coast, said to be based on Fast Castle in Berwickshire. A new political shift, however, has given Edgardo hope that the Ashtons may yet be made to return to him his birthright.

ACT ONE

SCENE ONE: The grounds of Ravenswood. An intruder has been seen and Normanno is sending out a search party. Normanno, Raimondo and Enrico stay behind and the latter confides his fears to the others. His fortunes are threatened but could yet be retrieved if only his sister will wed the rich and powerful Arturo Bucklaw, but she refuses. Raimondo suggests that she finds it too soon after the death of her mother but Normanno denies this. He says that regularly at dawn, by the haunted fountain in the forest, she meets a lover and that it is none other than Edgardo Ravenswood, Enrico's bitter enemy. Enrico, furious, resolves to be revenged on both.

SCENE TWO: It is evening and Lucia, with Alisa, is awaiting Edgardo by the haunted fountain. Alisa is alarmed by the possibility of discovery but Lucia insists on adding to her terror by recounting the legend of the fountain, where a former Ravenswood once killed his lover who now haunts the place. Alisa pleads that they leave at once, but Lucia must stay to warn Edgardo that Enrico has discovered their secret. Alisa escapes as soon as Edgardo appears. He brings news of his own. He must go to France on political business but first wants to see Enrico, to ask for her hand and to heal the quarrel between their houses. Lucia persuades him that the time is not right. They exchange rings, plight their troth and promise to write.

ACT TWO

SCENE ONE: Enrico's chambers at Ravenswood. Months have passed. No word of Edgardo has been allowed to reach Lucia. Enrico, whose affairs have been going from bad to worse, has sent for her, determined to force her to accept Arturo, who is already on his way to Ravenswood. To break down her resistance, Enrico has forged a letter from Edgardo, reporting his betrothal to another. He explains his plan to Normanno who is sent off to meet Arturo as soon as Lucia appears. The plan fails however. Enrico pleads his own danger, he accuses her of betraying the family, he threatens her, he brandishes Edgardo's faithlessness but he succeeds only in making her more wretched. In the end, he has to retire defeated but Raimondo takes his place. Lucia trusts Raimondo. When he untruthfully tells her that he is sure that Edgardo received her last letter and has not bothered to reply, her spirit at last breaks. Believing herself abandoned, she consents to marry Arturo. Raimondo exults but Lucia, already showing signs of madness, collapses in utter misery.

SCENE TWO: The wedding guests are all assembled in the great hall, singing joyfully of this new alliance which will save the house of Ashton. Arturo pledges his support. Lucia arrives, weeping and supported by Raimondo and Alisa. Arturo is concerned for her but accepts the explanation that she is still grieving for her mother. All sign the wedding contract. No sooner done than a dishevelled Edgardo bursts into the hall. As he and Enrico furiously confront each other, all the main characters progressively join in a sextet, each expressing as appropriate, anger, astonishment, fear and bitter regret. Swords are drawn but Raimondo intervenes and shows Edgardo the contract. Stunned, he turns on Lucia, cursing her for her faithlessness. The company close threateningly upon him but, declaring his life of no value to him, he throws away his sword. The company divides between those concerned for the swooning bride and those pursuing her retreating lover.

ACT THREE

Scene One: We join Edgardo in his ruined keep at Wolf's Crag to which he has withdrawn but Enrico has followed him. After exchanging insults, the two agree to meet at dawn next day in the Ravenswood cemetery to settle their debts of honour.

Scene Two: Back in the great hall, the guests are happily celebrating when Raimondo appears. Hearing cries from the bridal chamber, he has investigated and found Arturo on the floor in a pool of blood with Lucia crouching beside him, dagger in hand, bloodstained and mad. Lucia soon follows Raimondo into the hall. All shrink back as she moves jerkily to and fro, singing snatches about her former happiness and love. Enrico returns and upbraids her but then he understands and is overwhelmed with remorse. Eventually, Alisa succeeds in leading her away. Raimondo turns on Normanno and curses him for revealing her secret.

Scene Three: Edgardo is awaiting the dawn in his forefathers' cemetery, longing for his adversary's sword to end his misery. But first a band of mourners arrives from the castle with news that Lucia has gone mad for love of him and is dying. A bell in the castle begins to toll and Edgardo starts to go to her but Raimondo appears. She is already dead. Edgardo, praying to her to look down upon him from above, draws his dagger and stabs himself. As his life ebbs away, he sings of his hope soon to be united with her by God.

The World's Wonder

Lucia is based on Janet Dalrymple, who was married on 12th August, 1669, apparently against her will, to David Dunbar the Younger, of Baldoon. Neither lived in the Lammermoors but in Galloway, in the extreme south-west of Scotland. Something went wrong that night, but it is not quite certain what, for those most closely concerned were never willing to discuss it. No-one was killed, but many people suspected that Janet's lover, Archibald, Lord Rutherford, was somehow involved. After the wedding, Janet and Dunbar remained for a fortnight in her parents' house, Carsecreugh on the moors above Glenluce, before moving to his home, Baldoon some twenty miles away. A little over a fortnight later still, Janet was dead. It was essentially a private tragedy and might have remained so, had Janet not had such celebrated and controversial parents. The seventeenth century was a period of instability and struggle between the Stuarts and their enemies, with fortune favouring first one side and then the other. Whilst many suffered for their loyalty, the Dalrymples seemed to benefit from the misfortunes of others, some of whom would use anything to harm them. Sinister rumours were soon being spread about Janet's wedding until it became quite a notorious affair.

It was one of these rumours that Sir Walter Scott adapted for his book *The Bride of Lammermoor*. In his preface, Scott discussed the public sources he used, and mentioned a private one too. By this he probably meant his mother, who was herself a Rutherford. Scott transposes the drama to Rutherford territory, the Lammermoors, south of Edinburgh. Ravenswood House, by Melrose on

their southern flank, must have provided Scott with some inspiration, but it had no part in the real story. The Rutherfords came
from Hunthill, by Jedburgh, a few miles further south.

The opera diverges both from the novel and from reality in one
important way. In it, Lucia's family, the Ashtons, are all com-
pressed into her one contemptible brother, Enrico. Janet did have
an elder brother, John, who had his faults, but he cannot in any
way be blamed for her misfortunes. Both in the novel and in real
life, the evil genius was her mother, Margaret Ross of Balniel, a
woman of steely character and immense ambition, who seems to
have dominated her family, including her husband. The Sir
William Ashton of the novel is a weak character anyway, but
Janet's real father, Sir James Dalrymple, was anything but. He was
a remarkable man, rising from modest beginnings to found much
of Scottish law, as well as a great dynasty.

Born in 1619, Dalrymple was a near contemporary of the Vicar
of Bray, who so often had to trim his beliefs to the changing political winds just to hang on to his parish. Sir James, who had to cope
with these same winds, had aims that were more ambitious and a
position that was more exposed. He was not just one of the most
eminent lawyers in Scottish history but a far-seeing politician. He
experienced periods of adversity but these always preceded each
successive political upheaval, each one of which he helped to
bring about. As a young man in the Civil War he fought for the
Covenanters against his King, but he soon became disillusioned
by Cromwell's Commonwealth. Within two months of the King's
execution, he was part of a delegation which went to Holland to
pave the way for the Restoration of Charles II. At the same time,
under the protection of General Monk, he was able to pursue his
legal career in Scotland, becoming a judge in 1657.

When, in 1660, Charles II was restored to the throne, Dalrymple
naturally benefited, becoming a baronet, a judge of the Court
of Session[1] and a privy councillor. He soon found that it was not
easy to work under so arbitrary a king as Charles II, but, as one of
his contemporaries commented, he had a "freedom from passion,
which was so great that most men thought it was a sign of
hypocrisy." His career therefore developed steadily. He became a
Member of Parliament and President of the Court of Session, and

he accumulated a large fortune and much land. Even so, as the persecution of Presbyterians grew harsher, Dalrymple began to get into deep trouble and, in 1682, he had to escape to Holland. Leaving his wife to guard their now considerable possessions, Sir James spent six years in Leyden, writing legal treatises and, no doubt, plotting how the bigoted King James might be got rid of. When he returned in 1688, it was aboard King William's own ship and soon afterwards he became the first Viscount Stair. He had benefited from each successive turn of the political wheel.

Many people accused him of being the most shameless turncoat, but, as he pointed out in a written apologia: "Let my enemies show how many they can instance in this nation that did thrice forsake their station, though both honourable and lucrative, rather than comply with the corruption of the time." There was truth in his defence, but lawyers, however great and good, are not always easy to love. One who had managed so profitably to climb the heights could expect the hatred of those who, like the Ravenswoods in the opera, had lost their footing, their wealth and, in some cases, their heads. They could expect too that their enemies would be continually at work to reverse the situation, and, like the Ashtons, they had good reason to feel insecure.

In real life, Dalrymple never dispossessed Janet's lover Rutherford of any property, but he did acquire land pretty ruthlessly, particularly at the expense of the Kennedy family. Just as the Ravenswoods had been big landowners in the Lammermoors, so were the Kennedys in Galloway. It had once been written:

> *Twixt Wigton and the toun o' Ayr,*
> *Portpatrick, and the Cruives o'Cree,*
> *No man need think for to bide there*
> *Unless he court with Kennedie.*

Ironically, Dalrymple's wife Margaret had first married a Kennedy, no doubt with great expectations, but he died. She may not have pined for long for the Kennedys began to get into political difficulties and lose their wealth. In the meantime, her second husband, James Dalrymple, soon proved himself quick to profit from it. To quote McKerlie:

When it is considered that the connection with the district commenced with James Dalrymple's marriage with Margaret Ross in 1643 and that he

succeeded to Balniel on the death of her father in 1655 . . . to have
acquired, in addition, such an extent of landed property as we have shown
as possessed in September 1677 is really astounding . . . His career was an
extraordinary one and gives insight to the new road for success in the
adoption of the law as profession.

The list contains many former Kennedy properties. Dalrymple
was undoubtedly a forerunner of those villains of Victorian
novels, the lawyers who have acquired the hero's title deeds. Such
a role was no less unpopular in the seventeenth century but hos-
tility towards Dalrymple did not reach its peak until late in his life
when he and his son John were implicated in planning the massacre of Glencoe. All in all, he was never short of enemies.

Nor did his wife's character mitigate the situation. Margaret
Ross of Balniel was better bred than Dalrymple. When they married in 1643, she brought him the dowry, including the farms at
Balniel and Carsecreugh, which first gave him the financial independence so essential for an ambitious politician. But she brought
much more. Should his ambition ever falter, hers was there to
drive him on. Boundless in her energy, it was her resolve that
together they would found a family greater even than the
Kennedys. In an age when women were expected to be subordinate, she must have been egregious. For instance, until her husband became a peer, she seems to have continued to use her
maiden name, adding only the prefix Dame, which was her right
as the wife of a baronet. There is no doubt that she was a formidable woman, so formidable that many of her contemporaries suspected that she must be a sorceress. Witchcraft was still believed
in in the seventeenth century; in fact, even to doubt its existence
was a punishable offence. Belief in Scotland was particularly
strong. Howell, the chronicler of Charles II, wrote: "Scotland
swarms with them, now more than ever and persons of good
quality are executed every day." Furthermore, Scottish witches
were believed to be especially virulent. Another contemporary
wrote, not without a hint of pride: "Our Scottish witch is a far
more frightful thing than her supernatural coadjutor on the south
side of the Tweed."

Dame Margaret came to be known as the Witch of Endor, and
was suspected of all sorts of supernatural and malevolent prac-

tices. Why, during epidemics, was she never ill? How was it that her enemies so often had misfortunes while her friends and her family prospered? Others pointed to the strange tragedies that overtook her family, like Janet's death. So much could seem sinister in an age when so little could be explained. It is possible that she half believed in it herself. After her death and at the height of her son John's unpopularity after Glencoe, an anonymous writer published an apologia, intended to justify and explain the family and its members. About Dame Margaret, he wrote:

> She lived to a great age, and at her death desired that she might not be put underground but that her coffin might be placed upright on one end of it, promising that while she remained in that situation, the Dalrymples should continue in prosperity. What was the old lady's motive for such a request, or whether she really made such a promise, I cannot take upon me to determine; but it is certain her coffin stands upright in the aisle of the church of Kirkliston, the burial place of the family.

Dame Margaret died at Kirkliston because her son had acquired by marriage the nearby estate of New Liston just outside Edinburgh. He too is buried there but the property was sold soon afterwards. Their coffins are still in the family vault there, which has long since been bricked up. It was last entered in 1880; apparently Margaret's coffin, by then, was lying flat like all the others.

In the meanwhile, witchcraft featured in several of the stories that started to circulate concerning Janet's wedding. The earliest of these on record is that which appears in *Law's Memorialls*. The Reverend Robert Law had once been a pupil of Dalrymple. His treatise is much concerned with witchcraft, and he devotes a passage to the Dalrymple family. He would have us believe that Janet, "being married, the night she was a bride in, she was taken out from her bridegroom and harled through the house and afterward died." To be harled was to be dragged by evil spirits. Kirkland Sharp, who edited and commented on Law's work, is dubious about the evil spirits, clearly seeing the mother as sufficiently evil without recourse to the supernatural.

In Sharp's version, the headstrong Janet insists on marriage against her mother's wishes [though he does not make it clear to whom]. Eventually, Dame Margaret relents and gives her consent with the words, "Weel, ye may marry him but sair shall ye repent it." On the wedding night, she locks the bridal couple into their room – a normal practice in those days to protect them from drunken wedding guests – but soon bloodcurdling shrieks are heard through the door. She is strangely unwilling to unlock it, however, and when eventually she does, the bride is found dying in a pool of her own blood while the bridegroom crouches insanely cackling in the corner of the chimney.

There were not only many witches troubling Scotland at this time but also enthusiastic rhymers. A favourite form of abuse was the pasquill, usually in that style of verse which reached its finest hour quite recently with the works of William McGonagall. We owe some versions of Janet's story to these pasquills, perhaps the most poisonous coming from the pen of Sir William Hamilton of Whitelaw[2]. Sir William was another lawyer and his feelings about the Dalrymples were not improved when Janet's younger brother Hew was preferred over him for the post of Lord President of the Sessions.

Hamilton hated the whole Dalrymple family but reserved his most particular venom for Dame Margaret. On her death in 1692, he wrote a long pasquill starting:

> News, news, my muse, on Friday be it said
> It's now confirmed the Witch of Endor's dead
> And all men wonder what kind of devill is this
> Of such a monster have bereaved us;

He ends with an epitaph;

> Here lyes our auntie's coffin, I am sure
> But where her body is, I cannot tell.
> Most men affirm they cannot well tell where
> Unless both soul and body be in hell.
> It is just, if all be true that's said
> The Witch of Endor was a wretched sinner
> And if her coffin was in the grave laid
> Her body's rosted to the devil's dinner.

Before dealing with Janet's marriage, he establishes that the whole family is infected.

> Stair's neck, mind, wife, sons, grandson, and the rest,
> Ary wry, false, witch, pests, parricide, possessed.

He then goes on:

> *In al Stair's offspring we no difference know,*
> *They doe the females as the males bestow;*
> *So he of's daughter's marriage gave the ward*
> *Like a true vassal, to Glenluce's Laird;*
> *He knew what she did to her suitor plight,*
> *If she her faith to Rutherford should slight,*
> *Which, like his own, for greed he broke outright.*
> *Nick did Baldoon's posterior right deride*
> *And, as first substitute, did seize the bride;*
> *Whate'er he to his mistress did or said,*
> *He threw the bridegroom from the nuptial bed,*
> *Into the chimney did so his rival maul,*
> *His bruised bones ne'er were cured but by his fall.*

Hamilton's hatred comes through more clearly than his version of what happened, but he seems to suggest that the devil, at Dame Margaret's bidding, seizes Janet for breaking her word to Rutherford and, in the process, so mistreats Dunbar that his bruises are with him until his death [thirteen years later]. Hamilton's nephew and editor, William Dunlop, felt it necessary to add an explanatory footnote: "She had betrothed herself to Lord Rutherford under horrid imprecations, and afterwards married Baldoon, his nevoy, and her mother was the cause of her breach of faith." This is the only hint that Rutherford and Dunbar might have been related.

Since it is no longer a crime to doubt the existence of witchcraft, we may safely discard these superstitious tales. In his novel Scott denies the mother any supernatural powers, but he does fill it with baleful family omens, bewitched fountains and mumbling old hags, including an old Ravenswood retainer called Alice who seeks to warn Lucy of her peril. This is a reasonable course. While agnostic himself, Scott accepts that such superstitions could have influenced Janet and her contemporaries. We see this well demonstrated in the second scene of the opera. The educated Lucia only half believes the legend of the haunted fountain but her ignorant companion Alisa is terrified by it.

At the other end of the scale there are versions of the story which simply deny that there is any mystery at all. The most sceptical is the Reverend Andrew Symson, Minister of Kirkinner, the Dunbar family church, and author of both a book, *A Wider View of*

Galloway, and an elegy about his laird, David Dunbar. He describes him as the very paragon of men, sincerely mourning his young wife's early death. Since Dunbar, as the prototype of Arturo, is one of the main characters in the opera, let us see how Symson describes him:

> *His body, though not very large or tall*
> *Was sprightly active, yea, and strong withal:*
> *His constitution was, if right I have guessed*
> *Blood mixed with choler, said to be the best;*
> *In's gesture, converse, speech, discourse, attire,*
> *He practised that which wise men still admire –*
> *Commend and recommend. "What's that?" you'l say.*
> *'Tis this: He ever choosed the middle way*
> *'Twixt both the extremes. A'most in everything*
> *He did the like, 'tis worth our noticing,*
> *Sparing, yet not a niggard, liberal,*
> *And yet not lavish nor a prodigal,*
> *As knowing when to spend and when to spare,*
> *And that's a lesson which not many are*
> *Acquainted with. He bashful was yet daring*
> *When he saw cause, and yet therein but sparing;*

It is to be wondered at that Janet should object to marrying such an ideal man and Mr Symson did not believe that she really did. In his version:

> *A virtuous lady, not long since a bride,*
> *Was to a hopeful plant by marriage tied*
> *And brought home hither. We did all rejoice*
> *Even for her sake. But presently our voice*
> *Was turned to mourning for that little time*
> *That she'd enjoy. She waned in her prime,*
> *For Atropos, with her impartial knife,*
> *Soon cut her thread and therewithal her life.*
> *And for the time we may it well remember*
> *It being in unfortunate September,*
> *Just at the equinox; she was cut down*
> *In th'harvest, and this day she's to be sown,*
> *Where we must leave her till the resurrection.*
> *'Tis then the saints enjoy their full perfection.*

No conflict, no madness, no dagger here except that of Atropos – simply the sad and premature death of a young bride with just the hint in that phrase "even for her sake" that thus far, she had not been as enthusiastic about her good fortune as Symson felt she should have been. The local tradition in Galloway follows this line – that while there was a tragedy, there was no drama. The lover, the poniard, the madness are all held to be a myth, but this will do hardly better than the stories of Dame Margaret's sorcery. It is too bland.

We know that Symson was totally dependent on David Dunbar, his laird. He was not as agile as the Vicar of Bray, and, at one time, Dunbar was the only person willing to attend his kirk. When, in 1682, Dunbar fell off his horse and fatally injured himself, Symson finally lost his parish. He moved to Edinburgh to scratch a living by writing and publishing. It was not without feeling therefore that he wrote ruefully of his dead patron:

> *He used, and that most commonly to go*
> *On foot. I wish that he had still done so.*

Symson is a biased witness on the subject of Janet's death. He wrote as Dunbar would have wished him to, and Dunbar's wish had been to hush the whole thing up. He had always absolutely refused to talk about it, and he even made it known, that, if any gentleman so much as questioned him thereon, he would take it as a mortal insult for which he would demand satisfaction. It is one thing to grieve and want to be left alone with one's sorrow, but Dunbar's vehemence was such as to arouse more suspicion than it suppressed. If there was nothing to cover up, why make such a fuss?

The Dalrymples have also been extremely reticent about the whole affair. The family tradition does not deny that something untoward occurred. Not much seems ever to have been put in writing on the subject but there is a correspondence, dated 1823, between two descendants of Janet's younger brother Hew. In one letter, the story is retold. The husband, Dunbar, is described as "a less amiable but much more opulent suitor" than the lover, Rutherford. The writer regrets, however, that Sir Walter Scott seems to have been unaware of a local theory:

Namely, that from the window having been found open, it was
conjectured that the lover had, during the bustle and confusion occasioned
by the preparations for the wedding feast, and perhaps by the connivance
of some servant of the family, contrived to gain admission and to secrete
himself in the bridal chamber, from whence he had made his escape into

the garden after having fought with and severely wounded his successful
rival – a conclusion strengthened by the fact of young Baldoon having, to
his last breath, obstinately refused to give any explanation on the subject.

Both the novel and the opera are based on a version of the story
which is slightly different from any of these. While Scott had
access to most of the sources already quoted and clearly makes
partial use of them, he claims also to have had family sources of
information not available to us today. He quotes, for instance, an
informant who had spoken to Hew, Janet's younger brother. This
is quite possible since Hew did not die until 1737 and Scott was
born in 1771. Furthermore, Hew moved to North Berwick, closer
to Edinburgh and to the Rutherfords at Jedburgh. It would have
been natural, after all the passions had cooled, for members of the
two families to compare notes as to what had really happened,
and Hew was one of the last eyewitnesses. Scott obviously knew
that his story, with all three protagonists dying romantically, did
not really happen. In his preface he explains what he thinks did.
He, too, puts the blame on Dame Margaret for her imperious
nature and raging ambition, but not for any sorcery. It was simply
a clash of interests between the family and the individual,
between romantic love and dynastic planning.

He does not comment on how Janet and Lord Rutherford came
to know each other, and to make their secret pact of love. It was
certainly not by an enchanted fountain in the Dalrymple's park.
The barren moor round Carscrough would better suit the witches
in Macbeth than lovers' trysts. Anyway, Rutherford lived miles
away. The truth is probably prosaic. Janet's father had to spend a
good deal of the year on his legal and political affairs in Edinburgh, and the couple could have met at a social occasion there.
What is remarkable is that they should have so pledged themselves in an age when it was normal for marriages to be arranged.
Did Janet accept Rutherford, unaware that another match was
being planned for her, or did she do so to ward off such a match?
Was it a wilful act of disobedience, or was there something else
about Archibald Rutherford to which Dame Margaret objected?

The Rutherfords were a very old Border family. Their name
appears in the chronicles as far back as the days of King David in
the twelfth century. Members of the family had served under Wal-

lace and at Bannockburn, and had been involved in countless border feuds and battles with the English, who never tired of reducing
to rubble the Rutherford castle at Hunthill. Archibald's great-
grandfather had been known as the "cock o' Hunthill", perhaps
because he had so many children. Archibald was descended from
his eldest son, who had inherited the properties. The other fourteen
boys and girls had had to shift for themselves, and one had become
a sea captain, based in Leith. This man's son, Andrew, became a soldier of fortune in the French service. By 1660, he had risen to the
rank of lieutenant-general. He was married to a Frenchwoman, but
they had no children and, at his age, it did not seem likely that they
would. Knowing that, on his restoration, Charles II would need
loyal and experienced soldiers who had not been involved with
Cromwell, Louis XIV offered him Andrew Rutherford, and Charles
accepted with alacrity. To demonstrate his pleasure, he immediately
made Andrew a baron, gave him a regiment and put him in charge
of the negotiations with the French regarding the future of Dunkirk.
The King was so delighted with the settlement achieved that he
promoted Andrew to Earl of Teviot and commander of the garrison
of Tangier. Alas, he did not have long to enjoy his new honours, for
in 1664 he was killed leading his troops in a sally against the Moors.
The earldom died with him but he had been granted the right to
nominate any member of his family to inherit the barony. Before
sailing, he chose as heir his relative, Sir Thomas Rutherford of
Hunthill, head of the family and Archibald's elder brother. Sir
Thomas also did not last long and, in 1669, Archibald found himself
Lord Rutherford, the third of that name although the title had been
created but barely eight years earlier.

For a yeoman family on the make like the Dalrymples, Rutherford should have been quite a catch. He may not have had as solid
a fortune as young Dunbar, and not being a local man, was perhaps less to be trusted. He came, however, of a proud old family,
quite as distinguished in the Borders as the Kennedys were in Galloway, but Dame Margaret may have felt that these old families
were now in decline, not agile enough to cope with the changing
times. After all, she had been married to a Kennedy, and may have
decided that they were yesterday's people, to be exploited rather
than cultivated. But if this is what she believed, she greatly under-

estimated their resilience. It was in our own century that a Rutherford first showed how the atom might be split. In 1992 there were
still Rutherfords at Hunthill.

There could have been other considerations. At this early stage
in the Dalrymples' rise to greatness, Dame Margaret's first
endeavour might well have been to consolidate the family's position in Galloway, where the Dunbars were influential. She may
also have felt that the Rutherfords were too publicly attached to
the Stuart cause, and who could tell when the wheel might turn
again? Or perhaps she did not like their religious views. Dame
Margaret was a dedicated Covenanter. She must have known
Rutherford if Janet did, and may have distrusted his proud and
fiery spirit. There is no evidence, however, of the long-standing
feud between the families which is at the heart of both the novel
and the opera. The Dalrymples had not injured the Rutherfords in
any way. Quite possibly, Dame Margaret was just furious that the
two young people should have committed themselves without
her sanction, and was determined to stamp out such subversive
behaviour before Janet's younger sisters could be infected by it.
She was not the sort of lady to let her authority be flouted.

It seems certain that she misjudged Janet's spirit. It is difficult,
three centuries after the end of a short life, to fathom Janet's character. Perhaps she was one of those rather weak people who find it
hard to resist any proposition put to them with sufficient force. She
does not seem to have been naturally aggressive or even articulate,
but she must have had some obstinacy to have resisted her mother
for so long. Most probably she had her share of the family spirit, but
it is not easy for two strong-willed people to cohabit and Janet, in
the subordinate role, must have had to learn to suppress her views.
The effort may have affected her mental stability so that when the
test came she had no resource but to retreat into a nervous breakdown. People do this under much less provocation than Janet.

When the marriage to Dunbar was proposed, however, she
found the courage to cling to her engagement to Rutherford. Her
mother brushed this aside as a childish aberration, and demanded
that she write to him to break it off, but Janet and Rutherford had
plighted their troth, and had broken and shared a gold coin, each
taking half as a symbol of their pledge. She would not write. So

her mother did, informing Rutherford that such an engagement, unsanctioned by family approval, had no validity. She implied that Janet had accepted this, but Rutherford certainly did not. Nor would he believe that Janet had done so unless he heard it from her own lips. He insisted that he see Janet. Rutherford's name and connections were too important for Dame Margaret to ignore such a demand, so she granted his wish, but she insisted that she should be present throughout the interview.

According to Scott, the interview took place at Carsecreugh but Janet seems to have taken little part. All the argument was between Rutherford and her mother. It seems to have been both furious and learned. Dame Margaret based her case on the Bible, quoting the book of Leviticus: "If her father disallow her in the day that he heareth [of her vow]; not any of her vows or her bonds wherewith she hath bound her soul, shall stand: and the Lord shall forgive her, because her father disallowed her." Rutherford was probably not so well supplied with biblical quotations, but he was not impressed by all this. Nothing Janet's mother could say or quote would move him. He and Janet had plighted their troth, and they loved each other. He was as bound to her as she to him, and only a mutual and voluntary agreement could release either of them. Janet remained silent. Rutherford desperately wanted her to confirm their love but she could not. She seems to have been so in thrall to her mother that, despite his entreaties, she could not speak. Nor, on the other hand, would she obey her mother's demand that she deny his suit. She just sat speechless, motionless and miserable. Only when her mother sternly ordered her to return Lord Rutherford's golden pledge did she mutely extend it towards him. Dame Margaret had won, but Rutherford did not leave without heaping maledictions on her and her daughter. In the doorway, he turned to say one last bitter, prescient word to his lost love. "For you, madam – you will be a world's wonder."

Janet was probably already insane. All reports from this stage on indicate that her behaviour was completely obedient but torpid, as if in a trance. The wedding to Dunbar went ahead with all despatch and much festivity. It was a great occasion. Relations on both sides and many of their friends came to Carsecreugh to celebrate with feasting and dancing. Rutherford did not, as in the opera, burst in to disrupt it. Janet remained in a state of total apathy. Her younger brother Hew later vouched for the fact that her hand upon his as they rode to church was deathly cold. The wedding certificate, signed by Janet and David, the two fathers and four witnesses was still extant in the papers of Dunbar's descendants in the late nineteenth century, but seems since to have perished in a fire. However, the couple's signatures had been reproduced to illustrate the Stair family annals.

The wedding did not take place in some grand Dalrymple castle hall but in the village church. Local tradition maintains that this was the Glenluce church and that the family came down from Carsecreugh, some three miles up on the moors above the village. There is a nagging doubt about this. McKerlie states that the family had not yet built their house at Carsecreugh and were still living at Balniel, above New Luce fifteen miles up the Luce valley. It does not really matter. Both churches illustrate the small scale of the whole affair. Nothing is left of Margaret Ross's Balniel today. There is a modern stucco farmhouse with some old and rather fine stone outbuildings. Only one turret now remains of the house Sir James built at Carsecreugh but it must have been quite impressive in its day, although the Reverend Symson's view was that "it might have been more pleasant if it had been in a more pleasant place". Once established as the local grandees, the Dalrymples moved to Castle Kennedy and let Carsecreugh fall into ruin. It had been an unlucky house for them. Janet's was not the only tragedy it witnessed[3] and the family were said to be heartily glad to abandon it. Producers of the opera who have taken the trouble to go back to its source have generally been shown Castle Kennedy, also now a ruin but a grander place and much more in keeping with the opera's stage directions.

Janet continued in her apathy throughout the evening's festivities and, when the time came to retire, she went meekly to the bridal chamber. As custom prescribed, she was locked in with Dunbar, not by Lady Dalrymple but by the best man. It was he who, when shrieks were heard from the chamber, was unwilling to yield up the key, suspecting perhaps some practical joke. When he did open the door it was no joke that met his eyes. Dunbar lay bleeding on the floor, while Janet, evidently insane, crouched in a corner. "Tak up your bonny bridegroom," was all she would say.

Up to this point, Scott's novel, albeit highly coloured, follows his sources fairly closely. From now on, however, the ways part, for Scott ties it all up in a crescendo of challenges, deaths and suicides, none of which took place. Janet and Dunbar remained at Carsecreugh for a fortnight after their wedding. No-one offers an explanation why, but, if it was to let Dunbar recover from his wounds, they cannot have been very grave. The couple then moved to Baldoon and it was not until a fortnight later still that Janet died. Symson does not tell us what she died of. Given that he was writing many years later, and had a splendid opportunity to counter with facts all the lurid rumours which had for some time been circulating about it, it is perhaps significant that he did not do so. One is left to presume that her death was in some way a consequence of her wedding. Most plausible is the theory that she had some sort of mental breakdown, which would be consistent with the known facts. Janet is presumably buried in Symson's church at Kirkinner, but there is no sign of her grave there today. In one corner of the graveyard stands a ruined family tomb, romantically overgrown and entirely suitable for a staging of the last scene of the opera, but there is nothing to connect it with the Dunbar family, and, in fact, it is probably of a later date.

Dunbar may not have suffered too long from the physical wounds he sustained but, judging by his unwillingness to allow it to be mentioned, the affair must have damaged his spirit. He did not attempt to marry again for many years but eventually did so, and had several children. He seems to have spent most of his time in Baldoon helping his father, who was a keen farmer. To quote Symson again:

> He knew full well how to behave at court
> And yet but seldom did thereto resort,
> But loved the country life, choosed to inure
> Himself to past'rage and agriculture

He was however in Edinburgh, riding through the Quarrelholes, when his horse stumbled and fatally threw him. His grave is in Holyrood Abbey.

After his rebuff, Rutherford took up a commission in the Household Guards. He died in 1685. He never married but, unlike Edgar Ravenswood, he was not the last of the line. His brother Robert succeeded him but when he died in 1724, he also left no heir. Nevertheless, the title continued to be claimed by a variety of distant relatives for many years to come, and at one stage, there were two rival Lord Rutherfords. These claims never received convincing support and by the end of the eighteenth century, they had ceased.

Dame Margaret died in 1692. She was a proud, ambitious and domineering woman, much hated by her contemporaries. In his preface, Scott evidently does not think his harsh portrait of her in *The Bride of Lammermoor* is unfair. He is at great pains, however, to point out that the contemptible Sir William Ashton is a travesty of the great Sir James Dalrymple. All they have in common is that both were lawyers and somewhat in awe of their wives. There was no real life equivalent of the loathsome Enrico although Janet's brother John was evidently rather ruthless. He, too, was a lawyer, a politician and a great achiever. In due course he was created the first Earl of Stair. His son was a distinguished soldier and diplomat. Furthermore, several of Janet's other brothers achieved distinction, mostly at law but one became a physician and another an antiquarian. Several became baronets in their own right and Dalrymple landholdings soon spread far beyond the borders of Galloway. If it was truly Dame Margaret crouching in her coffin who supervised all this, it certainly was powerful magic. Today we may suspect that the real magic was in her genes. After all, even Janet, her one failed child, has become "a world's wonder".

NOTES

1 The Court of Session is the supreme civil court of Scotland. In the Outer House, judges sit singly to hear cases. The Inner House, which is mainly an appeal court, has two divisions, each of four judges. The Lord President presides over the First Division.

2 Hamilton was not a very satisfactory character, and was himself the butt of scurrilous rhymes, including the following obituary:

> *Old Nick was in want of a lawyer in hell*
> *To preside o'er his Court there of Session,*
> *So old Whytlaw he took, for he suited him well*
> *For tyranny, lust, and oppression.*

3 In 1682 a second tragedy occurred at Carsecreugh when the Dalrymples' eldest grandson, James, was accidentally shot dead by his younger brother, John.

UN BALLO IN
MASCHERA

Guiseppe Verdi

Libretto by Antonio Somma, based on Eugène Scribe

Dramatis Personae

Gustavus III, *King of Sweden*
Anckarstroem, *Chief Minister*
Oscar, *page*
Count Horn   )
) *conspirators*
Count Ribbing)
Christian, *sailor*
a judge
a servant

Amelia, *Anckarstroem's wife*
Ulrika Arvidson, *a fortune teller*

Courtiers, townspeople, conspirators, ball guests

Because of the censor's inhibitions about showing regicide on the stage, the earliest performances of *Ballo in Maschera* were not set in Stockholm, but in the colonial America of the seventeenth century. The role of the King was changed to Riccardo, the English governor of Massachusetts; Anckarstroem became Renato, his Creole adviser and so on. Although this version is still occasionally staged, the opera is about the assassination of King Gustavus III of Sweden in 1792.

ACT ONE

SCENE ONE: The court is assembled in the palace, awaiting the King, and all are singing his praises except for Horn, Ribbing and a few others. These hate him for the execution of some of their friends, and are plotting his death in revenge. Gustavus arrives with his page, Oscar, and is asked to deal with some petitions, but he is much more interested in the guest list for a proposed ball. Seeing Amelia's name on it, he is expressing his joy when Anckarstroem, her husband and his chief minister, arrives and sternly asks to see him in private.

When Anckarstroem says that he has made a serious discovery, Gustavus has a moment of guilty panic, but it is merely about a plot to assassinate him. The King refuses even to hear the plotters' names, so sure is he that the love of his people will protect him. Oscar now returns with a judge, who wants the King to banish Ulrika Arvidson, a gipsy soothsayer, but Oscar says she is harmless and diverting. The King recalls the court, and announces that they will all see her for themselves. While Anckarstroem worries about the risk and the plotters wonder if their moment has come, the King is delighted at the prospect of a little adventure.

SCENE TWO: Ulrika's den is a dim cavern full of tripods and bubbling cauldrons. She is working up her spells before an audience of simple folk, when Gustavus arrives disguised as a fisherman. Watching her foretell that Christian, one of his sailors, will soon become an officer, the King quickly slips a scribbled commission into the man's pocket. All, not least Ulrika, are expressing their astonishment at this instant fulfilment of her prophecy when a confidential client is announced. Ulrika asks all to leave, but Gustavus hides instead. He sees Amelia enter and ask for a spell to cure a forbidden love. Ulrika tells her to go alone at midnight to the gallows hill outside the town. There she must pluck a herb growing at the foot of the gibbet. Gustavus resolves to meet her there.

The courtiers now arrive, and Amelia slips out through the back door. Gustavus presents himself to hear his fortune. Ulrika is horrified. She sees only his murder ahead. He ridicules her, but his courtiers are filled with foreboding, except for the plotters who take courage. Ulrika goes on, predicting that Gustavus's assassin will be the next person he touches. All are shrinking from his outstretched hand when Anckarstroem arrives and, unaware, takes it, to everyone's relief. Anckarstroem is Gustavus's most faithful friend, and the last person in the world to want to assassinate him. The King now reveals his true identity, and the people, led by the grateful Christian, sing his praises.

ACT TWO

Amelia, veiled and terrified, is waiting for midnight on the gallows hill and singing of her fear, of her love and of her resolution. As the clock strikes, a figure emerges from the shadows. It is Gustavus and she forgets all about the herb. His ardour sweeps aside her protests, and they are rapturously confessing their love, when her husband appears. She barely has time to adjust her veil. Anckarstroem has followed the King to warn him that the plotters are even now on the hill, and closing in to kill him. He urges Gustavus to exchange cloaks with him, and to leave at once, but the King hesitates. He will only go when Anckarstroem has sworn to escort the unknown lady back to town, without trying to discover her identity.

The plotters arrive and Anckarstroem has to reveal his own identity. Angrily, they demand to know who the lady is, and, when he refuses to say, they threaten to attack him. Trying to intervene, Amelia lets her veil slip. The plotters' wrath dissolves into laughter, and they depart to spread the story round Stockholm.

ACT THREE

SCENE ONE: Anckarstroem is bitterly upbraiding Amelia in his study. He ignores her pleas of innocence, and swears he will kill her, but allows her one last look at her sleeping son. While she is out of the room, he addresses his resolve to be revenged on the King to the latter's portrait. Ribbing and Horn arrive. Anckarstroem tells them he has proof of their plot, but rather than report them, he wishes to join them. They are incredulous, but he offers his son's life as guarantee of his good faith. He has only one condition. He must be the one who strikes the blow. They cannot agree to this, and decide to resolve the problem by getting Amelia to draw a name from an urn. She is extremely suspicious, all the more so when she draws her husband's name, but at this moment Oscar arrives with invitations to the ball. Amelia pleads indisposition, but her husband insists that they will both go, adding to her suspicions. All express their hopes and fears for the coming evening. The plotters agree to wear blue dominoes and red sashes and to use the password "death". Amelia wonders how to warn the King without betraying her husband.

SCENE TWO: Gustavus is in his study meditating about the impossibility of his love for Amelia. While sounds of dancing float into the room from the adjacent ballroom, he decides he must send Anckarstroem and Amelia abroad to Finland. He has just written the necessary instruction when Oscar arrives with an urgent letter for him, which he has just been given by a masked lady. It is an anonymous warning not to attend the ball. Gustavus refuses to heed it. He is not a coward, and this will be his last chance to see Amelia.

The scene is transformed to the ballroom, and he and Oscar join the dancers. The plotters emerge from the throng. They are having difficulty identifying Gustavus, and Anckarstroem is suggesting that perhaps he has decided not to come, when he sees Oscar. The page confirms that the King has come, but teasingly refuses to reveal his disguise, until Anckarstroem angrily explains he must see him urgently on matters of state. Oscar confides that the King is in a long black cloak with rose-coloured ribbons on the shoulder.

The plotters disappear into the crowd just as Amelia and Gustavus emerge from it. She is pleading with him to leave, but he will not, and when he discovers who she is, all thoughts of prudence fly away. Confessing once more his uncontrollable passion, he starts to tell her about Finland when Anckarstroem steps between them, and stabs him. A menacing crowd forms, but Gustavus restrains them. He tells Anckarstroem that Amelia is blameless, and that he, Gustavus, though stricken with love, had decided to send them abroad. All are filled with horror and remorse, while the King's life ebbs away.

1. Simon Boccanegra: effigy from his tomb

2. Jorge Manrique

3. Alvaro di Luna

4. Jaime de Urgel

5. Triboulet, by Clouet

6. François 1er, by Clouet

7. Diane de Poitiers, by Flandrin

8. Saint-Vallier, by Clouet

9. Elizabeth, by Clouet

10. Don Carlos, by Coello

11. Charles V , by Rubens after Titian

12. Philip II, School of Titian

13. Prince and Princess Eboli

14. Gustavus III, by Roslin

15. Anckarstroem, a posthumous portrait by Arnberg

16. Ribbing, by Sparrgren

17. Horn, by von Breda

18. Marie Duplessis at the theatre,
by Camille Roqueplan

19. Antoine-Agénor
de Guiche

20. Alexandre Dumas
fils, engraving after
photograph by Salomon

21. Franz Liszt, by Lanchert

22. Count Stackelburg,
engraving after Isabey

23. Café Momus in 1819,
by Thomas Boys

24. Bougival in 1850

25. Henri Murger, by Gavarni

26. Alexandre Schanne, from the frontispiece of his autobiography

27. Champfleury, by Lemercier

28. Marie Roux (seated) with her sister Antoinette

A Shining Sort of Man

If Gustavus III of Sweden is not as well remembered as he deserves to be, it is largely because of timing. His assassination in 1792 coincided with the Terror in France, and, as sensations go, a little splash of blood in Stockholm could hardly compete with the scarlet rivers running through the streets of Paris. Moreover, although his achievements were extraordinary, they were mostly ephemeral, because his ideals were obsolete. He believed in absolute monarchy and that Sweden should be a great power, ideas with which too few of his subjects agreed. His dynasty did not long survive him. All in all, everything conspired to bury the memory of this brilliant man. To understand him, it may help to recall a little Swedish history.

Gustavus was a Vasa, a family which, in the sixteenth and seventeenth centuries, produced an astonishing series of great soldiers. Sweden had neither a large population nor great wealth, but Swedish armies ranged throughout much of central Europe and deep into Russia, winning victory after victory, establishing client states in Prussia and Poland, intimidating her neighbours and making the Baltic into a Swedish sea. Sweden's traditional enemies were Denmark and Russia, while her main support came from France. The last of these great soldiers was Charles XII, who was killed in battle in 1718 aged only 36, after a life of breathtaking adventures. He left behind no satisfactory successor, and Sweden's battered neighbours and exhausted people agreed that enough was enough. With foreign encouragement, Sweden's aristocrats seized power, and would have declared a republic had they dared, but the Vasas were still revered by the population; so they allowed Charles's sister, Ulrika Eleonora, to succeed him with much curtailed power. Having accepted these terms, she then ignored them so that, after a year, she was deposed in favour of her husband, Frederick of Hesse, whose main policy was at all costs to avoid a confrontation with these imperious nobles. He died in 1751 and was succeeded by an amiable nephew, Adolph Frederic of Holstein, Gustavus's father, who was quite unfitted to be king. A timid man, he had married Louisa Ulrika, the brilliant if capricious sister of Frederick the Great of Prussia. A group of admirers soon gathered round her who felt that more power should be restored to the monarchy, but they were easily defeated, and it was reduced to even more humiliating impotence.

Amongst other things, the King and Queen were informed, in odiously servile terms, that they were not considered fit to bring up their own son. Gustavus therefore had an unusual education at the hands of a series of eminent noblemen. The first of these, Count Tessin, found the boy responded best to unconventional ways of teaching. For whole days, lessons would take the form of a dramatic dialogue, as though the two of them were actors on a stage. They also carried on a correspondence which resulted in a fascinating book called *Letters from an Old Man to a Young Prince*. Although the boy proved a brilliant pupil, he began to cause anxiety because his tastes would have been more appropriate in a girl. He did not like riding or hunting, but loved dancing and pretty clothes and even playing with dolls. All agreed, however, that he could master with ease anything that interested him. He adored the theatre, and after a performance could often remember and recite whole sections, mostly of the heroine's part. At the age of eleven, aware of their anxieties, he wrote a dramatic satire in which he mocks a tutor, Dr Barbarissimus, who upbraids his young pupil for being too girlish and fond of fine clothes, and who is made to look a fool. Gustavus also showed great liking for anything French, which he soon spoke better than Swedish, and he thoroughly steeped himself in the literature, philosophy and culture of that country. His main enthusiasm, however, was history and the study of great heroes, mostly classical, French or Swedish, with whom he readily identified. Although patchy this education produced a highly civilised young man with a mind of his own. Concerning politics, despite all their efforts, his tutors succeeded only in teaching him how sorry was the state of a nation where kings were mere puppets and selfish aristocrats held sway. Gustavus became so convinced about this that he actually converted his last tutor, Count Scheffer, into a monarchist.

Gustavus was brought up during what came to be known as the Age of Liberty, but the aristocrats in charge of it were proving singularly inept rulers. The source of their power was the Riksdag, a parliament with four chambers dedicated to the nobility, the clergy, the burghers and the farmers. The noble chamber, called the Riddarhus, was the largest and was dominant. Years of warfare had led to the creation of a disproportionately large and privileged noble class. The Riksdag did not sit continuously but had to be re-elected and convened whenever momentous decisions were needed. In between, the Riksdag appointed a Senate which in turn supervised appointments to the various ministries. The composition of the Senate was therefore of critical importance, not only to the country, but also to its neighbours. Quite quickly a rudimentary form of party politics developed. The Caps, which was short for night-caps or sleepy people, stood for financial prudence and peace, and were largely in Russian pay. They were opposed by the Hats, who were more adventurous and expensive, and financed by France. The only issue that could unite the two parties without fail was the need to keep power in aristocratic hands. On everything else, their mutual antagonism soon became more interesting to them than good government, and their disunity was aggravated by blatant foreign interference and corruption. In particular, there were periods of Cap dominance when the most powerful man in the land was the Russian ambassador. The consequence was disastrous. The economy was a shambles, with banknotes inflating at a different rate to the coinage. The armed forces were so demoralised that on one occasion Russian troops had to be requested to defend Sweden from the Danes. On another, in mid-campaign in the Seven Years War, the army's officers abandoned their soldiers to return home to vote in the Riksdag. The lower orders were so impoverished that they longed for a return to the old days when Sweden had been firmly governed and a great power. As Gustavus grew up, he watched all this with patriotic anguish. He suffered when his father, rather than sign decrees over which he had no influence, abandoned his last constitutional duty, and gave the Senate a rubber stamp of his signature. He suffered when his mother, driven too far when the Senate claimed the right to check her jewellery, tried to organise a coup which failed, costing several of her friends their lives. He suffered too when his parents were forced to betroth him to a princess, Sophia Magdalena, from the hated Danish royal family. This marriage was part of a Cap policy to prevent an anti-Swedish alliance between Russia and Denmark. Sophia-Magdalena was a pleasant, placid and quite pretty girl, simple, pious, dull and cripplingly shy. Her character and interests were so opposite to those of Gustavus that anyone who knew them both advised against the match, but it was forced through. The prince was prejudiced against his bride from the outset, but when he met her, he softened, and wrote to one of his former tutors that he believed she might suit him. He was wrong. He soon lost all interest in her. He failed to protect her from the malice of his mother who hated her, and when his neglect became so scandalous that members of court remonstrated with him, he replied that he could not put up with "the boredom which follows wherever she goes", and that, while the State might require him to give her his hand, his heart was not at its command.

Gustavus was not the only Swede with grievances against the Caps, but they could be removed only by a new Riksdag, which they naturally refused to call. The Hats were so frustrated that they abandoned the aristocratic unity on which the Age of Liberty was based, and formed a tentative alliance with the Court. In 1769, after a particularly deplorable instance of Cap corruption, Gustavus, with Hat support, persuaded his father to abdicate, and to ban the use of the rubber name-stamp. No one had dreamed that Adolph Frederic had such courage in him, and it took the Senate totally by surprise. Without the use of the King's signature, the Senate had no power. There were still many Hats powerfully placed in the ministries, who refused to obey unsigned orders and, for a week, there was no government. Tremendous pressure was put on the King to resume the throne, but Gustavus managed him as a ventriloquist his dummy. Once, as he hustled his father out of the chamber lest he should weaken, one of the Senators, Count Gustav Ribbing, so far forgot himself as to follow them out and shout down the stairs, "It's that damned young thief that's spoiling everything!" In the end the Hats prevailed. The Riksdag was summoned and the King graciously agreed to resume his throne, but not before Gustavus had negotiated with the Hats an improvement in the royal position. The Hats were duly returned to power when the Riksdag met, but then broke their word. Instead, they voted a generous sum to enable the Crown Prince to tour Europe and especially to visit France.

Gustavus's visit to France was a triumph. He won all hearts, not just of the ladies and the court, of the King and his ministers, but also of the poets and philosophers whom he made a point of seeking out. Rousseau so far overcame his prejudices as to express his wonder at the prince's quickness of wit and comprehension, while Voltaire actually wrote him an ode. Gustavus was less impressed with them, and wrote to his mother: "I have already made the acquaintance of all the philosophers, and their writings are much more agreeable than their persons." He became the hero of all the salons, being likened to those ideals of French gallantry, François I and Henri IV. He naturally frequented the opera and the theatre, and feasted on all those civilised things which were in such short supply in Stockholm. But it was not all pleasure. He was busy in the meanwhile sounding out French political opinion towards a redressing of the balance of power in Sweden, and a switching of French financial support from the Hats to the monarch. When on 1st March, a courier from Stockholm brought the news of his father's sudden death, he redoubled his efforts, and he left Paris on 25th March with a promise of 300,000 *livres* and much sage advice to be cautious. This was repeated by his uncle, Frederick the Great, when he visited Berlin on his way home. Frederick informed Gustavus that, together with Denmark and Russia, he stood guarantor of the Swedish Constitution, and would be prepared to use force to defend it. He agreed that his nephew had a virtually impossible task to heal his country's divisions. "If there were Swedes in Sweden," said the old man, "they would soon agree to bury their differences; but foreign corruption has so perverted the national spirit that harmony is impossible."

When Gustavus reached home, he was met with immense popular enthusiasm, which he proceeded to encourage. He spent much time touring country areas, and talking to ordinary people who had no defences against such charm. He also started to hold regular audiences open to any of his subjects, regardless of class and party, who felt they had a grievance. He had the most extraordinary ability to send everyone away happy. Even though he was not always able to solve their problems, he made them feel he cared and gave wise advice. In the meanwhile, a new Riksdag had been elected to oversee the coronation. It was more divided than ever and in a more sinister way. While the Hats still had a majority in the noble house, the lower orders were all Cap. The scene was set for the party struggle to become a class struggle, with the lower orders disputing the dominance of the aristocrats. At first, this was blatantly encouraged by Count Osterman, the Russian ambassador, but eventually even he began to fear the genie he was coaxing out of its bottle. In the meanwhile, for various reasons, the funds promised by France had not arrived. Gustavus made several honest attempts to mediate between the factions but failed. His good faith was not accepted by the Caps, whose aims were not only to teach the Hats a lesson but to make sure that Gustavus could never repeat his father's abdication tactic. Their chosen weapon was the wording of the oath that Gustavus would be required to swear at his coronation. Unable to influence the situation, and secretly resolving that, no matter what oath he swore he would not reign in impotence, Gustavus withdrew from politics and devoted himself ostentatiously to frivolities. Delegations from the Riksdag would find him at his embroidery, feigning utter indifference to whatever they might put in his oath. When the Caps presented their text, he signed it without reading it. Having pinioned the King, or so they thought, the Caps staged his coronation all the more lavishly because it was only a charade. In the meanwhile, they went on to complete their triumph over the Hats so vindictively that they actually played into Gustavus's hands. They made too many enemies whose only recourse was rebellion, and whose only rallying point was the very monarchy that the Caps sought to prostrate. The Crown was now the only part of the constitution not firmly in Cap hands. The leading Hats mostly withdrew in a sulk to their country estates, leaving the King apparently isolated and friendless.

The Caps had every reason to feel confident but desperate situations discover desperate men. The anti-Cap plotting which now started involved men who had never been prominent in politics. One, a soldier named Sprengtporten, had been an obscure Hat deputy. Another, named Toll, had also been a soldier but, feeling himself unappreciated, he had left the army and studied law, only to find his career once again blocked. He was witty and sharp but lazy, a combination which may have made his contemporaries like him better than his superiors did.[1] He and Sprengtporten began to work out a plan. One problem confronting them was the disposition of the army. Only regiments with aristocratic officers of proven loyalty to the government were stationed in or near the capital. The conspirators would have to rely on subverting troops stationed on the frontiers. Sprengtporten was a Finn and could at least count on his own regiment stationed there. Toll would try what he could do in the extreme south in Scania. Assuming they were successful, they would co-ordinate their mutinies and march at once on Stockholm, hoping to arrive simultaneously with the news of their rebellion. If they were too slow, the capital would be defended, civil war would ensue, and Sweden's neighbours would intervene. But news travels faster than armies. It would be a desperate gamble, and some cover plan had to be found to distract and calm the government for just long enough to delay their reaction until it was too late. The only solution they could think of was to involve the King. If he remained in Stockholm, behaving normally, it might make the government doubt the rumours they were hearing, and hesitate for the vital few days. Could they trust him in such a critical role? Could they trust him at all? He seemed rather a fop and had not shown much resolution about the coronation oath, but they had no choice. In any case, they would need his written authority if they were to persuade any troops to rebel in the first place.

In fact, Gustavus was already casting about for some way to mount a coup, for he was not prepared to preside helplessly over his country's ruin. He joined their conspiracy with enthusiasm. Furthermore, he had just the qualities needed for the job – charm, acting ability, quick wits and, so it proved, steel nerves. This was just as well because, from the start, nearly everything that could go wrong, did so. First, a letter from Gustavus to Louis XV seeking his support, fell into the hands of the English,[2] who passed it at once to the government, but wisely Gustavus had worded it too vaguely to amount to proof of any plot. Worse, the promised French funds failed to turn up. Worse still, the uprising in the south misfired and Toll, far from being able to march on Stockholm, found himself on the defensive in Christiansand. Worst of all, although the mutiny had gone well in Finland, Sprengtporten was held back by adverse winds. The King was totally isolated amongst his enemies whose suspicions grew daily more acute. The English ambassador constantly urged the senators to arrest him, but they had no proof of his involvement. He was so relaxed, so collaborative, apparently so shocked himself by these rumours of mutiny. He attended their meetings, urged on them security measures, applauded the summoning of the ultra-Cap Upland Regiment to reinforce Stockholm, and the recall of his own brother Charles from military duty in the south. He even suggested that loyal garrison troops should be issued with live ammunition, just in case. For the rest he continued his frivolous pursuits but, in reality, he was in anguish. He had been secretly warned that as soon as the Uplanders reached Stockholm, he was to be arrested and all would be lost. With barely twelve hours to go and his own forces still days away, it was time to throw the dice. He could have fled to his nearest forces but that would have meant civil war. Characteristically, he decided to see what he could do on his own.

That night, Gustavus gave a party at the palace to which all, including his greatest enemies, were invited. He was carefree and charming as ever and never once betrayed the tension he was under. The main event of the evening was the first performance of an opera in the Swedish language, *Thetis och Pélée* by Uttini, for which the King had contributed the libretto. It was a great success, but the subject on every tongue was the mutiny, and every eye was on the King as he sauntered from room to room. Several tried to make him betray himself. In one room, he came upon a group listening to his arch-enemy, Senator Ribbing, who turned insolently to him. Had the King heard that the officer on duty at Christiansand had said that the mutiny was on his Majesty's orders? Quite calmly the King replied that he had heard the same story except that it had not been an officer, but a simple sentry who made the statement. An officer would have known better. As he circulated, he let it be known that he would go down to the Artillery Yard next morning to watch the parade, as he often did. After his guests had left, he went through his papers, destroying anything that could incriminate others. He wrote to his brother Charles, asking him not to avenge him if he fell. He still had no money, which was alarming since he might need to bribe. He sent out Beylon, a Frenchman on his staff, to try to raise some, and Beylon managed to borrow 5,000 ducats from a Dutch banker. He locked a scribe into one of the rooms, and gave him a draft constitution to copy out. He then went out and accompanied the night patrol of the Burgher Guard Regiment on its round of the city.

The King did have a number of supporters amongst the junior officers in the town, and as he rode to the parade next morning, some of them joined him along the way, so that he collected a following of sympathisers. After the parade, he inspected the troops before they marched back to the palace. He then announced that he would return home on foot, which was the pre-arranged signal, known to his sympathisers, that the coup was on. As many as were initiated therefore walked with him. When they reached the palace, he found that the Senate was already in session, discussing the resolution calling for his arrest and impeachment. He sent two officers, Count Frederick Horn and Ensign Lars Hjerta, to keep them inside their council chamber, while he went alone to talk with the soldiers on guard duty. To his horror, he found that their captain was an ardent Cap, called Cederström; for a moment his heart failed him, and he could not get the words out. However, he pulled himself together and, with some passion, explained to the men what was happening. They rallied to him, and even Cederström agreed not to interfere, offering his sword to the King, who returned it saying he had too good an opinion of its owner to imagine that he could make bad use of it. While this was going on, one of the senators looked out of the window. Turning to his colleagues, he said, "Gentlemen, are you aware that the King is talking to our guard?" They tried to intervene, but it was already too late. They were prisoners. Not all the King's enemies were caught so easily as the Senate, but there was more panic than effective action. One man, General Pechlin, kept cool and nearly turned the tables. He went straight to the docks intending to turn the guns of the fleet on the city, but he got there minutes too late. Frustrated, he left Stockholm, hoping to rally his own regiment in the north, but he failed and was lucky to escape arrest. In the meanwhile, the King was riding triumphantly through the city to the cheers of his loyal subjects. By the time Toll and Sprengtporten arrived, he was in complete control. No-one had been hurt, but the Age of Liberty was over. The Gustavian Era had dawned.

It lasted for twenty years. Politically its theme was the aristocrats' struggle to regain what they had lost, a story with twists and turns enough to fill a book. In the end, it was because of their lack of success that they killed their King. The Era is better remembered today for its cultural impact. Gustavus brought Camelot to Stockholm. There was no form of artistic activity that he did not encourage, often by importing foreign exponents, many of whom left when he died but their impact remained. And in some fields, the Gustavian Era was a golden age of native Swedish talent – in poetry and sculpture, for instance. His chief delight, however, was in performance – pageants, theatre, music and especially in the opera – anything that involved dressing up and fantasy. Soon after his accession, he organised a medieval tournament, more brilliant for its cavalcades and costumes than for its skill at arms.[3] Frequent *divertissements* were held, usually on some historic theme, such as the court of Queen Christina, with fancy dress, *tableaux vivants* and banquets of the period. He loved to act and to produce plays himself, and he wrote for the stage. Ceremonial also fascinated him and he liked nothing better than to design court uniforms and to work out an etiquette for all occasions. He even devised a ritual for the royal playing of cards which required the courtiers to stand in a ring and bow each time the Queen played a card. And he loved balls, especially masquerades. He was his own master of the revels. One of several poets who flourished under his encouragement wrote afterwards: "Gustavus III came among us like spring and, in an instant, all the hidden forces of life were opened and poured forth their abundance and melody awoke on every side."

After he died, the grey mists rolled in again, and the Swedes, looking back, wondered what had inspired them so to forget their normal inhibitions. They came to realise, once it had gone out, that what they had taken for the sun, had but been their King. Carlisle called him "a shining sort of man". It would be hard to think of a better description. Not all his subjects shared his enthusiasms, however, and many, especially of the Cap persuasion, were convinced he would ruin the country with his routs as surely as his forebears had with their victories.

Verdi, who based his opera on a play by Eugène Scribe, captures brilliantly this side of Gustavus's character – his charm, his gaiety and his high spirits. It also catches something of his moral courage but not his great political gifts. It hovers around his sexual ambivalence, with Oscar supplying a hint of homoeroticism. The opera is certainly misleading in so far as it portrays him as a womaniser. He did, all his life, cherish a romantic attachment to the Countess d'Egmont, a French lady he had met in Paris. It was probably always platonic and certainly was latterly, for her death did not abate it in the least. He continued to neglect poor Sophia Magdalena until, quite suddenly, in the mid-70s, he was seized with the thought that he must have an heir. After some fifteen years of unconsummated marriage Gustavus was perplexed to know how to go about it, and sought the advice of one of his equerries, named Munck, who was said to be capable at this sort of thing. While all Sweden fell about with laughter, the two men collaborated to such good effect that a son was soon born, and the Vasa dynasty assured. The Swedes laughed quite a lot about their eager young King, the echo of which we hear in Act II of the opera.

Immediately after his coup, Gustavus found himself with absolute power, but, mindful of his Uncle Frederick's warning, he used it with a restraint which was entirely in character. He had several confrontations with the nobility during his reign, and got the better of them each time, but, afterwards, his first concern was always to conciliate, to smooth ruffled feathers and to restore self-respect. Some historians suggest that he might have lived longer had he been sterner, but that was foreign to his nature. He was a monarchist because he believed that only monarchs could be truly benevolent, could rule impartially and unite all their people, but he abhorred the thought of ruling by fear. He now offered his new constitution, which redressed the balance of power but left the Riksdag with much control over the finances and with the ability to forbid an aggressive war, which must have comforted those countries which had suffered most from Sweden's aggressions in the past. Although several mobilised, none of them intervened to uphold the old constitution.

Wildly popular, the first few years of Gustavus's reign were one long honeymoon during which he could do little wrong in the eyes of most of his people. He at once abolished the political parties, believing that Swedes should be Swedes, and not Caps or Hats. He also abolished torture, and established the freedom of the press. He reorganised the armed forces and rebuilt the navy. He reformed the judiciary. There was hardly a part of the Swedish government which was not improved. Most important of all, he reformed the currency. Under Gustavus, foreign loans and subsidies were used to stabilise the economy and not to corrupt politicians. His most important step was to choose an obscure junior councillor, Liljencrantz, as his Finance Minister. Gustavus had great flair for picking the right man for a job, and Liljencrantz turned out to be not only a financial genius but honest also. Perhaps the King's most outstanding gift was his oratory. Time and time again his speeches turned a hostile audience so that they forgot their resentments and shared in his patriotic enthusiasm. Only afterwards, when the votes had been counted, did they look at each other and wonder what sort of spell he had cast on them. He had many more qualities than Verdi's hero but three hours in the theatre are not enough to portray all aspects of so complex a man.

Gustavus was not infallible. One of the Swedes more uncouth habits was their drunkenness, which was catered for by a cottage industry of distilleries of uncertain quality, whose combined demands on the economy were massive. Sweden has a hard climate, and crop failures and famine were not uncommon, but no matter how hungry the people might be, the distilleries still took huge amounts of grain. Gustavus felt that this national weakness harmed his beloved countrymen, and lowered their potential as citizens. No doubt it did. Liljencrantz meanwhile saw brandy as a potential source of money which could be used for the benefit of the country as a whole. Between them, these two men of genius developed a plan to come between the poor and their main source of comfort in a harsh world. In 1776 they banned private distilling and introduced a nationalised industry which proceeded to demonstrate all the shortcomings that have ever since typified nationalised industries the world over. While the government distilleries lost money, private distilling increased both in volume and profit, despite ever stronger efforts to suppress it. The suppression eventually provoked a peasant uprising, engineered by none other than the King's old enemy, Pechlin. It was put down forcibly, and did untold damage to the King's popularity, which he may not have immediately realised because the Riksdag, which was held soon afterwards, was almost sickeningly obsequious. Whether Gustavus knew it or not, the honeymoon was over, and there was one who did know it. General Pechlin, whose antennae picked up the slightest whiff of anti-royal sentiment, quietly returned to Stockholm where his house became a meeting place for anyone who wanted to grumble about the King amongst kindred spirits. In the meanwhile Gustavus, believing that all was well, set off on a prolonged tour of sight-seeing throughout Europe.

Gustavus's second and much worse mistake came a decade later. This was his war with Russia in 1788–90. He had, shortly before, had a shock at the hands of the Riksdag which he had called in 1786, and which brought the growing discontents of his people to the surface. Gustavus felt an almost mystical love for his subjects, but he needed theirs in return. Their love seemed to be weakening, or perhaps the aristocrats were coming between them again. He began to worry that his early lenience might have opened the way for a detested factionalism to return. Looking back to the days when the Swedes had united so fervently behind his forebears, he pondered whether a war might now re-animate their patriotism. In 1788, an ideal opportunity presented itself. The Russian Empress, Catherine II, was pre-occupied with wars in the south, and had left St Petersburg almost undefended. Although it was barely more than a day's march from the Swedish border, she believed that Gustavus could not attack without the sanction of the Riksdag. Even if he could get this, it would involve weeks of argument during which she could organise a defence.

Anyway, she regarded Gustavus as clever but effete. It did not appear such a risk, but it was.

Gustavus did not entirely ignore his own constitution, but he lied to the Senate, telling them of massive Russian preparations for an invasion of Sweden. The Senate believed this fabrication, and unanimously authorised the King to take appropriate counter-measures. On this basis, Gustavus went to Finland to lead the attack. Mindful of history, he embarked on the exact day on which the great Gustavus Adolphus had first landed in Germany, 150 years before. But Gustavus was not Gustavus Adolphus, and when he ordered the advance into Russia, his officer corps mutinied. Some feared that the Vasas were reverting to type, while others sensed an opportunity to regain power for their class. They refused to march to the frontier, and even sent a delegation to negotiate with the enemy. The Anja Conspiracy, as it was called, almost brought the country to ruin. Catherine ignored the con-spirators' delegation and, while she gathered her forces for a counter-stroke, there was an impasse. Gustavus was in a terrible position. He could not leave the front, since to do so would be seen by all as, at best, an admission of defeat or, worse still, cow-ardice. What the next Riksdag would do to him did not bear think-ing about. In the meanwhile, so long as he stayed in Finland, he was little better than the prisoner of his mutinous officers, and exposed to their insults. And who knew what would happen as soon as Catherine was ready to exploit his plight? He was saved by his arch-enemies the Danes. Thinking to profit from his help-lessness, they invaded southern Sweden. When Gustavus heard the news, he exclaimed joyfully, "I am saved!" He had his excuse to leave Finland.

He did not go back to Stockholm but to central Sweden, to the mining districts known as the Dales, where a sturdy breed of patriots lived. Two hundred and fifty years before, Gustavus Vasa had sought the help of the Dalesmen to reclaim Sweden for the Swedes, but since then, their robust patriotism had generally been considered too meaty for everyday use. They were no respecters of rank or nobility, and, once allowed out, would they ever go back to their Dales again? Always mindful of historical symbols, Gustavus followed exactly the route taken by his great ancestor. It was as though time had stood still. He soon had 20,000 volunteers drilling with the antique muskets which were all he could provide. With no more time to spare, he rushed on to Gothenburg, Sweden's second city, which was about to be besieged by the Danes. With dilapidated defences and faced by 12,000 invaders, the commandant of Gothenburg had already decided to yield without a fight, when, exhausted and muddy, Gustavus arrived. He had ridden 250 miles in forty-eight hours, but there was no time to lose. He set the people to digging earthworks. He remounted the antiquated cannons on the ramparts. He organised a people's militia. He deployed the first units of Dalesmen as they arrived. He burnt the bridges across the Gota river. In no time, the situation was transformed and Gothenburg stood defended, not by the best equipped of garrisons but by one clearly intending to exact a high price for their city. Disconcerted, the Danes hesitated, which allowed the English ambassador to attempt mediation between the two sides. As a result, the war was called off, Sweden was saved, and Catherine was furious.

Gustavus had many exceptional qualities as a leader, not the least of which was the knack of being at the right place at the right time. He had already displayed this during the critical twenty-four hours of his first coup. He showed it again by saving Sweden from dismemberment virtually single-handed in 1788. And yet he was not conventionally brave. He hated violence. His closest friend, General Armfelt, once said of him that "he is the biggest poltroon in the universe but that does not stop him from leading a forlorn hope against positions which we ordinary souls regard as impregnable." This was true. Time and again Gustavus took risks that no ordinary man would have thought sensible, but it was not through bravado or pugnacity. His courage, like his stamina, came from will-power. When necessary, he could drive himself to prodigies of strength and endurance which more strongly built men could only wonder at. There is no doubt that his conduct during the war retrieved much of the love of his people that he had lost through his interference with their drinking habits.

This became apparent when Gustavus recalled the Riksdag. With the Danish danger past, he did so because a means had to be found to resolve the impasse in Finland, to stiffen the nation's resolve to bring the war with Russia to a satisfactory conclusion and to vote the funds needed for that purpose. This time, when the four chambers assembled, the King found he had the support of the three lower chambers but not of the nobles. Despite an opening speech from the throne appealing to their patriotism as Swedes in time of war, it was soon clear that Gustavus was in for trouble. He therefore did something arbitrary. He arrested the leading troublemakers in the house of nobles. After this, it was relatively plain sailing to get what he wanted from the rest of the Riksdag, but the damage had been done. The aristocrats were outraged. The King had broken his own rules, and he was never forgiven. The supposedly enlightened monarch was no better than a tyrant. From this moment there was a distinct increase in the number of visitors to General Pechlin's dissident dinner-table.

The last act of the war was the second battle of Svenskund, a magnificent naval victory, in which the Swedish fleet, under the King's personal command, crushed a far more powerful Russian one. The treaty which followed was fair to both sides, and reflected a draw, but a costly one. There was not enough money in the Treasury even to celebrate the King's victory at Svenskund properly. Gustavus, however, now had a new preoccupation. The revolution in France had been increasingly obsessing him, and especially the plight of Louis XVI and his family. He had always regarded Louis as a fool, but he was nevertheless a king, whose person was sacred. France had always supported Gustavus, and his admiration for everything French had never abated. Then there was a special obligation. It was Marie-Antoinette's Swedish admirer, Axel von Fersen, who had engineered the family's attempted escape, the disastrous flight to Varennes. When that failed, Gustavus threw himself into all sorts of rescue schemes and warlike plans which greatly alarmed his less quixotic countrymen, and which diverted his attention from their growing discontent.

One delicate problem was to decide how best to deal with the Anja conspirators. They had many sympathisers but their mutiny had been far too serious simply to be forgotten, as Gustavus might have wished. In particular, there was a group of middle-rank officers, who had not only been ringleaders, but, led by one Colonel Hastesko, had once come to the King's tent to taunt and humiliate him, calling him "little Mr Red-shoes". This group was singled out, tried and condemned to death. A programme of public executions was planned. One by one, on separate days, the guilty were left to prepare themselves for death, until, at the last moment and with a typical Gustavian touch of theatre, their sentences were commuted. When the day came for Hastesko, therefore, it was a rather festive crowd that gathered round the scaffold, to picnic in the sunshine and enjoy a thrilling little melodrama. Hastesko, too, mounted the scaffold quite jauntily, and laid his head on the block; but where was the King's messenger? There was not even a distant cloud of dust! Before anyone had time to betray his feelings, the colonel's head was off, and the crowd reduced to a stunned silence.

Many things were combining to bring about a change of atmosphere at the court at this time. It was no longer a place of carefree revelry. Since the mutiny and the subsequent Riksdag, the King seemed preoccupied, even careworn. He was still charming and considerate. He still pursued his pleasures, but not with the same exuberance. The sunlight was already dimmer. There were still parties at the palace, but many people began to stay away, especially after Hastesko's death. It is undoubtedly about Hastesko that the conspirators are muttering in the first scene of the opera. The affair caused great bitterness, and recruited new visitors to Pechlin's house. At this stage, however, their grumbling did not amount to a conspiracy. Their host listened sympathetically, but took care not to make any compromising remarks himself. As a conspirator, Pechlin was a professional who knew how to minimise his own risk. When the real plotting started, he saw to it that it should evolve at two levels. While he and his friends philosophised, two younger members of the circle, Count Horn and Count Ribbing, were encouraged to think of action, but, at first, they were not thinking of assassination. The talk was of paying the King back in his own coin, of kidnapping him, and holding him in custody, while the Riksdag repealed all the acts he had forced through it. In the opera, Horn and Ribbing have shadowy roles, becloaked, baritone and barely distinguishable one from the other, although Ribbing, true to life, is made slightly the more aggressive of the two. It is he, for instance, who in Act II insists that Amelia should remove her veil. Both were in their late twenties, and both, in the heady times of the Anja Conspiracy and the subsequent Riksdag, had got themselves into difficulties by rashly resigning their army commissions. There the similarities ended.

Claes Fredrik Horn was the scion of one of the great families of Sweden. His grandfather had been Chancellor of the Realm and a founder of the Caps. His father was a distinguished soldier, and had initially supported Gustavus, but he had later reverted to opposition and had been one of those taken into custody during the recent Riksdag. The son had felt unable to go on serving a king who could do that to his father, and had abruptly sacrificed a promising military career as a fortifications expert. He was an able man, even brilliant, but a little unstable. An almost ludicrous tendency to panic under stress made him less than ideal as a conspirator. He had a very pretty young wife and children whom he loved dearly, and perhaps it was soft thoughts of them that sometimes unravelled his resolution.

Two years younger than Horn and still a bachelor, Adolf Ludvig Ribbing was made of sterner stuff. His father, Gustav, had been a constant thorn in the King's side and the family, all passionate Caps, had never reconciled themselves to the new order. The son had already served as a volunteer with the French army in the American War of Independence, and had picked up some fairly republican ideas on his travels. Since leaving the army, he had followed his father's example in politics and had been one of the King's most outspoken critics. But while his motives appeared entirely political and honourable, he had a private grievance. He had been rejected by a beautiful heiress, Mlle de Geer, who had then married Essen, one of the King's favourites. Ribbing blamed the King's influence for her preference. Whatever his motives might be, he was tougher-minded than Horn, but even Ribbing did not contemplate assassination until Anckarstroem arrived.

Anckarstroem was quite a different kind of man. He was not remotely like the trusty minister of the opera. He was a member of a respectable but minor noble family, thirty years old and married. His wife was not called Amelia but Gustaviana, and was a rather formidable woman, one of whose merits was that she had brought him a nice little dowry. One can understand why Verdi changed her name to Amelia – anything but Gustaviana – but the real Gustaviana has nothing in common with the imaginary Amelia, apart from being married to Anckarstroem. She certainly never had an affair with the King and, years afterwards in exile, she sued the playwright Scribe for saying that she had. Not only was the King far from being a womaniser, but he had probably never even met Gustaviana. All the society tittle-tattle of the time was about his liking for handsome favourites like Armfelt and pretty pages like Oscar, though there is not one of that name in the records. The page who brought Gustavus the warning letter at the ball was called Tigerstedt.

Shortly before the events in the opera, Gustaviana Anckarstroem had had an affair with a man named Runeburg, one of her husband's few close friends. Anckarstroem decided not to make an issue of this, probably because Runeburg owed him money, and he did not want a quarrel with him. In addition, both Anckarstroem and Runeburg were facing charges of sedition, arising from a trip they had made together during the Russian War to the front-line island of Gotland. Anckarstroem's talk there had been so rash that they were both arrested as spies, and subjected to a long, inconclusive and, in Anckarstroem's view, unjust trial. Although the King had personally intervened to stop the trial, this had in no way mollified Anckarstroem. Indeed, it had added to his obsession with killing the King. But his hatred for Gustavus must have had other sources.

A cantankerous and crossgrained man with a massive chip on his shoulder, Anckarstroem seems to have been cut out to be an assassin from the beginning. He lost both his parents while a boy, and was brought to the court as a page. Judging by the surly ugliness of his posthumous portrait, it is unlikely that he was ever one of the King's favourites, which might have sown the seed of his hatred for Gustavus. He did not stay long at court. Aged thirteen, he entered the army as a cavalry trooper, but, being a noble, he soon obtained a commission in the guards. It is not known why he resigned this at the age of twenty-one. Regiments have their ways of ridding themselves of misfits, but he was given an honourable discharge with the rank of captain. He next had an unsuccessful spell as a farmer in his native province in the north, where he is

reported to have quarrelled with everyone in the district. Thereafter, he moved southwards by stages, leaving behind a trail of ill
will, until he arrived in Stockholm with his family and a few cows,
intending to sell milk. His main livelihood came from usury,
based on Gustaviana's dowry. It had thus far been a rather bitter
life, full of disappointment and rejection. With anti-Gustavian fer-
ment all around him, it was perhaps easy for him to blame all his
misfortunes on the King and the King's supposed oppression of
the nobility. It was Horn's need to borrow some money that first
brought the two into contact at the end of 1790.

Although unbalanced, Anckarstroem had some redeeming features. He was apparently a loving, if stern, husband and father.
Furthermore, while much of his hatred for the King was irrational
and based on personal spite, he did convince himself that the King
was a dangerous tyrant, and that to kill him would be a noble
deed, which would earn him the gratitude of his countrymen.
There was certainly no hint of venality in his action. On the contrary, a crazed sense of mission seems to have strengthened him in
his struggles with his own conscience. In an apologia after the
event he wrote:

> All this time, the thought kept on occurring to me; is this right or is it not
> rather a sin? Nay, I would answer, 'tis thy bounden duty to love thy
> neighbour as thyself. If I were persecuted, I should wish others to help me,
> consequently I ought to help others. If I did the deed from selfish or
> malicious motives, it would be wrong, but now, it is the only comfort I
> possess in my most wretched state, which, with the help of the Great and
> Gracious God, will soon be changed into a most happy condition of things.

Later, he goes on:

> I bethought me much if perchance there was any fair means of getting the
> King to rule his land and people according to law and benevolence but
> every argument was against me . . . The King is more than gracious
> towards individuals but, if anything is demanded or required for the
> common weal, he gets nasty and everything turns out as he wills it . . . The
> misfortune that happened to me personally at the end of 1790 [i.e. his trial]
> . . . knit together my resolves rather to die than live a wretched life, so that
> my otherwise sensitive and affectionate heart became altogether callous as
> regards this horrible deed.

Anckarstroem's apologia reveals much of the confusion of his
mind, and goes some way to explain why the King's clemency

failed to mollify him. Muddled or not, he did not lack courage. He alone of all the conspirators did not flinch from the dangerous task of murder, and remained calm throughout. Later he bore the barbaric punishments meted out to him with great fortitude.

There are two other named characters in the opera. One is the sailor, Christian, through whom the King arranges a little free advertising for Ulrika Arvidson, the soothsayer. He is fictional but she is not. Mamsell Arfvidsson was no gipsy living in a cave on the seashore, but a society astrologer, much consulted by the gentry and even by the King. She is said once to have warned Gustavus to beware the next man he met wearing a red waistcoat, who turned out to be Ribbing. The operatic King laughs at Ulrika's warning, but the real one might have taken it seriously. He was quite superstitious, and had a particular premonition that March was an unlucky month for him. Although not afraid of death, he had a horror of assassination. He once said, "If I am to die a violent death, I pray that it may be publicly on the scaffold, not by the hand of some Damiens or a Ravaillac."[4]

By the autumn of 1791, the scene was set, and the key characters had been assembled for the assassination. All were poised for action, but, as in the opera, it was some time before the right moment arrived. Anckarstroem was to try several times to kill the King. The first opportunity, in December 1791, had arisen unforeseen, during an armed reconnaissance by Horn and Anckarstroem into the park of the Haga Palace. Its purpose was to verify whether or not abduction would be a practical alternative to assassination. There was a little isolated pavilion in the park where the King was believed to work late into the night. Stealthily, they crept through the shrubberies until they came upon it, and, sure enough, there he sat in the candlelight, only a few feet from them. There were no guards. Like Olof Palme nearly two centuries later, the King does not seem to have felt them necessary. He was at their mercy, but, although they had already discounted the idea of abduction, Horn had not yet prepared himself psychologically for murder. And then, while they watched, the King suddenly slumped in his chair, as if overcome by a seizure. Horn panicked, and did not stop running till he got back to his horse outside the park, leaving the bewildered Anckarstroem to trudge after him.

Next, two days later, Anckarstroem went alone to the opera. Gustavus was sure to attend, since it was a performance of that same *Thetis och Pélée* which he had first presented on the night before his coup. The King kept two boxes, the main one in the centre behind the pit and the other just to the left of the stage. He liked to divide his time between the two. They were connected by a long dark corridor behind the public boxes, open to anybody, but normally deserted when the curtain was up. There, Anckarstroem planned to ambush him, but he waited in vain. That evening the King never left his main box. This was so unprecedented that some of the conspirators became temporarily unnerved, wondering whether some divine spirit was protecting him. Others began to grumble that Anckarstroem and his friends were all talk and no action, and probably did not have the courage to do the deed.

Just before Christmas 1791, the conspirators' plans were thrown into turmoil when the King called a session of the Riksdag. No one had expected this and the King did so unwillingly, dreading a repeat of the hateful experience he had had with the previous session. The truth was, however, that the Government was almost bankrupt. The war had cost much more than anticipated, and subsidies promised by allies, like the Turks, had failed to arrive. France, of course, was now no help at all. On the contrary, Gustavus desperately needed funds to help Louis. There was no alternative to another session, but Gustavus decided it would be too dangerous to hold it in Stockholm. Instead, he selected the little town of Gävle which had a staunchly royalist reputation.

The conspirators were divided in their reactions to this development. Some welcomed it, feeling that the King was bound to antagonise more people during this meeting, which would help when the moment for revolution came. They counselled delay. Others were extremely worried that the King might be planning to do the nobles some new mischief. Why had he chosen such an obscure town? Why was he taking so many troops there, specially picked for their loyalty to him? Ever cautious, Pechlin decided it was better to wait and see what happened, and Anckarstroem, who was longing to get at the King on one of his unguarded evening strolls through Gävle, had to restrain himself.

In the event, the composition and humour of the Riksdag were much more favourable to the King than at the previous session, reflecting, no doubt, the country's admiration for his behaviour during the war. Furthermore, he surpassed himself in his handling of it. It was a *tour de force*. He got what he wanted, his opponents achieved nothing, and, although there were tense moments, they were always resolved with such good humour, wit and charm, that no-one could take offence. At the very last moment, perhaps out of mischief, the King announced that he wished to bestow the Order of Vasa on one of his most implacable opponents, a man called Frietsky. Frietsky was absolutely mortified by this distinction, and at first could only stutter in confusion, but his presence of mind returned, and he found words to refuse the honour on the ground that he had once vowed never to accept it. This he had done, he said, lest anyone should believe that his zeal to serve his King stemmed from an ambition for such favours. The scores were now even and there was an awkward silence, but then the King smiled, made a graceful little speech in reply, and closed the session. Gustavus had certainly not made any new enemies, but nothing he did now would soften any of the conspirator's hearts. Their plot had already gone too far. Too many people knew about it.

The Riksdag closed on 24th February, 1792. Everybody wanted to go home, not least Gustavus who was longing to get back to the pleasures of Stockholm before Lent put an end to the season. He was in a high good humour again. The conspirators followed close behind. Their best chance of success, they felt, was to do the deed quickly, while the King's most loyal troops were still in Gävle, but they were to be disappointed. No obvious chance presented itself until, on 2nd March, the papers announced that there would be a masked ball at the opera that very night. This took everyone, including the conspirators, by surprise since Lent had now started. Evidently, after a month of austerity in Gävle, the King was not going to be denied one of his favourite amusements. Religion was never one of his strong points. Horn agreed to go to the ball with Anckarstroem, and sent a message to his beloved wife that he was having to take a lady to it and would be home late. We do not know exactly what the countess replied, but it caused Horn to decide that, as far as he was concerned, the revolution would have to wait. Ribbing was located and he went with

Anckarstroem instead. Horn was not the only one with a prior engagement. The conspirators found that the opera house was nearly empty. They would be almost on their own with the King, if indeed he came. It was too dangerous and they decided to wait for another chance. But with Lent had come bitter weather in which few people ventured out if they could help it.

The failure of the ball had, of course, also been a great disappointment for the King. Not a person accustomed to being thwarted, it began to obsess him that he must have a masquerade. On the following Wednesday, notices again appeared in the papers announcing a ball for the next Friday. These balls were not by invitation, as implied in the opera, but open to anyone who applied for a ticket. People who wanted to please the King felt obliged to attend frequently, and two days warning gave them plenty of time to make the necessary arrangements to do so. A good crowd was to be expected. The conspirators agreed that the deed would have to be done this time. With the attempt so imminent, the leaders had been taking more and more risks, sounding out people who might support the revolution they all believed would automatically follow the King's death. Action was urgent. Thus resolved, the intrepid band wound up their courage yet again. Alas, it was not to be. Friday was so cold that at the last moment the ball was cancelled.

Panic now really began to seize the fainter hearts. At any moment and without warning, the arrests might start because someone somewhere had talked, but nothing happened. It is difficult to believe, in fact, that the authorities knew nothing. Perhaps they discounted it as the usual daydreaming of the usual gang of dissidents, and did not tell the King, knowing his distaste for this sort of report. More likely, the King knew all about it and dismissed it, confident that the love of his people would protect him. At all events, he was not to be deflected from holding a masked ball. On the following Wednesday another one was announced for Friday, 16th March.

Some of the stories surrounding the events of that day may be apocryphal, but it seems that at the last moment an element of farce invaded the drama. First, Horn's nerve more or less cracked. In the plan, the only one to go armed to the ball was to be Anckarstroem.

The others were going only to cover him, and confuse the situation. But Horn began to have visions of an angry mob hunting down the miscreants, and felt he too must have not only pistols but also a sabre. Unfortunately, he had left his sabre in the country. He scoured Stockholm for one to hire, which was easy enough except that no armourer could be persuaded to sharpen one in peacetime. Eventually he borrowed one from a cousin, and hid his weaponry in some builders' rubble just outside the opera house. Anckarstroem, meanwhile, had been quarrelling with a gunsmith, who had promised but failed to repair one of his pair of pistols. After a bitter argument, the man did what was needed, but made note of the incident. Ribbing also made a contribution by deciding that, for purposes of identification, they should all be identically dressed, not in the blue dominoes and red sashes specified in the libretto, but in black hats and cloaks, white masks and, according to some accounts, "shoes with square toes". He sent Anckarstroem round to the costumiers with a multiple hire order. Altogether it would seem that they were determined to leave nothing undone that could help the police to trace them. What further follies might they not have committed had there been yet another postponement of the ball! But Friday, 16th March dawned fair and mild. The ball was on. At the very last minute, however, one conspirator did crack.

Colonel Lilliehorn does not figure in the opera but he had an important task. He was not going to the ball, but would keep watch outside. As soon as he received the signal that the deed had been done, he was to deploy sympathetic troops to occupy key points in the city. He was an aristocrat, and believed that the King had done great damage to his class, but he had a problem with which many were wrestling. The King had been a fount of kindness and generosity to him personally. Gustavus had made a special friend and favourite of Lilliehorn, and gave him a regular allowance out of his privy purse. At the last moment, Lilliehorn decided to warn him. He wrote a long and rambling anonymous letter, full of clumsy attempts to disguise his own identity. Early in the evening, he gave it personally to a street urchin, a butcher's boy, with instructions to deliver it to one of the palace household, but the King had already left for the theatre, from where he would go straight to the ball.

Masked balls at the opera officially started at 10.30 pm, but no-one usually turned up so early. The opera house attendant was therefore quite surprised to see a figure in a black Venetian cloak and black hat, prowling about at least half an hour before he had expected the first guest or even the orchestra to arrive. More amazing still, this figure was soon joined by several more identically disguised figures. He does not seem to have noticed whether their shoes had square toes, but did remark that none appeared to have brought a lady with him. They stood in a group together, talking intensely and ignoring the other guests when they began to arrive. Even when the dancing started, they showed no inclination to join in, and remained in a conspicuous group.

The King, with two equerries, Essen and Loewenhjelm, came straight from the theatre to the opera house, and, as usual, went first to his private suite to dine. It was during dinner that the page Tigerstedt brought Lilliehorn's letter, saying that it contained urgent information. The King read it twice, and then sent young Loewenhjelm off to join his sweetheart, who was waiting for him on the dance floor. He showed the letter to Essen, who begged him to take heed of it, but Gustavus just laughed. He had had such warnings before, and to leave would be cowardly. Instead, after dinner, they both went undisguised to a box overlooking the ballroom, and stood in full view of all, contemplating the festivities. They saw a group of identically-clad men come together, approach to just below where they stood, and then disperse. After several minutes, the King turned to Essen and said, "They have lost a good opportunity for shooting me. Come! Let us go down. The masquerade seems bright and gay. Let us see whether they will kill me."

They returned to the private suite, where the King chose as his costume a black cloak with a large feathered hat, to which a face mask had been sewn. It was barely a disguise since the cloak did not cover his tunic, on which the orders of Seraphim and the Gun had been conspicuously embroidered. Thus attired, he emerged with Essen, and mingled with the dancers on the floor. Passing by Loewenhjelm, he whispered to the girl, "The pretty mask should be kind to her cavalier tonight. He was in quite a hurry to run away from me to join her!" Then, still with Essen, he threaded his way through the crowd up onto the stage, and thence into the refreshment room on its left hand side. While he stayed there for a few moments, the conspirators gathered outside, and when he emerged, they crowded round him, obstructing his progress. Horn distracted him, tapping him on the shoulder, and saying, "Bonjour, beau masque!" while Anckarstroem pressed his pistol into his back. Whether it was because of Horn's address or something else, the King turned, causing Anckarstroem's aim to waver. The pistol discharged itself obliquely into the right buttock, high up, a flesh wound which did not even cause the King to fall. Anckastroem had brought the second pistol plus a barbed and sharpened knife for just such an emergency, but, as he said afterwards his surprise flustered him, and he failed to use these.

People standing quite close by seem to have been unaware of what had happened, although one or two said later that they thought it was some form of practical joke. One guest was heard to say "I didn't know they allowed shooting at these balls!" The leader of the band also heard something unusual, and marked his score at the moment it happened, but they went on playing. Loewenhjelm heard it too, with more anxiety. He abandoned the pretty mask, and rushed to assist the King, clearing a space round him with his sword. But otherwise the dancing went on as if nothing had happened.

The King, of course, knew that something had. He asked Essen quietly to give him his arm, and suggested that they might make their way back to his suite. Understandably, he had not identified his assailant. Anckarstroem and the other conspirators had already melted away into the throng by the time Loewenhjelm arrived. Some of them, believing they had succeeded, made for the exits, and started to shout, "Fire! fire!", the prearranged tactic intended to confuse the hue and cry they thought would follow. But as there was neither hue and cry nor fire, they succeeded only in puzzling a few onlookers in the foyer.

In the meanwhile, the King and his companions were reacting calmly and efficiently to the situation. The guards were promptly ordered to close all doors, and allow no-one to leave. Messages were sent summoning the chief of police, Liljensparre, and naturally enough, doctors. The King's wound soon began to bleed seriously, and the first numbness to wear off. Nevertheless, he behaved throughout with cheerfulness, even with gaiety.

As rumours started to run through the city, an anxious crowd gathered in the square outside, the courtiers and diplomats began to arrive. First on the scene was the Russian ambassador, Count Stackelburg. He chided the King for his foolhardiness, but Gustavus just smiled. "Thank you, dear Count," he said, "but when a madman has made up his mind to sacrifice his own life to obtain yours, he must succeed in the long run."

Soon the King was holding court, sitting awkwardly, but greeting each new arrival with his normal urbanity and humour. Some he even had to comfort, sending for water and seats when they went white and swayed at the sight of the blood, now oozing and bubbling its way down his leg. Then, leaning on Stackelburg's arm, he attempted to walk out, but he found that he could not, almost fainting with the pain. He was placed on a chair and carried shoulder-high through the crowd, joking as he went that now he knew what it felt like to be the Pope.

In the meanwhile, Anckarstroem, caught inside by the closing of the doors, decided to divest himself of his weapons, the pair of pistols, one still loaded, and the awesome knife. Sahlberg relates that Anckarstroem, consumed with anxiety, tried to find out what was happening. He went to the buffet, took a drink, and engaged the attendant in conversation.

"What is going on?"

"Haven't you heard?" said the man. "The King's been shot."

Anckarstroem looked shocked. "How terrible!" he said. "Did you see who did it?"

"Yes."

"Really? What did he look like?"

"Well," said the man after a long pause, "he looked just like you."

Other sources, however, say that the guests had little doubt that the regicide was one of this group of identically-disguised men, and gave them a rough time. In the confusion, perhaps there is some truth in both stories.

Liljensparre arrived and decided that only limited action could be taken that night. He ordered all guests to remove their masks which considerably embarrassed some of them, particularly an elderly moustachioed major in the guards who had come dressed as a woman. It also revealed who had been flirting with whom, and many considered that the police were behaving in a very high-handed manner. That did not worry Liljensparre. He had a table set up on stage, and sat down to take down the details of everyone in the building. No-one was to leave until this was complete. In the meanwhile, he had the building thoroughly searched. It did not take them long to find the weapons.

While this was going on, the conspirators waiting outside were becoming confused. Colonel Lilliehorn realised that his warning letter had not worked. On the other hand, the assassination did not seem to have worked either. A handful of guests had emerged but with inconclusive news. There had been a shot but no-one had seen the King fall. And then the doors had been shut, and various members of the King's entourage had been seen speeding off on errands. Lilliehorn decided to wait and see, and the moment for action passed. Loyal troops occupied the key positions, and the coup fizzled out.

Next morning, the police summoned all gunsmiths, and at once discovered whose pistols they had found. Anckarstroem was arrested. He confessed, but insisted that he had acted entirely alone. No-one believed this, and the search was on. Horn, with difficulty, managed to retrieve his weapons, but he was soon under suspicion, as was Ribbing, if only because they had worn the same disguise. However, that was not a crime, and they were obdurate under interrogation.

The breakthrough came through Lilliehorn. It was no problem identifying him as the author of the warning letter, and the question naturally arose as to how he had known in advance about the crime. He first claimed that Mamsell Arfvidsson had foretold it, but the police were not much impressed with this explanation. Having none other, he soon broke down and confessed to a part in the plot which he had, after all, later tried to frustrate. Once broken, he told all. Horn and Ribbing, betrayed, could not hold out any longer, but Pechlin and his circle were another matter. Under Pechlin's lead, they had been careful to keep their tracks covered. Try as he might, Liljensparre could not break them, hampered ironically by Gustavus's abolition of torture. Pechlin taunted him, saying that, although innocent, he realised that no plot was complete without his arrest. Pechlin held out even when Liljensparre deprived him of his tobacco, but he never regained his freedom. Eventually, one of the minor conspirators, a rather nervous individual called Bielke, took poison and then panicked. Sending for a priest, he confessed all. Although the priest refused to reveal what he had heard in confidence, this suicide was taken as confirmation that a lot of people had been involved. A poignant little pot still exists in a Stockholm museum,⁵ containing parts of Bielke's stomach preserved in a mixture of arsenic and formaldehyde.

The King by no means shared his police chief's zeal. He could not bear the thought that one of his own subjects might have shot him, and clung to the hope that it was the work of one La Perrière, a French actor and known Jacobin who was then in Stockholm, but La Perrière had not been at the ball. Despondently, the King commented that "at any rate, the Jacobins must have suggested the idea. Swedes are neither cowardly nor corrupt enough to have conceived such a crime." He was an incorrigible romantic. As in the first act of the opera, he simply did not want to know who was involved, but, against his wishes, he was told when Anckarstroem confessed. He was stunned.

"It is only months since I saved him from a lawsuit," was his bewildered comment.

But the King was a realist too, and he knew better than anyone how badly he was hurt. The doctors had groped about in the wound – one put his whole hand in it – but they did not find all the nails and rusty metal with which Anckarstroem had filled his weapon. Nevertheless, they were optimistic about what seemed a superficial wound, especially when the King's condition remained stable for a week and his morale high. Gustavus was not reassured. Summoning his friend, Armfelt, he instructed him to form a regency council.

"Don't let's hope too much." he said. "This affair may be serious. I shall certainly grow much worse than I feel now."

In the meanwhile, he continued as though nothing much was amiss, greeting his many visitors cheerfully, and doing whatever his immobility allowed. But, after a week, gangrene set in, the pain rapidly became worse and a terrible cough began to wrack him. The King did not complain, but it was soon clear that he was sinking.

On the evening of the 25th March, almost ten days after the ball, he sent for his doctor. He asked him how much time he had left and was told it was only five or six hours.

"Then," said the King, "I've got until half past eleven."[6]

He sent at once for his closest advisers, and started to give them instructions and to make appointments. His own son was still too young to succeed, and he feared that his brother Charles might abuse his position as regent. He sent for him, nonetheless, and asked him to pardon the conspirators, but Charles drew the line at Anckarstroem. Gustavus then dictated his instructions regarding the appointment of a regency council, which would be sympathetic to what he had achieved and would act as a brake on his brother. The secretary was excruciatingly slow to write it all down and then, when the first copy was ready, he managed to upset the inkwell upon it. They started all over again, but the King's strength was running out. Perhaps the secretary was hedging his bets. Even the most faithful of servants must consider his own future when times are out of joint. Gustavus died before the second version was completed and Charles had no difficulty in getting it declared invalid.

Charles was a totally different character, weak and utterly without that seductive charm with which Gustavus could disarm his most resolute enemy. He dabbled in freemasonry and revolutionary ideas, and seems to have rather sympathised with the conspirators. Initially, however, there was such a wave of public anger at the assassination of the King that he had to ride out the storm. In particular, Anckarstroem was given an exemplary punishment. First made to stand on public display in the stocks, he was then brutally flogged, and finally he was taken to Skanstull where Amelia, had she existed, would have had to go to seek her magic herb. There, having had his right hand cut off, he was beheaded, after which his body was quartered and displayed to the multitude.

Four of the other conspirators, including Horn, Ribbing and Lilliehorn, were also eventually condemned to death but, before the sentences were carried out, the regent, Charles, had them commuted to perpetual banishment on the grounds that this had been Gustavus's dying wish. This was not entirely true. Gustavus's last wish had been to frustrate Charles's succession to power, but in this he had failed, and no-one was in the mood to argue. Lesser men were now in charge. They made haste to sweep away most of what the King had done, not so much because it was bad but simply because he had done it. It was not until the late nineteenth century that anyone again challenged the power of the aristocracy, and then it was not a king that did so.

Thus died Gustavus III of Sweden, victim of one of the more contemptible and stupid crimes in history. He tried to swim upstream, and was killed not because he had failed, but because he was succeeding. But then the stream carried everything away. He would have been much saddened by most of what happened afterwards, but he would have been enchanted to know about the opera.

NOTES

1 Apparently, as a young boy Toll was stupid and sullen. In his mid-teens, he was in his parents' house with some friends when one of them, in play, took an antique pistol off the wall, pressed it to Toll's forehead and pulled the trigger. It turned out to be loaded, but the ball skimmed past Tom's brain without doing lethal damage. What it did do, on the other hand, was change his personality. He became intelligent, witty and good-natured.
    Despite his false start in the army, he reached the rank of Field-Marshal and became a senior statesman but eventually fell from power. He was disgraced, arraigned and condemned, in the language of the court, to forfeit "life, honour and goods". He replied, disdainfully, "My life belongs to the Almighty, my honour to history and the only good I possess after long and faithful service to the crown is a good conscience of which no man can deprive me."

2 The story goes that it was Louis XV's mistress, Mme du Barry, who stole Gustavus's letter from under Louis's pillow and gave it to the English. This is not very likely. Gustavus had made a particularly good impression on Mme du Barry when he visited her, by presenting her favourite poodle with a diamond studded collar.

3 Although the conception of the tournament had mainly to do with mounted fancy dress, the King was determined to acquit himself well at the lists. For weeks beforehand, he rose daily at three and practised tilting until mid-morning. He spent the rest of the day studying heraldry and manuals of chivalry. He did virtually no state business during this period.

4 Damiens stabbed but failed to kill Louis XV in 1757. Ravaillac successfully assassinated Henri IV in 1610.

5 The Livrustkammaren in the Royal Palace.

6 The majority of the direct quotations are taken from R. Nisbet Bain's biography, *Gustavus III and his Contemporaries*.

LA TRAVIATA

Giuseppe Verdi

*Libretto by Francesco Maria Piave
after Alexandre Dumas*

Dramatis Personae

Alfredo Germont, *a young man from Provence*
Giorgio Germont, *his father*
Gaston, Vicomte de Letorières, *Alfredo's friend*
Marquis d'Obigny, *Flora's protector*
Baron Douphol, *Violetta's protector*
Dr Grenvil, *Violetta's doctor*
Giuseppe, *Violetta's coachman*
A messenger

Violetta Valéry, *a courtesan*
Flora Bervoix, *her friend*
Annina, *Violetta's maid*

Synopsis

ACT ONE

The curtain rises to reveal a party in progress in Violetta's house, with guests arriving, including Flora, d'Obigny and Douphol. Violetta has been ill, but cheerfully bids them all make merry, for the night is young. Gaston arrives and introduces Alfredo Germont as the unknown admirer who has been calling daily to ask after her health. She teasingly asks Douphol why he did not call, and he reacts sulkily, refusing her invitation to propose a toast. Instead Alfredo obliges, leading the assembled company in a drinking song.

A band strikes up off-stage, and Violetta is leading her guests to the dance floor when she falters, coughing painfully. She waves her guests on, but Alfredo anxiously stays with her. He tells her how he would like to cherish her, if only she will allow it. She does not at first take him seriously, but then he sings passionately of how he has loved her, ever since he first saw her. She warns him to beware. She has no love to offer, only friendship, but he persists. Relenting, Violetta gives Alfredo a flower, and bids him return when it is faded. He may visit her next day, but must promise to be obedient, and not talk of love. Transported with joy, he leaves, soon followed by the other guests.

Left alone, Violetta ponders. To be truly loved and cared for would be a wonderful new experience, and she wistfully repeats Alfredo's phrases, but then she pulls herself together. It is folly! Her vocation is pleasure, and she is resolving to stick to it when

she hears his voice again, protesting his love. Is he in the street outside or in her head? Either way, she cannot escape him so easily.

ACT TWO

SCENE ONE: Time has passed. Violetta has given up everything to
live with Alfredo in the country, not far from Paris. Alfredo, who
has been out shooting, enters through a french window from the
garden. He is singing happily about how much Violetta loves
him, when Annina enters in travelling clothes. Cross-questioned,
she admits she has been to Paris, to sell yet more of Violetta's
possessions in order to pay their bills. Ashamed, he too rushes off
to Paris.

Violetta enters and is surprised but relieved not to find him,
since she is expecting her lawyer. Giuseppe brings her an invitation from Flora to a party that night, and she laughs at the very
idea. A visitor is announced, but it is not her lawyer. It is Alfredo's
father, who at first treats her so disrespectfully that she dismisses
him. More politely, Germont insists he must stay for Alfredo is
ruining himself. Stiffly, she corrects him, showing him the receipts
Annina has just brought. He is astonished, but she explains that
love has transformed her. Changing tack, he tells her that she can
never escape her past, which will drag down not only Alfredo but
his family too. Already, his young sister's marriage is threatened
by the scandal. Violetta is appalled, and agrees to leave Alfredo
until after the wedding, but Germont wants more. Relentlessly he
points out that Alfredo's love for her will not last, and that eventually he will come to hate her for ruining his life. Utterly miserable, she concedes. Germont may tell his daughter that, for her
sake, she will sacrifice her own happiness. She will have to convince Alfredo that she no longer loves him. He will then need his
father's support – just as she does now. It will give her courage if
Germont will embrace her as a daughter, and promise to explain
everything to Alfredo when she is dead. But now he must wait in
the garden until he is needed.

Alone, she at once sends Annina with an acceptance of Flora's
invitation. She is trying to compose a letter to Alfredo when he
returns. She refuses to let him see it, and he tells her about an

angry letter from his father, who is coming to see them. Violetta says she must not be present when he does, but surely he will relent when he sees how much they love each other. Suddenly, overwhelmed by emotion, she clings to Alfredo, and implores him to love her, whatever happens, just as she loves him. She runs out of the room.

Alfredo still suspects nothing, even when he hears that Violetta has gone to Paris, but he starts to worry when a messenger brings her letter. Trembling, he opens it. With a cry of pain, he falls into his father's arms, but immediately rejects him, hardly hearing Germont's reminders of his loving family in Provence. Stalking angrily about, he finds the invitation, and resolves to go to Flora's. Germont now tries whether a little self-pity will soften his son's heart, but Alfredo is blinded by his jealous fury.

SCENE TWO: News of the lovers' separation has already reached Flora's party, where guests dressed as Spanish gipsies and matadors present a cabaret. A tense Alfredo arrives and dismisses questions about Violetta. He goes to gamble, and does not see her enter with Douphol, but she sees him. She begs to leave, but Douphol forbids her to do so or to speak to Alfredo. Alfredo's reckless remarks provoke Douphol to challenge him at cards, hoping to teach him a lesson, but Alfredo's luck is in. They agree to continue after supper.

The room is no sooner empty than Violetta rushes back in extreme agitation. Despite the ban, she has sent for Alfredo, who must leave, since Douphol is spoiling for a duel. Alfredo asks her if she takes him for a coward, or is she afraid that he will kill her new protector? He will only leave if she promises to come with him. She cannot, but cannot explain why not. He asks her if she loves Douphol. Brokenly, she says that she does.

Beside himself, Alfredo summons the guests to witness him insult her, and throw his winnings in her face. Now he owes her nothing. His father, in the doorway, has seen and disowns him. Alfredo is at once seized with remorse, Violetta sings of his cruelty and of her love, and all the other characters express their outrage in a swelling finale. During its course, Alfredo and Douphol arrange a duel.

ACT THREE

It is winter. Violetta is lying desperately ill in her darkened bedroom. Dr Grenvil visits and confides to Annina that there are only hours left. Violetta sends Annina to see if there are any letters, and, on the way, to donate half her remaining money to the poor, since she will not need it herself. Left alone, she pulls out a crumpled letter, and re-reads it aloud. It is from Alfredo's father. Alfredo, having wounded Douphol, had to leave the country, but now knows all, and is hurrying back to see her. Tottering across the room, Violetta gazes at her ravaged beauty in the mirror. If he does not come soon, it will be too late. Her reverie is interrupted by carnival noises from the street, and, moments later, Annina returns in high excitement, followed at once by Alfredo. In his arms again, hope revives, and soon they are talking of life together outside Paris, where fresh air and his love will revive her health. But even joy is too much for her to bear. She tries to put on a dress, and her strength fails. Alfredo realises just how ill she is. They send for Grenvil, who must cure her now that she wants to live. It would be bitter to die so young, and on the very threshold of happiness. Alfredo pleads with her not to leave him alone.

Grenvil and Germont arrive together. It is clear to all that Violetta is dying. She summons Alfredo to sit by her, and, giving him a miniature of herself, urges him to find and marry a pure young girl, and to give her this likeness of one who will be watching over their happiness from above. The others are all expressing their emotions when, suddenly, Violetta's pain eases, but as she starts to rise from her bed she collapses dead in Alfredo's arms.

Led Astray?

Violetta is based on a girl named Alphonsine Rose Plessis, who was born in Normandy on 15th January, 1824. She is called Violetta only in the opera. Alexandre Dumas *fils*, in his novel *La Dame aux Camélias*, called her Marguerite Gauthier, but Marie Duplessis was the name she chose for herself. She added the Du to Plessis to give it a little class and, with a touch of fantasy, because she hoped one day to buy a property called Plessis, near her home village of Nonant. Marie's childhood friend, Romain Vienne, who late in life wrote a book about her, once asked her why she chose Marie. "Because," she replied merrily, "it is the name of the Virgin." "An original idea!" he answered. "Do you intend to add Magdalene?" She laughed. "I don't foretell the future. Marie's enough for now. One day I may yet emulate Magdalene, but one doesn't think about that at twenty." Like St Augustine, she did not want to be redeemed quite yet.

Poor Marie, she had to cram all the events of her life into a much shorter time than the saint. She was barely twenty-three when she died on 3rd February, 1847. Even so, she had already become something of a legend and an icon of the Romantic Era, which was itself approaching its end. It so happened that Charles Dickens was in Paris at the time, and he wrote in disgust:

> Paris is corrupt to the core. For a number of days every question –
> political, artistic and commercial – has been neglected by the newspapers.
> Everything is wiped out by an event of the highest importance, the
> romantic death of one of those glories of the demi-monde, the celebrated
> Marie Duplessis. You would have thought it was a question of the death
> of a hero or a Joan of Arc.

How a poor peasant girl, wretchedly brought up, could become so celebrated is one of the marvels of her story. It was not so much Marie's beauty that brought her fame but her talent, her charm, her character and, it must be said, her romantic death. She owes her immortality to Alexandre Dumas *fils* and to Verdi; it is due to them that she is still so familiar today. But they owe a debt to her as well, especially Dumas, whose book about her made his name. How much of the real Alphonsine lives on in his Marguerite Gauthier and in Verdi's Violetta? In the opinion of Liszt, perhaps her greatest love, "Dumas understood her very well. He did not have to do very much to recreate her again."

Dumas had also been one of her lovers, scarcely disguised in his novel as Armand Duval, and becoming Alfredo Germont in the opera. Indeed, when she died, he was on his way home from a foreign tour undertaken at least partly, to help him forget her. Unlike Alfredo, he did not arrive back in time to console her in her last moments; given his hurtful treatment of her, perhaps it was just as well. He did attend most of the obsequies. His reactions were lachrymose. First he poured out a lot of mawkish poetry, published as *Péchés de Jeunesse*, which he subsequently regretted and tried to have suppressed. Then, written in white-hot haste, he produced his *chef-d'oeuvre, La Dame aux Camélias*. This was so successful that it was soon turned into a play. Verdi attended the first night in 1851 and was much moved. Involved in his affair with Giuseppina Strepponi, he was easily able to identify with the lovers destroyed by bourgeois morality.

Once Marie's star had been firmly, almost respectably, fixed in the heavens, many others who knew her were keen to record their impressions of her, competing for a corner in her growing legend. Their memories often conflict over the detailed events of her life, and the confusion is compounded by their cautious tendency to use false names for her admirers. Happily, while there is disagreement about times, places and people, there is hardly any argument as to what sort of a person she was, except perhaps in one important detail. Did she *really* have a heart? Both Dumas's novel and Verdi's opera only work on the assumption that she did. They would have us believe that not only does she first offer to sacrifice her wealth and career for the love of an obscure young man but, when confronted with the damage this could do him and his family, she is prepared to sacrifice all her own hopes of happiness for theirs. Dumas, who insisted that his book was basically true, did not quite credit her with this. "Marie Duplessis," he wrote later, "did not have all the pathetic experiences which I gave to Marguerite Gauthier, but she would have asked for nothing more. If she sacrificed nothing for Armand, it was only because he did not ask her to do so. To her regret, she never got beyond Acts I and II." In the narrowest sense, he was certainly right, but the problem with Dumas is that as he got older he came to regard Marie as his own creation, almost his own property. And he was concerned to maintain his own part in her legend, as the handsome young lover who alone could awaken her latent capacity for love and self-sacrifice. In reality, of course, Dumas was never her only, or even her greatest love. That she made no sacrifices for him did not mean she made none for others.

Nonant is a very small village near Saint Germain-de-Clairefeuille in Orne. Marie's mother was called Marie-Louise-Michelle Deshayes, a soft-hearted and apparently very pretty girl of poor but respectable stock. Her great-grandfather, Du Mesnil, had been a squire with a picturesque manor house in nearby Argenteuil, but the family's fortunes had declined. Her grandmother had married one of the servants. Marie's father, Marin Plessis, was a terrible man. His parents had been a defrocked priest and a prostitute; he was himself an itinerant pedlar, good-looking and rather dashing in the eyes of the young village girls, but definitely no good. He was a feckless, violent drunkard. He married Marie-Louise in 1821, and Marie was the second child. She had an elder sister, Delphine. On marrying, Plessis gave up his travelling, and joined with his wife in a little draper's shop in Nonant, but it failed. So did the marriage. After ten years of ever more barbarous treatment, Marie's mother had had enough. She abandoned her husband and children and, after a few days in hiding, found a place in the service of an Englishwoman named Lady Yarborough. She died two years later in Geneva. Delphine was put in the charge of a distant uncle, Mesnil, and apprenticed to a laundrywoman. Marie was still only eight, and went to live with a cousin, Agathe Boisard.

Agathe Boisard was extremely poor, and already had three children of her own to feed. She undertook to look after Marie until she had taken her first communion, but after a year or so she found the burden too great. She asked Plessis to help, but he would not. Nor would anyone else. When Marie was about ten, Agathe had to tell her that she must fend for herself as best she could as far as food went. This meant begging. The child was soon hanging around the gangs of farm labourers hoping for a crust, and listening wide-eyed to their bawdy talk. Her curiosity soon got the better of her. One evening she waylaid a young man named Marcel, a servant to one of the village worthies, and, still barely eleven, she seduced him. The word *traviata* means led astray and, applied to Marie, may be a little charitable. Agathe, thankful for an excuse, sent Marie back to her father.

Plessis placed Marie with a laundrywoman named Tontain, and for some time she worked well. But the Marcel incident had set her father's mind to work. Marie was already very pretty, and she used to visit him every other Sunday. One Sunday, he took her to see Plantier, a rich old man of the neighbourhood. She did not get back to Mme Tontain until quite late on Monday, and, when she did, she had twenty francs in her pocket. No-one believed her story that her father had given her so much money. She began to visit Plantier regularly, and her work suffered. Worse still, she started to entertain the village girls with spicy stories, until their parents forced Tontain to sack her. Marie, now aged fourteen, went to live with Plantier. In later life, she would never say what transpired there, but after a few months, she escaped and sought refuge with a decent couple called Denin who had an inn. They took her in, and gave her a job as a servant for sixty francs a year. According to Romain Vienne, it was here that Marie first met Clémence Prat who was to become her confidante and procuress in Paris. Her father meanwhile was being investigated by the police for immorally exploiting his daughter, but he managed to talk his way out of it.

In the autumn of 1838, Plessis arrived at the inn and removed Marie. She worked briefly for an umbrella manufacturer, but again her father returned, and took her away. She disappeared for a fortnight but then reappeared, and set off with her father to walk to Paris. He had a sack of rabbit skins which he intended to sell, and it was thought he had the same intention towards Marie. Afterwards she liked to claim that she had been sold to gipsies, but strict veracity about her past, or indeed about anything, was never her strongest point. She used to say with a giggle that "telling fibs makes your teeth whiter."

Her father was indeed seen in hard negotiation with some gipsies, and there is that missing fortnight to explain, but whatever his intention, no deal went through because she was still with him when they reached Paris. Plessis left her with some cousins called Vital, who had a grocery stall in the rue des Deux Ecus, saying he would return to collect her after he had finished some business in Picardie. He went straight home, however, where he found that his few possessions had been taken to the rubbish dump. He spent the rest of his life living rough, and died within a year or so, a pariah.

The Vitals had no place for their fifteen-year-old niece, but found her one with a laundrywoman called Barget in rue de L'Echiquier. Mme Barget had two well-brought-up daughters, and when one Sunday the three of them came upon Marie in a compromising situation with a young man, she concluded that she had allowed a viper into her nest. The long-suffering Mme Vital came to the rescue and found a more worldy-wise friend, who had had a hard life herself. Mme Urbain had a fashionable draper's shop on the corner of the rue St Honoré and the rue de l'Arbre Sec. Marie, aged sixteen, became a seamstress and a *grisette*. Working for Mme Urbain gave Marie her first direct experience of *le beau monde*, of elegant ladies in unimaginably expensive clothes. She learned about good taste and city ways. She quickly adapted her Normandy burr to something more genteel, and learned how to wear her own clothes, such as they were, to best effect. She learned too, to dream of how things might be so much better, but like a hundred thousand other young working girls in Paris at that time, the gulf separating Marie from a better life seemed unbridgeable. The *grisettes*, the little grey people, were exploited. At a time when a skilled labourer's wage might be about twelve francs per week, a *grisette* could expect only twenty to thirty sous per day, enough, if she lived at home, for her to be nourished, and still able to save a little towards a shawl or some ribbons to cheer up her grey dress. If she had to fend for herself, as did Marie, a mean room cost so much that there was not enough left over to eat and buy the minimum needed to maintain a respectable appearance. Under these circumstances, it was difficult for a girl to remain respectable at all, but for Marie all went well, if frugally, for some six months. She settled down to work hard and learn all she could. She liked Mme Urbain, who was kind but firm, and knew all about the danger of having a pretty face. It was during this period that a young man-about-town, Nestor Roqueplan, first saw Marie. She was standing gnawing a green apple and looking longingly at a fried potato stall on the corner of the Pont-Neuf. She was dirty and dishevelled but exceedingly pretty, and he was touched by her. On an impulse, he bought her a bag of potatoes, and watched her wolf them and lick the paper when they were gone. The next time he saw her she was in very different circumstances. Much later still, in 1851 and now an impresario, it was Roqueplan who first discussed with Verdi the commissioning of a work for the Paris opera.

To survive, many *grisettes* were tempted to look for a protector, often, like Mimi in *La Bohème,* seeking one amongst the students of the left bank. It is not known what little adventures with men Marie may have had at this time, but she made firm friends of two girls. One, Hortense, also worked for Mme Urbain, while the other, Ernestine, was employed in the nearby Magasin du Louvre. One day, the three friends decided that by combining their savings and borrowing a little, they could afford a Sunday outing to St Cloud, but on the great day it poured with rain. They met in their damp finery at their rendezvous in the Palais Royal, and decided to make do with a tisane and a patisserie in one of the cafés in its colonnades. It was a fateful decision. As they sat in the corner they were noticed by the restaurateur – or at least Marie was.

In his memoirs, Romain Vienne calls the man Nollet, but he uses only false names and this is one that has never been deciphered. All we know is that he was forty, a widower, quite handsome, and that he too was from Normandy. He came over and sat with the girls, commiserating and being generally friendly until it was agreed that they would try again, the following weekend, to

spend the day at St Cloud as his guests. And so they did. It did not
rain, he was jollity itself, and he treated them right royally. At the
end of a day of huge meals and much laughter in the fairground,
he drove them all home in a chaise. He dropped the others first at
their lodgings, and then took Marie to hers. There he gently
detained her, and asked if he might see her again. She did not
object. It was agreed that after work next day she would come to
his restaurant at the Palais Royal.

It started in a conventional way. As often as he could, he would
take Marie out, and for the first time in her life she began to taste
some of the luxuries that she had never been able to afford. She
was no longer always hungry, and she began to accumulate lots of
little gifts. The big surprise came after a month. The restaurateur,
now totally captivated, decided to celebrate by asking out all three
girls from the first encounter and providing escorts for the other
two. At the end of the day the couples went their several ways.
Marie went with her restaurateur but he did not take her home.
Instead, they went to an address in the rue de L'Arcade where he
led her upstairs and ushered her into an apartment, furnished in
every detail down to a little maid, sitting in a back room and waiting for a mistress. Opening a drawer, he showed Marie three thousand francs which would be for her immediate needs, if she
would consent to accept this apartment.

Marie hesitated. A few days later she confided everything to
Ernestine, and the day after that she did not report to work. Several days later she did return, splendidly dressed, to pay her
debts, and say goodbye to Mme Urbain. They cried a little, and
Marie asked her to accept a silver ring that had belonged to her
aunt. She did not have the courage to face Mme Vital. Instead she
wrote asking for forgiveness, which she did not get. Mme Vital
wrote in reply: "If ever you cross my threshold, I will chase you
away like vermin."

He may not have been the romantic hero of her dreams, but
Marie had arrived. She was now *une femme entretenue*, free for the
first time from the hunger and deprivation of her life so far. It
seems a little unjust that the man who first discovered her should
remain anonymous. Nor was he given long to enjoy his discovery,
for things soon went wrong. Romain Vienne has been the best

guide to Marie's childhood, which he witnessed. After she reached Paris, he remained her friend, but saw her only intermittently and becomes less reliable as a source. His memoires were written forty years later, without the help of his personal papers which he had lost in the great fire of San Francisco. Some of his stories are therefore secondhand but, according to him, it was Marie's ability to spend that dismayed her restaurateur. His first gift of money went in no time, then a second and a third until the poor man was forced to call in reinforcements. Vienne says that it became a sort of relay race in which the restaurateur and his friends tried to keep up with her spending until, quite soon, they all gave up and Marie was momentarily left high and dry. This may be true. Her *insouciance* with money is not the least part of her legend. More credible, however, is the theory that she began to get bored. Perhaps her protector was a little ridiculous; perhaps he tried too hard to keep her in a cage. She apparently suspected that her maid had been put there as much to spy as to wait on her. Although she was now living in luxury, she was not having much fun, pent up except on days when the restaurant was closed. No wonder she urged him to let her make the most of these days, and take her to exciting places she had heard about. And no doubt he liked to go there too, and to show off the lovely creature on his arm. His vanity was his undoing. One evening at the Prado, a popular dance hall, a young aristocrat came slumming and spotted her. At this point, the restaurateur disappears from Marie's story.

Although others later claimed to have discovered Marie first, this young aristocrat was probably Antoine Agénor, Duc de Guiche and son and heir to the Duc de Gramont. He was certainly her first real lover and her Pygmalion. Much the same age as Marie, he was lively, talented, extremely handsome and rich. His blood was of the very bluest, his family being not just dukes but also peers of France, which put them in an exceedingly ancient and exclusive class. He later became a successful diplomat, and as Minister of Foreign Affairs under the Emperor Napoleon III, he had the dubious distinction of declaring war on Prussia in 1870. His first and less disastrous contribution to history was Marie. To say that he created her would be going too far, but he certainly drew out and polished all those extraordinary graces and talents which so distinguished her from others of her profession.

De Guiche moved Marie to a new apartment at 28 rue du Mont Thabor, and then, assisted by his grandmother, he took charge of her education in all the accomplishments that were expected of a young lady. He tackled her problems with reading and writing, grammar and elocution. She proved marvellously diligent and apt, and soon could write well, albeit with the occasional howler. Christiane Issartel quotes a charming letter from Marie to de Guiche, written much later when they were no longer lovers, in which, after many a prettily turned phrase, she suddenly writes *sel* instead of *celle*. Even more eagerly, Marie plunged into the arts, into literature and music, seeking to acquire in weeks all the cultivation and the polish most girls needed a childhood to develop. In keeping with the times, her taste tended towards the romantic, but she seems to have had an innate feel for quality. An English friend, recalling Marie later, wrote that "her inbred tact and instinctive delicacy compensated for an absolutely inadequate education. Whatever she recognised as admirable in her friends, she strove to master herself so that her natural appeal was enhanced by the flowering of her intelligence." Thus, she learned to play simple things on the piano and to sing. She could ride prettily and her dancing was one of her glories, which other couples on the floor would often stop to watch. Perhaps most remarkable of all, she learned the art of intelligent and cultivated conversation so that an intellectual, like Arsène Houssaye, could say of her: "When you are with her, you don't want to leave."

Marie soon became a leader of fashion. She not only dressed expensively; she chose her clothes with originality and flair, and wore them with an exquisite grace. Romain Vienne assures us that no matter how ravishing her costume, it was she who embellished it rather than the other way round. She undoubtedly soon adorned her young duke's arm most elegantly and with decorum. To be sure, she was still a little diffident and did not talk much, but when Roqueplan met them soon after he was as impressed as he was astonished. "The count had on his arm a most charming lady, very elegantly dressed, who was none other than my little gourmande of the Pont Neuf. She is now called Marie Duplessis."

What was she like? Curiously, there are not many representations of her, which the poet Théophile Gautier regretted. "What a shame," he wrote, "that so exquisite a person did not find her Praxiteles or her Raphael . . . or that none of these gilded young men who filled her boudoir with treasure chests and rare vases ever thought to put a handful of gold in the way of a sculptor, to capture such beauty in marble." Of the three authenticated portraits, the best known is the life-sized oil by Vienot. It is striking, but hardly supports the near idolatry with which she is mostly described. Perhaps it is too constricted by the conventions of the time; the ringlets *à l'anglaise*, the rather prissy little mouth, the bottle shoulders. At the same time, there are the huge velvety black eyes, the swan neck, perfectly flawless features and a gaze which is langorous and inviting in equal proportion.

The other two pictures are a little more animated but still leave us mystified. One, a sketch by Chaplin, shows her in her peignoir with her hair tumbling to her waist. She looks up wistfully with just a touch of mischief, but there is no elegance. In fact it makes her rather lumpish. It is said to be a copy of a lost portrait by Vidal, but that artist, whose livelihood largely depended on portraying respectable society women, hotly denied it. The other is a watercolour by Camille Roqueplan of Marie in her box at the theatre. She looks thoroughly matronly, yet all the men in the audience are looking at her while all the women are looking away. There is one other picture which some say is of her. It is by Anäis Colin and entitled *Le Maître à Danser*. It is full of movement and charm, and does look quite like her, catching her love of dancing and her determination to learn to do everything well.

None of these portraits attains the lyricism with which her contemporaries wrote about her. Dumas describes her in his novel as:

> tall and slender almost to a fault, she had the skill to improve even on nature by the way she wore her clothes . . . Her head was small – very striking with a hint of intimacy and allure. Her mother, as de Musset might have said, seemed to have made it small so as to make it perfect. Her oval face had an extraordinary grace with two dark velvet eyes under perfectly arched brows and veiled by lashes so long that when lowered they seemed to cast shadows on her cheeks. Her nose was small but spirited with nostrils slightly flaring as if scenting something sensual in the air. Her mouth was regular; her lips smiled bewitchingly to reveal

milk-white teeth. Her skin was like an untouched peach . . . Two
undulating bands of hair framed this charming face, allowing just a
glimpse of her ears before losing themselves behind her slender neck.

Dumas was, of course, writing in the first agony of young love
lost.

As Dickens complained, the Paris press seems to have been
quite carried away by emotion when she died, with journalists
competing to write the most lyrical obituary. Jules Janin, who
contributed the preface to Dumas's novel recalled seeing her at
the opera:

> It was her! But this time she was in full evening dress and with all the
> glittering accessories of a successful and fashionable woman. Her
> beautiful hair was dressed to perfection, intertwined with flowers and
> alive with diamonds. Her arms and shoulders were bare but loaded with
> necklaces and bracelets – emeralds. She carried a bouquet of flowers but of
> what colour? I know not. You need to be very young to note the colour of
> the flower over which leans such a lovely face. At our age we see only the
> cheek, the sparkling eyes.

Matharel de Fiennes, in *Le Siècle*, wrote:

> I feel I can see her still – huge black eyes, vivacious but soft, a little
> astonished even anxious, combining innocence with a dreamy desire –
> eyebrows of black velvet arching delightfully to divide the downy white of
> the forehead from the lustre of these eyes . . . in short, an effect so charming
> and so poetic that no matter who saw it, be he monk, octogenarian or
> schoolboy, he could not but fall hopelessly in love with her.

There must have been a glamour and a vivacity to Marie difficult to catch, either on canvas or in words. De Guiche took so
much trouble with her education, that one must wonder whether
he did not contemplate making her his duchess. Many an ancient
family has refreshed its blood from the chorus line. When the
summer came, and he felt she was ready, he took her away from
Paris to tour the German spas where all fashionable Europe met to
take the waters, to socialise, to dance, to gamble and, no doubt, to
flirt. It does not seem to have been a total success, at any rate in de
Guiche's view. Perhaps she was still a little too unsophisticated for
such company. Perhaps also her immediate enthusiasm for gambling with large sums of his money may have alarmed him,
although she seems to have been a lucky gambler. That, of course,
might have alarmed him even more, but gambling bored him any-

way. One way or another, there is just a hint that by the time they returned to Paris he was reconsidering his first enthusiasm. She, on the other hand, had been discovering the delights and the uses of money. She had no doubt received many compliments, and become aware of her power to attract and of the glittering future that was beckoning her. Inevitably, they had not been long back in Paris before de Guiche's monopoly was challenged.

Emerging one morning from her apartment, Marie found awaiting her a magnificent carriage, drawn by four English bay horses and complete with coachman. It was the offering of a young friend of de Guiche and fellow member of the Jockey Club, Comte Fernand de Monguyon. Marie got into the coach without hesitation, but not entirely without shame. A day or so later, out enjoying her new toy, she encountered de Guiche on horseback who, with mischievous gallantry, insisted on escorting her. "Cocher!" she called out, "please tell M. le Duc that I am not here!"

This must have been a giddy time for Marie, with all the gilded youth of Paris vying for her favours. She was the toast of the Jockey Club, a recently established meeting place for the young, the fast and the rich. Her name is even recorded as a signatory to some of the club's more facetious motions which she could not have signed herself. Like Danaë she was showered with gold and with gifts, each more extravagant than the last. There is a story that, in an effort to bring some order into this stampede, seven young men agreed to syndicate her, each sponsoring one day of the week. They even had made a beautiful dressing table with seven drawers into which she could segregate their gifts. Poor de Guiche could not compete, but as de Monguyon told him, "Friends of kept women must not be jealous." He seems to have taken it well. He never quarrelled with her or complained, and remained her life-long friend, but he left Paris. With him went any prospect that Marie might one day become the Duchesse de Gramont, if such a prospect had really existed.

Hidden in the shadows of this sunlit scene, it seems that Marie's first love affair was being brought rather brutally to an end. According to Romain Vienne, she found she was pregnant with de Guiche's baby, a situation which powerfully concentrated his family's thoughts. De Guiche's father, the Duc de Gramont, was by no means so bewitched by Marie as was his son, and seems to have had a hand in getting him to leave Paris. Furthermore, there is a strong possibility that, like Alfredo's father, he paid her a call to make sure no illusions were lingering in her mind. Whatever happened, she was given no choice in the matter, and she sat down to write de Guiche a sad little letter . . .

> Adieu, my beloved angel. Try not to forget me too much, sometimes think of one who loves you . . .
>
> Marie.

According to Vienne, she gave birth to a son who was taken from her, and brought up by the de Guiche family. Needing to recuperate and wanting to see her uncle Mesnil, who had become her guardian since the death of her father, she went home to Nonant, taking the road she had trudged with her father three years before. This time she was in a coach with her maid, Rose. She spent some time in Nonant, seeing old friends, including Marcel. She must have enjoyed showing off her finery and her sophistication, but they had not made her conceited. It is one of her most endearing qualities that while princes and dukes, poets and famous pianists paid her homage, she never forgot old friends from her childhood in Nonant, nor from her days of poverty in Paris. Ernestine and Hortense remained close to her; they too had become *femmes entretenues* though not on such an extravagant level as Marie. Both had accepted the protection of their squires from that fateful outing to St Cloud.

It would not have occurred to Marie to feel superior to her friends; she seems to have viewed her own good fortune almost as a sort of charitable fund, to be shared freely with others. She certainly never forgot what it was to be poor. Ernestine and Hortense were often in despair at her prodigality, and Georges Soreau suggests that she got through as much as 20,000 francs a year in gifts large and small to the needy. At a time when an artisan might be pleased to earn 500 francs a year, this seems a little exaggerated. Perhaps it just felt like that to some of the young men trying to keep up with her expenditure.

While Marie was in Nonant, she was able to renew her relations with her sister Delphine. Delphine too had had a difficult childhood, though she had not been quite so badly abused as Marie.

She had reacted in a very different way, becoming not only prudish but sour and cantankerous, so much so that she found it hard to keep a job, even as a washerwoman. Romain Vienne comments on the contrast between the two, pointing out that while Delphine could never make a friend, Marie "made friends with everyone who approached her because she never said an unkind word about anyone." Delphine was engaged to marry a weaver called Plaquet, and she was most unwelcoming to her fallen sister. Marie tried to persuade her to come to Paris, which she said was full of marvels, but Delphine would not. She merely berated Marie for her waywardness, for having had a bastard, and for bringing disgrace to their name. Marie persisted in trying to be friends with Delphine who, for all her principles, did not reject the little presents that sometimes came her way, but their relationship remained cool, as is shown by the following letter from Marie.

My dear sister,

I was very pleased to receive the letter you so kindly wrote to me for it is a long time since I had news of you. May God be thanked that you are well and also your family. It was a very pleasant surprise that the gentleman gave me when he visited my native district and came to see you, leaving you ten francs for a dress. Always write to me addressing your letters to this gentleman for I am expecting to leave for Baden before long where he will kindly forward them to me.

We do not know who "this gentleman" was, but he may have been a connection of a young man whom she met soon after her return to Paris, who was to play a considerable role in her life. He was Edouard, Vicomte de Perregaux, the grandson of one of Napoleon's financiers, a Swiss banker who had been rewarded with a fortune and a title. Edouard's father had been the banker's son and heir, but one of his aunts had married Marshal Marmont and become Duchesse de Ragusa, with the result that she now considered herself head of the family. It was a rich and influential family, although by no means in the same aristocratic class as that of de Guiche. Edouard's father had recently died and had appointed a guardian for his son. Edouard seems to have needed one. After an undistinguished period of active service with the army in North Africa, summed up by his colonel as "reasonably competent but somewhat immature", he had left the army, apparently because his father refused to enable him to meet certain debts of honour. However, by the time he got back to Paris, his father had died, and de Perregaux found himself suddenly rich. He plunged into fast Parisian society, becoming an enthusiastic member of the Jockey Club and riding his own racehorses with considerable success. He seems to have started an affair with a celebrated model, Alice Ozy, a beautiful but more brazen member of Marie's profession. She inspired the poet de Banville to compose an admonitory couplet:

> *Les demoiselles chez Ozy – menées*
> *Ne doivent pas songer aux hy-menées.*[1]

Alice had a wonderful figure, and was much in demand by artists, especially Chasseriau who was her lover. There may be something of her in the character of Flora Bervoix. While rather grasping she was not insensitive. When she died many years later, she left a sad little legacy to a man she had known, because "he had once greeted me openly while he was in the company of an honest woman."

Before considering Marie's affair with Edouard, it will be as well to consider the gulf separating polite society and the demi-monde, a word coined to describe the top of a hierarchy of prostitution. Despite the Government's efforts to bring it under control, prostitution had a golden age during the reign of Louis Philippe. The police had 30,000 registered whores on their books, working under cruel conditions in the *maisons de tolérance*, but these did not include a vast number of *filles de barrière* walking the streets on their own account. Then there were the 100,000 *grisettes*, many of whom were forced by poverty to find support in whatever way they could. Slightly further up the scale came the *lorettes*, concentrated round Notre Dame de Lorette where the upper classes would go whoring. At the top of the tree were the great courtesans, women of character, beauty and talent, but also known as *mangeuses d'hommes* or *grandes horizontales*. In her brief career, Marie became perhaps the greatest of these. No Russian archduke or Polish count would regard his visit to Paris as complete without calling on her, and leaving some costly offering. Marie's salon was an exclusive club, however, to which not everyone was admitted. To quote her English friend again; "In her view, money alone did not justify any pretension to her favour unless allied with style and background. It was on her discernment of these qualities that she selected her circle." Perhaps, but money was still important, for gallantry forbade any opting out of one's share of the lady's dues. She might sometimes take as a lover a young man, like Dumas, with no fortune, but, while flattering in a way, his position was invidious. There was a slang term for such fancy men – *maqereau*, literally mackerel, but meaning gigolo.

Sometimes Marie's lovers became so infatuated as to suppose that they could introduce her into society but a letter, first published in 1907 in *Mercure de France*, reveals the true situation:

> My dear Arvers,
>
> d'Anthoine has just told me that M. Roger de Beauvoir is to bring Mlle Marie Duplessis this evening. Without wishing to seem prudish, my friend's lady guests would perhaps prefer not to meet Mlle Duplessis. He has asked me to ask you to arrange with Roger that it does not happen. See you later – in great haste.
>
> Baudemon.

There was one curious episode, recounted by Romain Vienne, when Marie *was* invited across the divide. A group of society ladies formed a desire to meet this young Normande who was so fascinating their menfolk, and arranged through one of the latter to invite her to a party to raise funds for charity. Marie, who was patroness of an orphans' home, agreed to risk a little humiliation for their sake. It went very well. The ladies were captivated by her modesty, dignity and charm, and were impressed by her generosity which, they discovered, seemed to exceed their own. The initial party was such a success that Marie was persuaded to call on other great ladies, and wherever she went, they were forced to admit that, at any rate, their men had good taste. Once everybody's curiosity had been satisfied, the gulf opened up again and the invitations ceased, but Marie was happy to have raised 24,000 francs for her orphans.

Marie did have one woman friend who was "honest". This was Judith Bernat, the well-known actress. Marie, who loved the theatre, admired Mme Judith very much, and once when Judith was ill, she went every day with flowers for her, leaving them anonymously like Alfredo in the opera. As soon as Judith felt better, she asked her maid who had left the flowers, and was told "a very beautiful lady from high society." The next day, Judith gave her maid a note for this lady, to which Marie replied:

> Mlle,
>
> My admiration for your talent caused me great concern for your health so I am very happy that you are now better and that I may soon be able to applaud you again. Forgive me for concealing my name. I feared that if you knew it you would refuse my flowers. I fear that now that you do know it, you may regret having accepted them. Your devoted and unworthy admirer,
>
> Marie Duplessis

The two became firm friends. Marie was deeply moved and grateful because Judith was prepared to walk openly with her, arm in arm, in the Bois de Boulogne. But Judith was an exception, and Marie clearly had no illusions about her own status. She was a professional, and did not hesitate to take Edouard de Perregaux away from her competitor Alice. Probably Marie had little choice because Edouard fell completely in love with her, and she seems to have loved him. He was not another de Guiche, but he was handsome, witty, and heir to a vast fortune. His father, knowing his son well, had left the bulk of it in trust, under the control of the guardian, but he still had enough to impress Marie and was incapable of denying her anything, whether he could afford it or not. She seems to have been happy to become exclusively his.

To get Marie away from her dissipated life, Edouard bought a little house in Bougival. Much later, with Dumas too, she was to spend a week in lodgings in Bougival, but the real basis for Act II of the opera must be this first springtime with de Perregaux. Bougival was then a little village on the banks of the Seine, some way downstream from Paris. The railway had recently brought it within range for citizens wishing to spend a day in the country. It became the fashionable place to visit, and so Marie and Edouard went there too. While they were wandering round the lanes, they came upon the little house for sale, and, on an impulse, he bought it. Their retreat to Bougival was not quite the rustic idyll of Violetta and Alfredo. Marie and Edouard often received friends from Paris, or came up to town for a first night, a ball or the races. Marie retained her apartment in Paris and her expensive habits, while he pursued all the activities of a young man-about-town. Far from simple and cheap, their life was exceedingly extravagant. One day, when Marie went in her carriage to watch him ride at Chantilly, the gown she wore was said to have cost 10,000 francs. In the summer, they toured the spas in Germany together. This was probably the best time of Marie's life. She was now at home in such high society, and accepted as one of its most spirited and graceful adornments, her beauty the more bewitching for its aura of wickedness. She had everything she had ever wanted, and a rich lover who doted on her, indulged her most extravagant whims, and did not complain about her gambling. Her illness, if she was yet aware of it, was still a distant cloud. Her cup of happiness brimmed full to overflowing. It was too good to last.

Towards the end of their tour, Edouard began to fret. When they returned to Bougival, he got worse. The atmosphere was quite altered from their previous time there in the spring. He would often be away for whole days in Paris, and would not tell Marie where he was going or what he was doing. In fact, he was trying to recoup some money by gambling, but he did not share her luck at it. The truth eventually had to come out. They had been spending in a month his allowance for the year. With his expectations, he had been able to borrow, but now he was appallingly in debt. One evening he confessed to her. Their idyll was at an end; he could no longer afford her. Her reaction stunned him. If they could not afford them, why did they not sell the houses, the carriages and horses, the jewels and all the other unnecessary things, hers as well as his, and go away to live quietly in the provinces? They could get married. Bemused, he agreed.

But Edouard's guardian and family were not bemused, and were not going to allow the silly young man to throw himself away on a whore. They manoeuvred cautiously, trying to avoid a premature confrontation, for how could they know which way such a fool would react? Not realising that Marie was quite open about it, they investigated her background. Friendly people visited Nonant in search of damning evidence. It may have been one of these scouts who was the subject of Marie's letter to Delphine, already quoted. Edouard's guardian and his aunt began nagging him about his recklessness. When they were ready, and felt that he was too, they offered him a deal. They would clear all his debts, and give him an allowance of 24,000 francs a year, provided he gave up Marie. If he would not, he would be disinherited. Edouard accepted, but lacked the courage to tell Marie. Instead, one afternoon when she was alone in Bougival, his guardian called on her, and told her brutally that it was finished. It was the end of all her dreams of domesticity.

She had probably known it in her heart all along, and perhaps there had been some calculation in her offer. He was still a very rich man even if temporarily short of cash. Even so, the contrast between the cynicism of the deal and her own trusting proposal must have hurt her. She refused to mope, however. From now on, there would be no more romantic dreaming. She returned to her Paris apartment, and threw herself into the hectic life once again. Edouard did not, like Alfredo, follow to create a scandalous scene, but slunk away with his tail between his legs.

Marie built a new circle around her salon, this time not so much of hedonistic rich young men, but of artists and authors, men such as de Musset, Balzac, Gautier and Arsène Houssaye, the smart and celebrated rather than the great and good. She resumed her round of the theatres and the opera, and gave cultivated dinner parties and soirées. In the words of one observer: "She made vice decent, dignified and decorous." All was not well, however. In the first place, poets and authors may be witty and intelligent, but they are not often rich. She was leading her normal extravagant life but on her savings, or more accurately, on debts. She was the despair of prudent friends like Romain Vienne, but as she once told him: "As soon as I clear one set of debts, I hurry to contract a new lot – to justify the old ones and to keep in practice; it's stronger than me . . . " She had a principle that she would never wear with one lover jewels given her by another, which meant that she was rarely short of things to pawn. Before some employee of the opera house coined the name *la Dame aux Caméllias*, she was sometimes known as *la Reine du Père-Lachaise*. Secondly and even more worrying, her tuberculosis was beginning to give her real trouble. She may at first have blamed her illness on her disorderly way of life, and let fatalism and necessity drive her on. Throughout the winter, she behaved as recklessly as ever, but, when the summer came, she made a serious effort to repair her health. She went alone to Germany, choosing the quieter resorts and trying to keep away from the gambling tables and the balls.

One day in Spa, as she sat on a promenade reading in the sun, an elegant old man introduced himself. He was a Russian, or more accurately a Pole, Gustav Count Stackelburg. He had had a distinguished diplomatic career in the service of the Tsar. He was the same Count Stackelburg who over fifty years earlier, as ambassador in Stockholm, had lent the stricken King Gustavus his shoulder as he tried to hobble out of the opera house. Later, he had represented his country at the Congress of Vienna, where he had given some memorable parties. That was already twenty-five years ago and he was now long since retired. He was in mourning because the last of his three daughters had recently died of consumption, and he had no-one left to brighten his remaining days and on whom to spend his immense wealth. He had followed Marie, he said, because she so singularly reminded him of this daughter. Would she consent to take her place? "I know it is more usual to get portraits painted of people we have lost," he said, "but you could be a living portrait of my daughter. I know all about your way of life, which I have inquired into. Would you be able to give it up? You could decide yourself your income, and I will undertake to give it to you."

Marie did not hesitate. She badly needed the money. In addition, the romance of her glamorous new life was already beginning to turn to ashes. After the collapse of her affairs with both de Guiche and de Perregaux, she must have abandoned any hope of domestic security. The only alternative was her expensive salon and the endless series of short and empty affairs, without which she could not finance it. Further ahead, her looks fading, lay decline and perhaps a return to the grinding poverty she had once known – if she survived. She already recognised the conflict between her dissipated life and her health, and the old count offered her a way out.

There may be something of Stackelburg in the operatic character of Douphol, but Douphol is too young and too unpleasant.

Stackelburg is more easily identifiable in Dumas's novel as the "old duke", playing, albeit in the background, precisely the role described. There is some doubt as to whether the arrangement really was platonic. Mme Judith says that Marie herself told her it was so, but Marie may have been fantasizing. Johannes Gros, however, quotes others who believed the story – Nestor Roqueplan and an Englishman of her circle, Sir Richard Wallace. On the other hand, Dumas claims that it was make-believe, saying: "The story of the consumptive daughter whose double the Duke discovered in Marguerite Gauthier is sheer invention. The Count, in spite of his great age, was not an Oedipus seeking an Antigone but rather a King David looking for a Bathsheba."[2]

If so, Stackelburg is to be admired for his vigour because he was well over eighty. However great his ambitions, he cannot have overtaxed Marie physically, and he seems genuinely to have wanted her to give up her wild life. Whatever his motives, his generosity was boundless. Soon after they returned to Paris, he collected Marie in his carriage, and took her to a sumptuous new apartment he had bought and furnished for her. It was on the first floor of 11 Boulevard de la Madeleine [now number 15], a highly fashionable address.

This was her home for the rest of her life and it is in this apartment that the first and last acts of *La Traviata* take place. It was designed and furnished throughout in the most fashionable taste, and might seem today to have been a little vulgar. The ante-room was devoted to flowers. Its walls were covered in gilded trellis up which creepers climbed from rosewood jardinières. There were also baskets of flowers in profusion, many of which were changed daily. Her bills from the florist are of an extraordinary extravagance. It is not true however that she liked only camellias. No doubt she did like them; they were amongst the most expensive flowers and Marie liked to spend ostentatiously. For this reason she may have often affected bouquets of camellias, and the bills confirm this. It is also true that when her illness was already well advanced she was advised to avoid scented flowers. It is probably not true that she would always carry white camellias when "available", and red ones when having her monthly period, but it is a nice idea which would have amused her. She liked earthy jokes.

Out of this bower of an ante-room, a door on the right led to her dining room, rather severe with leather wall-coverings and a heavy carved oak table with twelve chairs, covered in green velvet to match the curtains. There were cabinets and candelabra and statuettes and *objets* enough to satisfy the cluttered taste of the time. Her bedroom was reached through the dining room, and was furnished in rosewood. The legend of the huge and vulgar carved bedstead, set on a dais, is not supported by the inventory of the sale, but there was a large carved and gilded mirror and a heavily ornamented clock that was said to have belonged to Mme de Pompadour. The room had a cerise motif, overlaid with plentiful embroidered muslin frills and furbelows. The grandest room was the drawing room, with white and gold boiserie, huge Venetian mirrors and three folding doors matched by three windows overlooking the Boulevard. The motif was once again cerise, and the room was lit by a massive antique Dresden chandelier for twenty-four candles. On the mantelshelf, two large candelabra flanked another impressive clock. Finally, leading off the drawing room was a card room, provided not only with gambling tables but also a divan and a couch, no doubt for guests with less intellectual games in mind.

Marie took great pleasure in all her possessions and became quite a connoisseur. She especially loved paintings, and had a large collection, mostly in the sensual styles of Boucher and Watteau. Although today the whole effect might seem fussy and oppressive, there was nothing which her contemporaries found vulgar and, when she died, the crowd in her apartment for the sale were not all there out of curiosity. They had come to buy.

But the greatest luxury cannot satisfy an ardent young spirit for long. For a while Marie revelled in the chance to rest, to read, to practise on the piano, but she found herself a great deal alone. She was to be seen daily driving to the Bois de Boulogne to exercise her three dogs. She very much enjoyed shopping, and she bought clothes wholesale as evidenced by the bills found amongst her papers. But she was a high-spirited girl who needed company. The old count came as regularly as he could, considering he still had a wife. He often took Marie to the theatre or the opera, sitting in the shadows at the back of her box, and watching her enjoy the admiration of at least half the audience. And enjoy it she did. Marie was more than a little bit in love with her own beauty, and certainly loved to dress up and be seen, and to feel the impact she was making on all around. But when the evening was over, and he had taken her home in his carriage, the old count did not often stay long. Marie needed more than admiration, and eventually she began to deceive her protector.

For all her sensibility, Marie was no shrinking violet. Certain of her own attractiveness and without any hypocrisy, she was quite prepared to accost anyone she fancied at a ball or a function. Men who sought introductions to her had no need to fear a coy reception, though they had to be ready to amuse her. With Stackelburg supporting her, their ability to pay was more a question of decorum than a practical concern. She did not want to drop her standards and gifts were still valued, especially if they were droll, as well as lavish. The visiting prince who first sent a diamond-studded key, then an ivory coffer, which it unlocked to reveal a dozen perfect oranges, each wrapped in a thousand franc note, obtained a charming welcome when, shortly afterwards, he arrived himself.

And so, despite her promises to the old count, other men came back into her life. She began to have little dinner parties when he was not coming or after he had gone home. Old friends reappeared, Edouard de Perregaux for one. He had gone away, and had almost accepted a commission in the Foreign Legion, but he could not quite cut himself free of her. Although she was still fond of him, things were now on a different footing between them. He irritated her, and found himself more and more treated as a sort of lapdog, a silly mooning fellow whose protestations had been proved unreliable. She began to seek out men she fancied, sometimes using her neighbour as a sort of procuress. This neighbour was Clémence Prat from Marie's home town. Clémence had once been on the game, but had become fat, blowsy and bawdy. She made hats which Marie would buy. It was through her that Alexandre Dumas obtained his first introduction to Marie.

Dumas had first seen Marie by chance two years earlier when he had just arrived in Paris from school in the provinces. He was in the Champs Elysées when she descended from her carriage and went into a shop. He was thunderstruck, and thought her the most enchanting thing he had ever seen, but he shrugged the thought away as absurd. He was just a poor young student, the unknown son of a famous but disreputable father. Although also only eighteen, she was already the famous courtesan, surrounded by the rich and brilliant. It was a hopeless situation and he decided to forget about her.

Two years later he was a struggling writer, trying to escape from his father's enormous shadow. He lived with his father, and had got to know many of the racy and artistic people in his circle. He made friends with a young man called Déjazet, the son of a famous actress. One day, having spent some hours riding together, they decided to go to the *Théâtre des Variétés*. Marie was there in her box with the old count in the shadows behind. By this time she felt sure enough of him to look boldly round the audience and greet any friends she saw. In particular, she kept smiling and nodding at the fat woman in the box opposite. All Dumas's longing for her came flooding back, and he confided his emotions to Déjazet. He absolutely had to meet her. Déjazet laughed. "You must be feeling very rich! If you want to meet her, it's not difficult. Go to her box in the interval. She's not shy!" Dumas, however, *was* shy. Instead, he asked Déjazet to go to see Marie's fat friend, Clémence Prat, whom he claimed to know well, and see what he could arrange. Déjazet returned in triumph. It was all settled. They would go to Clémence's after the theatre and wait there until the Count went home. Then they would go round and join Marie. Dumas always maintained that what occurred that evening is faithfully reported in his novel, on which the following dialogue is based.

The plan went almost like clockwork. Soon after Stackelburg left, they heard Marie calling for Clémence to join her. Marie was not alone. A young count was with her, possibly de Perregaux, for she treated him with barely disguised contempt. She had been playing the piano, but stopped when Dumas and Déjazet entered.

"But do go on!" said Dumas.

"Oh no!" she said, "not now that you and M. Déjazet are here. My playing is good enough for the Count, but I won't torture you with it."

The Count soon took the hint and left. Clémence upbraided

Marie for so insulting a rich young man who was in love with her.

"Ah," said Marie, "if I had to listen to everyone who is in love with me, I wouldn't have time to dine."

And dine they did, sending out to the Maison Dorée for chicken and champagne and drinking punch while they waited. It was not the *grande soirée* of Act 1 of *La Traviata*, but an intimate and rather bawdy meal, which grew more boisterous as the champagne flowed. Clémence was a fount of smutty jokes, and Marie was sometimes helpless with laughter. It was at such a moment that her laughter turned suddenly into a paroxysm of coughing. Unable to control it, she rose and fled into her bedroom. Appalled, Dumas followed, leaving the others to carry on the party. He found her collapsed on a couch, gasping for breath and he took her hand.

"Oh! It's you! Are you ill too?" she smiled.

"No, but what about you? Does it still hurt?"

"Not much. I'm used to it."

"You're killing yourself, Madame. I would like to be your friend and prevent you from harming yourself in this way."

"You mustn't alarm yourself. No-one else does because they know that there's nothing to be done for this sickness. I can't sleep and need distraction. Anyway, with girls like me, one more or less makes no difference."

She proposed to return to the table, but he would not move. For a while they argued, he earnestly and she flippantly. Clémence looked in, her dress in disarray, winked and withdrew. Marie wanted to end the conversation.

"Are you in love with me?" she asked abruptly. "If so, say so at once. It is much simpler."

"Maybe, but I am not going to say so now."

"It will be better if you never say it."

"Why?"

"Because it can only lead to one of two things. Either I won't accept you and then you will be cross with me. Or else I will, and then you will have a sorry mistress, nervous and ill, always either too sad or too gay. Come! We're talking nonsense. Let's go back to the dining room."

In desperation he was forced to confess. "If you knew how much I loved you!"

"Truly?" She looked at him steadily.

"I swear it."

She paused for a seeming age. "Oh, well," she said, relenting. "If you promise to do all that I ask you to without arguing, I might perhaps love you." She raised her lips to be kissed. It was all rather more businesslike than the opera. There was no coquetry with a flower nor serenading from the street, but the essence was the same. He had to persuade her against her better judgement, and he succeeded. Walking home, Dumas's feet hardly touched the pavement. Here he was, a young nobody, half-caste and a bastard as well, and the most celebrated beauty in Paris was to be his mistress. He called again next day.

Their affair lasted for about a year. Stackelburg continued to support her. He did stop eventually, but it is not clear exactly when. Meanwhile, Marie did not intend to cost her young lover what she knew he could not afford. She was genuinely touched by Dumas's solicitude for her, and felt once more that here, just possibly, was someone who loved her for herself. She called him "Adet". They were much together, and even spent that week in lodgings in Bougival. But she had to be careful not to do anything to upset Stackelburg. When they returned to Paris, Dumas was forced to wait once more in the street until the old Russian re-emerged from her front door and went home. Humiliated, he began to nag her to give up the Count, but she would not. He was her livelihood, and anyway she was fond of him. He alone made possible the kind of romantic fantasy in which she and Dumas were now indulging. She had made quixotic gestures before, and nothing but pain had come of them.

It was hopeless. Dumas could barely afford to buy her her bonbons at the theatre, but while she could protect his pocket, she could not protect his pride. It is not without a little bitterness that Dumas puts into Marguerite's mouth words that must have been on the tip of Marie's tongue as their love affair started to turn sour. "Lovers are a nuisance. We should only have passing lovers, able to satisfy our need to expand ourselves. Our own interests require that we should inspire ardour in others and feel ourselves only whims. We need to change our lovers when their purses run dry. Our other interest, notwithstanding, is to keep our friends."

In due course, the indignity of his position began to gnaw at Dumas. He was very young and ardent, and this was his first serious affair. He and Marie might be the same age, but they were a generation apart in worldly wisdom, in worldly weariness. Eventually he began to fret away her affection. She began to see other men as well as Stackelburg. One evening, when she had told him that she was too sick to see him, Dumas stood to watch in the street outside her house, and saw another man go in. Furiously, he went straight home and wrote her a letter:

My dear Marie,

I am neither rich enough to love you as I would wish nor poor enough to be loved by you as you wish. Let us forget, therefore, you a name that must be almost indifferent to you and I a happiness that is no longer possible for me. It is unnecessary to tell you how sorry I am because you know how much I love you. Goodbye, then. You have too tender a heart not to appreciate why I am writing this letter and too much intelligence not to forgive me for it.

Mille souvenirs.
A.D.
30 August, midnight

Dumas's Armand Duval in the book also writes Marguerite a bitter letter which he immediately regrets. It causes Marguerite terrible pain, and there are several emotional but abortive attempts at reconciliation. In real life, Marie did not reply. Possibly she had already had enough of her prickly young lover, and certainly by now she had other worries. Her health was going from bad to worse. While she struggled to remain bright in public and seductive with her lovers, she was consulting all the leading doctors without thought of expense, and faithfully following their various and often weird prescriptions.

Her favourite was Doctor Davaine, credited with the discovery of bacteria. Since he was at her deathbed, he must be the leading candidate for the role of Doctor Grenvil in the opera. Another in whom she placed much faith for a while was a terrible old quack called Koroff. He was a great character, known to all European society, and she used him to help her with her last great love affair. This was with the composer, Franz Liszt. They had met first at the *Théâtre du Gymnase*, theoretically by chance but probably by her design. Liszt was with Jules Janin the journalist, and Marie came straight across and joined them although she had never met either before. According to Janin, Liszt was immediately entranced, as much by her conversation as by her looks.

The next day, she asked Koroff to arrange a second meeting with Liszt, and they became lovers. Of all her loves, Liszt seems to have been the one who aroused her greatest passion, and she affected him no less. His engagements in Paris, however, could not keep him there indefinitely. He had to return to central Europe for some performances, and then later was engaged to go to Constantinople. They discussed the possibility that Marie might go with him. Just before he left she wrote to him, pleading. "I know I won't live. I am a strange girl in that I can't hold onto this life which is killing me. Take me away with you. Take me anywhere you like. I won't worry you. I sleep all day, you can let me go to the theatre in the evening and at night you can do whatever you want with me."

It was her last bid for love, but Liszt left without her, promising to come back in due course to take her to Turkey. He never did and he regretted it all his life, cherishing her memory and often speaking of her, of her grace, her artless charm and her enthusiasm. As an old man, he wrote: "I am not normally interested in the Marion Delormes or the Manon Lescauts, but Marie Duplessis was an exception. She had a great deal of heart, a great liveliness of spirit and I consider her unique of her kind . . . She was the most complete incarnation of womankind that has ever existed."

So Marie waited in vain. She turned for comfort to an old flame, Edouard de Perregaux. He had never ceased to sigh at her feet and irritate her, but she still had some affection for him. A few of her letters to him still exist, showing her changing mood. Some are peremptory instructions such as to get her a box for the theatre; others are just irritable. Once, when she was planning a journey to Italy seemingly with someone else, he stupidly proposed to meet her there. "Dear Edouard," she wrote, "Do you want to injure me? You know perfectly well that what you propose would damage my future which you seem resolved to make miserable and sad."

Now, in her loneliness, he could perhaps be some use. He did not have much to offer except for one thing, a title. In February

1845, they went together to London where, on the 21st, they were married in Kensington Registry Office. They returned at once to France and parted again, more at odds than ever. Most of her biographers declare themselves to be baffled by this reanimation of a dead affair, but the likely truth is that she just fancied the idea of being a countess, and cajoled Edouard into agreeing. He did not do so without qualms. Although such a marriage had no validity in France, and although they never lived together as a married couple, Edouard was clearly terrified he might have trouble with his guardian and his aunt. He irritated Marie exceedingly by needing more than her word for reassurance. She had to write to him:

My dear Edouard,

In all that you have written to me, I can find only one thing that I need to answer. It is this. You want me to put in writing that you are free to live as you like. I told you that you were the day before yesterday. I repeat what I then told you and sign myself,

Marie Duplessis.

Still, Marie was now a Countess. Duplessis became du Plessis and coronets began to appear on her carriage doors and her dinner service. She designed herself a coat of arms, a mixture of the de Perregaux arms, argent with three sable bands, and a fantasy of her own, a green lizard looking at itself in a golden mirror. This lizard represented a stuffed one that had been brought back from Italy by a friend who had got it from some gipsies. Marie treasured it as a talisman, saying that she had after all once been sold to gipsies herself. It went everywhere with her, even it seems in her pocket to the opera. The golden mirror shows a nice touch of self-mockery.

Marie knew, of course, that her title was just a bit of make believe, and she did not like it if old friends like Romain Vienne used it, knowing that they were teasing her. But it was harmless fun, and gave her no small pleasure in her last few months. That she knew it was invalid is clear from a newspaper report about a lawsuit in which she was involved in April, two months later. It concerned an unpaid lingerie bill of 4700 francs. The normally dry reporter from the *Gazette des Tribunaux* was moved to write:

Mlle Duplessis is very beautiful and was dressed with impeccable elegance. She explained perfectly the extent of the claim against her. The President asked 'Is it Mme or Mlle Duplessis that is before the court?' Mlle Duplessis hesitated. 'I think, M. le Président, that that has no bearing on the matter.' Told she must answer, she said, 'I am a spinster.'

That summer [1846] was her last, and she spent it in a lonely search for a cure in the German spas, which had already failed her so many times. Even at this stage, she could not entirely keep away from the dances and gambling rooms. As usual, she was very lucky and won several thousand francs which was as well, since Stackelburg seems by this time to have given her up, peeved perhaps by her passion for Liszt. But her health steadily got worse, and at times her spirits failed her. She wrote to Edouard a bleak and despairing letter.

Forgive me, my dear Edouard, I beg you on both knees. If you love me enough for that – just two words – your forgiveness and friendship. Write to me *post restante* at Ems in the Duchy of Nassau. I am alone here and very ill. So, dear Edouard, say quickly that you forgive me.

Adieu.   Marie.

In the autumn she had a partial remission, and when she returned to Paris felt well enough to go out dancing and gambling, but it was clear to everyone else that she was dying. Romain Vienne visited her in September, and found her praying. He forebore to tease her about Magdalene, but she admitted that she was increasingly finding comfort in religion. A report in the newspaper *Siècle* in November described her appearance at the opera:

When one saw this lovely spectacle with burning eyes, covered with diamonds and enveloped in a sea of lace and white satin, one felt as if Marie Duplessis had risen from the grave to come and reproach all this brilliant society of young fools and contemporary Ninons for their abandon and ungrateful forgetfulness.

Even so, when Edouard came calling to ask after her, she felt well enough to refuse to see him. Later, in December, she went to a ball where a guest wrote of her: "Her great dark eyes, dimmed and dark-circled, were slowly burning themselves away under her eyelids. In her broken but still voluptuous grace she was like a flower that had been trodden underfoot at a ball." Her last appearance in public was on 12th December at the *Théâtre du Palais Royal*.

She had to leave early, half-carried by her coachman, Etienne, and his son. The rest of her life she spent in the bedroom, where we see her in the last act of the opera.

Her final act of defiance was on 15th January, her twenty-third birthday. She got up, put on a ball-gown and all her jewels, and stood for some time looking at herself in the mirror. It was a gesture totally in character and it is recalled in the opera. By this time, she was too weak even to forbid Edouard to visit. Although she was using her savings, it is not true that she was destitute or that the bailiffs were stalking through the house. Dumas *père* was indulging his imagination when he wrote: "Poor girl. She died in sorrow and poverty as all these poor creatures do. Her creditors seized every article of furniture except the bed on which she was lying in her death agony. It is a beautiful law which forbids the seizure of the bed and bedding. But for that she would have died on the floor. The carpet had been taken away." It is true that there were unpaid bills towards the end, but that is not to be wondered at. Clothilde, her faithful maid, paid a lot of the smaller creditors from her own pocket, but recovered the money later.

Hearing in Spain of her illness, Dumas *fils* wrote: "Will you permit me to add my name to those who grieve to see you ill? A week after you get this letter I will be in Algiers. If I find at the *post restante* there a letter to me forgiving me the wrong I did you about a year ago, I shall return to France less sad – and entirely happy if you are better." It was a gesture, but it is unlikely that she kept it under her pillow or stained it with her tears.

On 2nd February, Edouard called and found Marie in an extreme state. Silly to the end, he decided that the best thing to do was to take her chemise to a clairvoyant for advice. He was told that she only had hours to live. Distraught, he hurried back to find Clothilde kneeling beside her holding her hand while a priest gave her the last sacrament. Dr Davaine and Stackelburg were both there, but departed with the priest, leaving Edouard and Clothilde alone with Marie. Opening her eyes, she saw him and said, "Ah. You have come to see me. Adieu. I am going." She did not die until three next morning when, in delirium, she sat bolt upright, gave three loud cries and collapsed, dead.

Marie's funeral was in the Madeleine on 5th February. It was quite a lavish affair, costing 1,350 francs. Reports vary as to who was there. Soreau talks of a large crowd, but that seems unlikely since not many were willing publicly to advertise their association with her. Her sister Delphine and Romain Vienne apparently came from Nonant for the service. Edouard and Stackelburg both followed the cortège to the cemetery of Montmartre together, accompanied perhaps by a handful of her past lovers and members of the Jockey Club.

Dumas heard of her death when he arrived in Marseilles, and he hurried back to Paris. He was too late for the funeral but was probably there a fortnight later to support de Perregaux who had decided to have Marie's body transferred to a better plot in the cemetery. This was a harrowing affair, since it involved opening the coffin and identifying the rotting corpse within. Dumas's description is so vivid that it is impossible to believe he did not see it. De Perregaux also provided the carved tomb with its marble camellias and inscription:

ICI REPOSE

ALPHONSINE PLESSIS

NEE LE 15 JANVIER 1824

DECEDEE LE 3 FÉVRIER 1847

DE PROFUNDIS

A porcelain ornament juts out from the cornice with the one word: *Regrets*. A cult has grown up around the tomb. Edith Saunders wrote in 1930 that she met her concierge setting off to visit it with a bunch of camellias. Visiting the grave myself over sixty years later, I found no camellias, but there were a dozen fresh red roses in their cellophane, two pots of chrysanthemums, a big display of anemones, some pansies and a tiny bunch of violets. All had clearly been left recently, but none indicated by whom. I could only conclude that many different people were still coming to pay Marie tribute, a hundred and fifty years after her death. Not far from Marie's grave, her lover Alexandre Dumas lies, like an elderly crusader on his marble four-poster. There were no flowers for him. Instead of his nose, a rusty screw points ludicrously upwards, presumably the remains of some unsuccessful repair.

Dumas was present in the crowd at the auction of Marie's possessions, which lasted four days, and was a great event. Dumas claimed he paid an exorbitant price for her favourite book, *Manon Lescaut*, but the auctioneer's catalogue does not support this. It does reveal that many of the more expensive items had been recovered from the pawnbroker for the purpose of the sale. The de Perregaux family, led by the formidable duchess, were out in force trying to recover what they could of the family heirlooms Edouard had given her. They met some stiff competition, however. In the end the auction realised 89,000 francs, a considerable fortune. Just over half of this was needed to clear her debts; the rest went to Delphine and her husband, who also took home with them the famous portrait of Marie in her peignoir of which only the sketch by Chaplin now remains.

Delphine and her husband were now rich by the standards of Nonant, and they brought a small estate, but within a few years it failed. They had to sell, and they reinvested what was left in an inn, a feature of which was Marie's portrait, which attracted sight-seers. Vienne relates that in the summer of 1869, a young man arrived at the inn, and asked if he could see the portrait. After gazing at it for some time and seeming to be much moved, he thanked them, told them his name was Judelet of Tours, and left. He had no sooner gone than everyone present remarked how much like Marie he had looked. They hurried out, hoping to question him before he left, but the coach was already on its way out of the village. Their inquiries discovered no trace of a M. Judelet in Tours. He seemed to have used a false name. Delphine had none of the qualities needed to make a success of an inn. In due course, that failed too and everything had to be sold, including Marie's portrait. The respectable Delphine had lost Marie's little fortune. M. Judelet had disappeared. Nothing remained of Marie except the remembrance of her, and that has stayed fresh ever since and made fortunes enough to make even her velvet eyes sparkle.

La Dame aux Camélias was the foundation of Dumas's career. None of his other books achieved such lasting success. He became steadily less sympathetic towards fallen women until, late in life, he seriously advocated that single women without means should be required to do forced labour, lest they lead men astray. He never seems to have had any regrets about Marie, or about his behaviour towards her, and one must doubt whether he ever really loved her. He probably thought he did for a while, but he was only in love and it did not last long. In the end, his interest in her seems to have become little more than financial. During his long life, he had to go to the cemetery at Montmartre on many occasions, but according to the keeper he never once visited her grave.

Most of those who knew or have written about Marie portray her as a marvellous heroine, even more enchanting in real life than on the stage. They make it seem only natural that the concierges of Paris should still be laying flowers on her grave. Marcel Pagnol was not exaggerating when he said: "It is impossible to write of Marie Duplessis without developing a passion for her." Nor are women immune. In her memoires, Marie's friend Mme Judith wrote:

> There was an extraordinary charm about her. She was very slight, almost too thin; but oh, so refined looking, so marvellously graceful; her face was of an angelic oval shape, her large dark eyes were full of seductive melancholy, her complexion was dazzling, and her hair, that resembled masses of black silk, was perfectly magnificent. She was very intellectual and her conversation was most captivating.

She relates how Marie showed her round her apartment, full of beautiful things – "more like what you would expect to find in a palace or a museum than in a private residence." Marie's delight in them was such that she was even singing a little snatch of song, when Judith took her hand. "Are you happy really?" she asked.

"Yes, of course I am," said Marie and then at once, "Oh no! I am not happy and you never supposed I was."

They sat down, still holding hands, and Judith waited. Marie went on. "Why do I sell myself? Because as a working girl I could never have earned enough however hard I had worked to obtain this luxury for which I crave. But despite what it may seem, I swear that I am neither grasping nor wanton. I wanted refinement, art, good taste, elegance and cultivated society. I've always chosen who would be my friends . . . and I have loved. I have loved very deeply but no-one has ever really responded to my love. That is what is horrible in my life."

She paused, struggling with her own emotions, and then went on. "Young people have sometimes confided their sentimental

woes to me and I have even shed tears with them over their ago-
nies; but not a single one has ever cared to enquire whether my
heart was suffering too. I once said to one of my lovers – 'You
know the love I give to you is true love. I should like to belong
only to you.' He was flattered but answered with a smile – 'I don't
ask as much as that!' And when this indifference made me sigh he
cried – 'You're not at all amusing when you are melancholy. Try to
be gay or I shan't come to see you again.' "

She paused again and then added "It is a mistake to have a
heart if you are a courtesan."[3]

_____

NOTES

1 *Young ladies once to Ozy carried*
  Should not dream of getting married

2 Romain Vienne was mostly away from Paris during Marie's life there
  and only saw her occasionally. Writing his memoirs many years after
  her death, he had to piece together her life during this period from what
  she and her friends told him. He makes no reference to Stackelburg at
  all, but relates a curious story which has some features that are similar.
  According to him, Lady Yarborough, whom he calls Lady Anderson,
  became very fond of Marie's mother during the short time she was in
  her service and, after her death, resolved that she would find and look
  after her favourite daughter. She tracked Marie down in Paris, and
  offered to adopt her as a daughter. She knew all about Marie's way of
  life, which did not worry her, though Marie would have to give it up.
  Lady Yarborough was a wealthy woman, much in society, and Marie
  would in due course inherit her fortune and her position. After much
  thought and with great tenderness, Marie refused, because she felt it
  would not work. For a few weeks, they might be very happy, but Lady
  Yarborough's friends would soon find out who this "daughter" really
  was, and would ostracise them both. Lady Yarborough's life would be
  ruined, for which Marie's gratitude and love could never compensate
  her. It is a charming tribute to Marie, but difficult to believe. No-one else
  mentions any direct contact between Lady Yarborough and Marie and
  they all agree that Stackelburg was for some time her protector.

3 This conversation between Judith and Marie is taken from Mrs Bell's
  translation of Judith's memoirs, published in 1912.

LA BOHÈME

Giacomo Puccini

Libretto by G. Giacosa and L. Illica

Dramatis Personae

Rodolfo, *poet*
Marcello, *painter*
Colline, *philosopher*
Schaunard, *musician*
Benoit, *landlord*
Alcindoro de Mitonneaux, *rich patron of Musetta*

Mimi, *artificial flower maker*
Musetta, *artists' model*

Pedlars, passers-by, peasants, sweepers, customs officials

Synopsis

ACT ONE

A garret in the Latin quarter. It is Christmas Eve and the rooftops outside are snowy.

Rodolfo and Marcello are too cold to work. Marcello says that the Red Sea he is painting is frozen like Musetta's heart. He suggests they break up a chair for fuel, but Rodolfo offers to burn his verse drama instead – a weighty manuscript. His play has been only half consumed when Colline arrives, followed soon by Schaunard, who is in the money. A wealthy English tourist has employed him and his piano to retaliate against his neighbour's noisy parrot.

Helped by two errand-boys, Schaunard brings fuel, food and wine. Scenting money, old Benoit, the landlord, arrives to collect the rent, but the Bohemians ply him with drinks until he starts boasting about his flirtations at the Bal Mabille. Pretending to be shocked, the Bohemians eject him, rentless.

Schaunard proposes that they conserve his provisions and celebrate Christmas Eve at the Café Momus. All agree, but Rodolfo says he will follow when he has finished his article. They leave, urging him to hurry.

Alone, Rodolfo is waiting for inspiration when there is a knock. It is Mimi; on the way up the stairs her candle has blown out and she needs a light. Exhausted by the climb, she suddenly staggers. Rodolfo catches her, and helps her, half-fainting, to a chair. Some water and a glass of wine restore her. As she is leaving she finds she has dropped her key. Somehow both their candles go out so they must feel for the key in the dark. Rodolfo finds it but hides it. Still searching, their hands meet. It is the start of romance.

Mimi's hand is cold. Rodolfo wants to warm it in his while he tells her who he is – a penniless poet but a millionaire in dreams. And who, he asks, is she? Mimi is poor too, scratching a living making artificial flowers, but she too has dreams, inspired by the roses she makes. Her name is Lucile but they call her Mimi, she does not know why.

Rodolfo's friends call impatiently from the street, and hoot with laughter to hear that he is not alone. They leave, bidding him hurry up. Side by side in the moonlight, Rodolfo and Mimi are suddenly flooded with love for each other. He wants to stay there with her, but she feels it is too soon for that. Let them go out together to join his friends. Arm in arm, they leave.

ACT TWO

The square outside the Café Momus is thronged with people – street-vendors, children, parents, students, working girls, waiters – amongst whom Rodolfo's friends are individually threading their way.

Above the general hubbub of the crowd now one, now another of the Bohemians can be heard. Colline has bought a coat, Schaunard bargains for a horn, Marcello is trying to pick up a girl. One by one the friends gather at the Momus, Rodolfo and Mimi last of all. He has bought her a little cap. He introduces her – if he is a poet, she is poetry. They welcome Mimi, but warn her that Rodolfo is no beginner at flirtation. At this moment, Marcello's composure is shattered by the arrival of Musetta with Alcindoro. They take the table next to the Bohemians. Marcello tries to ignore her, so Musetta starts to tease him, to the acute embarrassment of Alcindoro. Colline and Schaunard watch the contest with amusement, but Mimi is distressed – how much Musetta must love Marcello, she feels. Musetta's determination to recapture Marcello grows. Shrieking that her shoe is hurting, she sends Alcindoro off to get it eased by a cobbler. She and Marcello are joyously reunited. The Bohemians all go off to follow a passing military band, leaving Alcindoro to pay both bills.

ACT THREE

A year has passed. It is midwinter again and early morning. The scene is outside the customs post at the Barrière d'Enfer. On the left there is an inn, where Marcello and Musetta have been staying. They are working for their keep; he is painting an inn sign while she gives singing lessons.

Customs officials are letting country folk in through the gate when Mimi arrives, and asks a guard where Marcello is. She is shown the inn. Marcello comes out and invites her in, but she won't enter because she knows Rodolfo is inside and she does not want to see him. Rodolfo loves her, but his possessive jealousy has been poisoning their happiness, and they have decided to part. Marcello advises that they should either love less intensely, like him and Musetta, or part. He shows her Rodolfo sleeping inside on a bench. Mimi has a crisis of coughing, and Rodolfo starts to wake up. Mimi says she will go home, but instead she hides behind a tree to see what will happen next.

Rodolfo comes out and starts to tell Marcello his side of the story. He has loved Mimi. "I believed my heart was dead," he says, "but her blue eyes revived it." But now she bores him. Disbelieving, Marcello tells him to take love less seriously. Rodolfo concedes that he is jealous, but Mimi flirts with everyone. Seeing Marcello still sceptical, Rodolfo finally admits the real trouble. She is desperately ill, and he cannot afford to look after her properly. She must find a richer protector.

This is too much for Mimi behind her tree. Her sobs become audible, and Rodolfo rushes to her side. She will not go in, but Marcello, hearing Musetta flirting, does so. Left together, Mimi and Rodolfo talk over their situation. He is full of nostalgia, remembering all the good times, but she reminds him of all the quarrels, the jealousies and the reproaches. Gradually, the happy memories begin to overlay the bitter ones, and by the time Marcello and Musetta re-emerge from the inn, quarrelling furiously, Rodolfo and Mimi have half decided to give their love another try, at least until the spring comes. In the spring, it will be more bearable to be alone. Musetta flounces off, followed by Marcello's insults, but Mimi and Rodolfo stroll away in renewed harmony.

ACT FOUR

Rodolfo and Marcello are once again at work in their garret. It is now spring outside but not in their hearts. They have both been abandoned by their women, and are unable to concentrate, for their thoughts are elsewhere. They have been talking bravely about how little they care.

Each claims to have seen the other's girl living it up and each pretends to be delighted to hear it. But neither can keep up the pretence and, fingering their mementoes, they fall back into sentimental daydreams. They are rescued by the arrival of Colline and Schaunard who have brought some meagre provisions. They try to make the most of these by exuberant play-acting – it is a feast, then a ball, then a quarrel of honour, then a duel! In the middle of this horseplay, Musetta arrives. She has found Mimi in trouble, and brought her to her old friends. Mimi can barely climb the stairs. Rodolfo rushes to her aid, and half-carries her into the room, where she sinks onto the bed. Mimi is unsure of her welcome, but everyone is kind, and that makes her feel better. But kindness is all they have to offer her. They are penniless.

Mimi feels cold. Her hands are freezing. If only she had a muff! Musetta goes to fetch hers, having sent Marcello out to sell her earrings and buy medicine. Colline resolves to pawn his coat. He signals Schaunard to leave the two lovers alone. Rodolfo and Mimi talk over old times. He shows her her cap which he has been keeping, and they relive that evening when her candle went out, and she pretended not to have seen him hide her key. Suddenly she is overwhelmed by coughing, and he cries out in alarm. Schaunard rushes in. Mimi seems to sink back into sleep.

Mimi revives when Musetta and Marcello return. She thinks that Musetta's muff is Rodolfo's gift and chides him for his extravagance. As she drifts into sleep once more, Musetta starts to pray. Colline returns with some money, which he gives to Musetta. The doctor is on his way. Schaunard, meanwhile, has been observing Mimi more closely than the others. While Rodolfo is trying to fix Musetta's cloak over the window, Schaunard bends over her. She is dead. Rodolfo turns back. Looking from one to the other, he senses there is something wrong and what it is. With a despairing cry, he hugs her body to him.

Only Young Once

In April 1845, *Le Corsaire*, an obscure Parisian magazine, published a story called *An Envoy of Providence*. It was about the contrivances of two young artists, Marcel, who desperately needed to borrow a decent coat for the evening, and Schaunard, who providentially had a sitter wearing the very thing. The two young men in the story were based on friends of the author, Henri Murger.[1] Murger was not sure how his friends might take it, so he did not put his full name to the story, but he submitted it because he needed the fifteen francs he was paid for it. It may be that his friends were not too pleased, for he wrote nothing more about them for a year. Then necessity and M. le Poitevin Saint-Alme, the editor of *Le Corsaire*, combined forces to overcome his hesitations. Murger began a whole series of stories, breezily recounting his daily experiences in a harsh place called 'la Bohème', distinguished, he said, from the Bohème of Central Europe by the grave accent on its e. It lay "within the Department of the Seine: it is bounded to the North by the cold, to the East by hunger, to the South by love and to the West by hope."

Murger did not invent Bohème. Already people like Théophile Gautier, Alfred de Musset and Arsène Houssaye had talked of themselves as Bohemians, meaning artistic persons leading a free and unconventional life, but they had had some money to cushion them, and could later recall their Bohème with fond nostalgia. A decade or so later, Murger and most of his friends came from poor families, and had to survive on whatever they could earn while they learned their trade. They longed above all else to escape from this misery, and those who succeeded did not look back on Bohème with the slightest regret. Murger knew very well that his stories were misleading, making starvation into a joke and freezing seem an adventure. When his stories were later collected into a book, he wrote a preface warning romantic young people not to be seduced by the scene he depicted. Having traced the roots of Bohemianism back to Homer, he tried to tell his readers what it had really been like.

Every man who enters on an artistic career without any other means of livelihood than his art itself, will be forced to walk the paths of Bohème. It is a stage in the artistic life, the preface either to the Academy or the Hôtel Dieu² or the morgue. Like all societies, Bohème contains different classes.

Let us begin with the most numerous class, the unknown Bohemians, those poor artists who do not know how to attract attention, regarding art as a faith, not a profession. They wait for others to come and seek them out, believing in art for art's sake, deifying each other and scorning to give the slightest help to Fortune which does not even know their address. They wait for pedestals to arrive underneath them of their own accord. Absurdly stoical, they endure misery which would excite pity, did not common sense force you to reconsider it. If you remind them that this is the nineteenth century, that the 100 sous coin is mistress of mankind, and that boots do not drop ready polished out of the sky, they turn their backs on you, and call you bourgeois. Those who persist in this mad heroism often die young of no illness but misery, for lack of a few concessions to the stern laws of necessity. These merely clutter the ways of art, and hinder those with a real vocation. It is a mistake to pity their lamentations. Unknown Bohème is not a path, it is a blind alley.

There is another curious category of Bohemian which might be called amateur. They find the Bohemian life full of seductions – not to dine every day, to sleep in the open on wet nights, to wear nankeen in December – seem to them the height of felicity. They abandon the family home and the study that would lead to a safe career, but, as only the most robust can stand a way of life that would render Hercules consumptive, most soon give up, hurrying back to the family roast, marrying their little cousins, setting up as provincial notaries and recounting by the fireside the hardships of their artistic youth. Some, however, persist in their folly, and finish more wretched than the real Bohemians, who never having had any other resources, at least have intelligence. We knew one such amateur who, having quarrelled with his family, spent three years in Bohème before he died, and was buried in a pauper's grave. He was entitled to an income of 10,000 francs per year. Needless to say, these amateur Bohemians have nothing whatever to do with art.

We now come to the real Bohemians who are truly called by art, and have some chance of success. This Bohème, like the others, bristles with perils; two abysses flank it – poverty and doubt. Its inhabitants have already made some mark other than on the census list. To reach their goal, any roads will do, and they know how to profit from chance encounters. Their daily existence is a work of genius. They would have got money out of Harpagon[3] and found truffles on the raft of the Medusa[4]. If necessary, they know how to go without, but if fortune smiles, they know how to enjoy it in style, never finding enough windows through which to throw their money. And when it is gone, they will revert to improvisation, and to the hunt for that wild quarry, the five-franc piece. They cannot take ten steps on the boulevard without meeting a friend, nor thirty anywhere without meeting a creditor. It is a charming and a terrible life, with its victors and its martyrs. No-one should enter into it unless resigned to submit to the pitiless law of *vae victis*, woe to the vanquished.[5]

If Murger felt his own stories made Bohème seem too jolly, he would certainly have condemned the opera as too sentimental if he had seen it. It combines all the most pathetic and lachrymose episodes from his various stories. Even so, he would have recognised his old friends. The librettists, Illica and Giacosa, may have manipulated the plot, but they took great trouble to be true to Murger's characterisations. While all based on his friends, most of the characters are composites. Rodolfo is largely Murger himself but, especially in the opera, contains something of a sculptor called Joseph Desbrosses whom Murger greatly admired. Marcello, the artist, has elements of two painters, Léopold Tabar and Lazare, but there is a great deal in him based on another writer, Jules Fleury, better known as Champfleury. A religious essayist named Joan Gustave Wallon provided the model for Colline. The name Colline is a typical Murger play on words; Wallon sounds like *vallon*, a valley, so he called him Colline, a hill, retaining his Christian name Gustave to make sure everyone got the joke. Wallon was a great good-humoured bear of a man, continually smoking his churchwarden pipe, and he was indeed a walking library, but the famous overcoat belonged to another philosopher, Marc Trapadoux. Of the four friends in the opera, only Schaunard is taken unalloyed from life, something of which he was inordinately proud. His real name was Alexandre Schanne but his friends called him Schannard[6], which was accidentally altered to Schaunard by a printer's error. He was a painter and a musician.

The Mimi of Murger's stories also combines at least two women. One was Murger's first love, Marie-Virginie Fonblanc, who usually used her maiden name Vimal. The other was his mistress during most of the time he was writing the stories. She also used her maiden name, Lucile Louvet, although she had been briefly married to a carpenter called Paulgaire, which is the name on her death certificate. The operatic Mimi borrows a great deal from a third, purely fictional, girl called Francine. Francine only occurred in one story in Murger's book, but she was closer to his sentimental ideals than any woman he was able to find in real life. Mimi had been his pet name for his first love, Marie, and Murger tended to revive it when he thought he had found someone worthy of her memory. There were altogether four Mimis, but two occurred later in his life. Musetta's origins were not so complicated. She was based directly on a high-spirited young lady called Marie-Christine Roux, loved by many people but especially by Champfleury, who called her Mariette. Despite his great enthusiasm for women and their important part in his book, Murger does not mention them in his preface about Bohème. Perhaps for him they were just the truffles on the raft of the Medusa.

There were many others clinging to the raft, some of whom played important roles in Murger's life, but he could not put them all into his stories and they do not appear in the opera. Some survived the ordeal and even achieved a certain celebrity, like the painter Antoine Chintreuil and the photographer and pioneer balloonist, Felix Tournachon, better known as Nadar. Many more, such as Lazare, Privat d'Anglement, Vastine and Fauchery, failed and disappeared from view, remembered only because they inhabited Bohème at a time when it was being particularly well chronicled. Murger himself spent over ten years on the raft before his stories about it enabled him to escape. They were years of continual movement as the Bohemians struggled to survive, forming and reforming their groups and exchanging one garret for another, as fortune, or more often misfortune, dictated. Their abodes were mostly in the Latin quarter, and were always very cheap. As Murger himself once said; "I live on the sixth floor for the very good reason that there isn't a seventh."

Henri Murger was born in 1822 in rue Saint-Georges in Paris, but the family soon moved to 5 rue des Trois Frères where Henri's father, Claud-Gabriel, was the concierge, and made some money on the side using the skills he had learned as a regimental tailor in Napoleon's army. He came from Savoie, though Murger himself believed him to be of Prussian stock. The father certainly could behave in a Prussian manner. The son too had a streak of Teutonic sentimentality, but it was redeemed by a characteristically Parisian wit and good humour inherited from his mother, a seamstress named Hortense-Henriette Tribou. She had married rather beneath her and had rich relations. Henri, their only child, was the subject of violent quarrels. Delicate, he was much pampered by his mother, who, to her husband's disgust, resolved that her son would somehow rise above a labouring life. She dressed him as a proper little bourgeois, all in blue, and he soon became a favourite of the inhabitants of the building.

These were a remarkably cultivated lot. Jean Baptiste Isabey, one of Napoleon's favourite painters, lived there as did the well-known baritone, Lablache, whose daughter became a famous pianist. In another apartment lived Marcel Garcia, whose daughters, Pauline Viardot and Maria Malibran, were amongst the greatest singers of their day. The most useful to the young boy, however, was a literary academician, Joseph de Jouy. For all her ambitions for Henri, Mme Murger had not the resources to procure for him a decent education, and at thirteen he had to be sent into the world with his head full of ideas that he was ill-equipped to realise. His father felt Henri should learn a trade, and was sure that no good would come of it when his wife persuaded M de Jouy to find the boy a post as a messenger boy with a firm of notaries called Cadet de Chambine. Unfortunately, not long after this, she died, leaving father and son to get along as best they might–which was not very well at all.

Henri had no interest in law, but his errands took him all over Paris and into all sorts of company. He soon fell in with two young brothers called Bisson, similarly placed but burning to become artists. They persuaded him to try painting too, and introduced him to a circle of like-minded characters who were to become his companions in the first phase of his life in Bohème. He was readily accepted and when, soon after his arrival, they formed themselves into a sort of club, he became a member. They called themselves *les Buveurs d'Eau*, the Water Drinkers.

The Water Drinkers were a small group of young men, mostly, like Murger, from working-class families, but all with artistic dreams. Their headquarters was the hayloft of an old farmhouse in the rue d'Enfer just beside the Barrière d'Enfer where the third act of the opera takes place. The farmhouse belonged to Lazare, one of the painters incorporated into the character Marcello. The Water Drinkers were all desperately poor, and one purpose of the club was to pool what little they had in the hope that it would somehow go further that way. If it did not, then sharing their privation might make it more bearable. The underlying aim of the club was to help its members to remain true to their artistic ideals. Lazare was the conscience of the club. He was a fanatic who believed in art for art's sake, and condemned any compromise, even to ward off starvation. By no means all the group were so austere, but all accepted the rule that, when together, they would drink only water so as not to embarrass members who could not afford anything else. Perhaps Lazare irritated the others because presently the club transferred its headquarters to the hayloft of another farmhouse in the rue du Cherche-Midi. In winter, this had the advantage that a faint if rather ammoniac warmth rose from the cowbyre below, through a trapdoor around which they would huddle. In summer, however, they could all climb out onto the roof and conduct their debates perched astride the dormers and gables. Murger maintained to friends that the club had moved because the water was better in the rue du Cherche-Midi.

The Water Drinkers constituted themselves into a proper club with rules and officers. Murger, one of the youngest members, became its secretary; the president was an artist named Léon Noël, who was several years older than the rest. If Lazare was its conscience, the heart of the club was Joseph Desbrosses, one of two brothers who were the tenants of the loft. Léopold was nicknamed *le Gothique*, but they called Joseph *le Christ* because he was so unselfish. Eugène Pottier, who wrote the *Internationale*, was a member. He greatly helped Murger to improve his makeshift education, but spent too much time in trouble with the authorities over his seditious views to succeed in his artistic career. Another Water Drinker was the artist Léopold Tabar. It was Tabar who painted the famous *Pharaoh engulfed in the Red Sea*, the picture at which Marcello is forever dabbing in the opera. Although this picture did exist, it never became an inn sign. Instead, it underwent a long series of metamorphoses, changing its subject after each rejection by the Salon, until it eventually achieved acceptance in 1842 as *Niobe punished by the gods*. Its whereabouts today is not known, which is sad because it featured a heap of naked bodies representing Niobe's slain children, all modelled by the Water Drinkers. According to Schanne, the subject was chosen because it avoided the need to hire costumes for the sitters.

Two other Water Drinkers of importance to the story were the writer Adrien Lélioux and the photographer Nadar because, with Léon Noël, they wrote a book called *Murger par Trois Buveurs d'Eau* which is a key source of information about him. It may have been Lélioux who first persuaded Murger to abandon painting for poetry. At any rate, it was he who said that Murger's paintings made his hair stand on end. Another source of memoirs was Schanne. He was a Bohemian of the amateur category, having private means. His father owned a toy factory and was extremely proud of his artistic son. Schanne dabbled in both painting and music, and once was foolish enough to ask his friends on which he should concentrate. They were unanimous that he should pursue neither, but they valued him for his contributions to their larder. His main talent was for excruciating practical jokes. He once held a housewarming party at which the guests were tricked into eating roast cat, believing it to be rabbit. He was still chuckling about this over forty years later when he wrote his memoirs. Another Water Drinker was an engraver called Guilbert, remembered only for the malign role he played in Murger's life. He stole Marie Vimal, Murger's great love and first Mimi, against whom he measured all his subsequent loves, and found them all more or less wanting, even Lucile, the Mimi of his stories – indeed, perhaps especially Lucile.

Marie may have been Murger's first love, but she was not his first crush. This was his cousin Angèle Tribou, whose father was a successful supplier of heating equipment. Angèle did not share Murger's infatuation, and consistently humiliated him, but it was through her that he met Marie, who gave English lessons to middle-class girls. It grieved Marie to see him so rejected, and she let him understand that, unlike Angèle, she much appreciated flowers and poems, and would be happy if he wished to attend some of her English lessons. It was 1839, he was barely seventeen, she twenty-four and dissatisfied.

Murger had great problems with women. It was not that they found him unattractive. He is described at this time by Lélioux, as "beardless, rosy and round like an apple – round forehead, round chin, round cheeks, round nose – gazing out at us through great staring round eyes." His trouble was his shyness. With a little encouragement he could approach a girl, but how to get any further baffled him. While longing to seduce her, he would fall into a sort of high-minded romantic relationship, placing her on a pedestal, and subjecting her to a torrent of pretty feeble poetry. One of his earliest surviving works, inspired by Marie, went:

> *Ah, le bal, le bal,*
> *Plaisir sans égal,*
> *Que mon coeur adore*
> *Du soir à l'aurore!*

This must have been quite a new experience for Marie. Her life thus far had been harsh, and she may at first have found this boyish courtship charming. Some six years earlier, Marie had been seduced by and forced to marry a much older man, Benoit-Vidal Fonblanc. He was quite well educated but a criminal, who had already done time. Fonblanc embroiled Marie and her brother in his gang, but in 1834 he had a narrow escape when several of his accomplices were caught and given heavy sentences. Shaken, Fonblanc tried to go straight with some success, but it was not easy to escape his past. As they emerged from gaol, the gang reformed, and involved Fonblanc and perhaps Marie too in ambitious plans. An epidemic of burglaries followed, involving several houses where she taught. All this was going on while Murger knelt adoringly at her feet.

Their affair continued for some eighteen months, apparently with Fonblanc's acquiescence. At any rate, it was always Murger who took her to the Bals Masqués at the Opera, where at that time Parisians of all classes went in disguise to enjoy some wild goings on. In 1840, Marie and Murger never missed a ball, going dressed up like swells – he apparently borrowed Fonblanc's dress suit. The young concierge's son felt he was really living. A Bohemian friend saw him one evening in his tails, shouting at the cabbies delivering guests; "Have you got my women there? I'm expecting seven – all women in velvet!" As if velvet was all that was needed to prove their respectability! In fact, they were mostly disreputable women, and several were registered prostitutes. Still, their velvet differentiated them from the wild young girls in fancy dress, to whom the management gave cheap tickets to get the Bacchanalia going.

Perhaps Fonblanc did not care what Marie did, or simply could not bring himself to feel jealous of so callow a youth. If the latter, he judged shrewdly, for Murger never made any sexual advance beyond an ardent kissing of hands and other gallantries. He gave Marie things he could ill afford – a beautifully bound copy of Moreau's poem *Myosotis* in which he inscribed a little offering of his own; they exchanged rings and many protestations of affection. What Marie made of it all we do not know. She may well have become rather frustrated. When the bubble burst and Fonblanc went on the run, she turned first to Murger for help, but it was not long before she found someone a little more worldy-wise. Marie needed a hiding place at once which, of course, Murger did not hesitate to offer. Easier promised than provided! He could hardly take her home. The idea of explaining to his father that he was involved with a married woman, who was wanted by the police, made his blood run cold. But he had an inspiration. His friend and fellow Water Drinker, Guilbert, had both a studio and a hotel room. Could Marie live in one of these till she could find a permanent refuge? Guilbert agreed, and it seems that, at long last, Marie and Murger spent a night together.

Unfortunately, Murger could not also spend the days with her. He was now eighteen, and had left Cadet de Chambine. Joseph de Jouy had found him a part-time job as secretary to a Russian living in Paris, Count Jacques Tolstoi. Tolstoi was not demanding [and did not pay much] but he did expect Murger to turn up each day. Having no other source of income, Murger had to ask Guilbert to keep an eye on Marie, lest she get frightened alone by herself all day. Alas for our young idealist, Guilbert did his job all too well. A few days later, Murger returned to find the room empty, and a note from Marie telling him not to try to find her. Cross-questioning

Guilbert, Murger soon discovered his friend's treachery. He tells the story in *Les Amours d'Olivier*, describing how, after finding the note, he returned home, tried unsuccessfully to commit suicide, and awoke next morning to be thrown out by a father beside himself with rage.

According to Lélioux, with whom Murger now sought lodging, *Les Amours d'Olivier* gave a highly-coloured version of what really happened. He says that Murger had already been thrown out by his father some time before, but there is no doubt about his misery over Marie's treachery. It killed something in him. Not long afterwards, in January 1841, he heard of her arrest along with her brother and about a hundred other members of the gang. In August, when she came to trial, Fonblanc gallantly made a speech exonerating her and taking the blame on himself. As a result, she was acquitted, but the court, unmoved by Fonblanc's chivalry, sent him down for twelve years. Murger made no attempt to renew contact with Marie – but that is not to say he was cured. All he had left of his first love was a pair of gloves, a domino and a withered bouquet of flowers. Wherever he went during the rest of his life, these mementoes went too. He decided it would be too painful to keep the other thing she had not bothered to take with her, the little volume of *Myosotis*. He gave it to Lélioux, but later in the day had second thoughts and asked for it back. Next morning, however, he did give it to Lélioux, who found inside the fly-leaf a newly inscribed poem ending with the verse:

> *Poor Myosotis – if I throw you away,*
> *When your white pages seem to bid me wait;*
> *If I am cruel – forgive me, but you say*
> *Forget me not – and I want to forget.*[7]

It was now that the true life of Bohème started for Murger. The forty francs that Tolstoi paid per month, considerably less than he paid his cook, had been meagre enough while Murger lived with his father, who had taken thirty, leaving him ten for his tobacco and other wants. It was much more difficult to find everything out of the forty francs. For the next few years, Murger was so poor that he even considered joining the navy. His friends dissuaded him without too much trouble.

Despite his poverty, he did not stay long with Lélioux in rue

Montholon. The winter of 1841 was bitterly cold, and Lélioux's room had no stove; Murger found himself a lodging at 3 rue de la Tour d'Auvergne where he was to stay for three years. Already, Lélioux noticed, he was starting to lose his youthful looks. His chubby cheeks were sinking and becoming sallow, and although only nineteen, his hair was receding and he was starting to grow a long, variegated but lustreless beard. In fact, Murger was not well, and later in the year had to spend a month in hospital, the Hôpital de Saint-Louis, the first of many stays there. His problem was said to be purpura, a condition in which his whole skin became inflamed with a burning red rash. The doctors blamed it on his addiction to coffee and his generally disordered way of life. For Murger was discovering that he had a disorder. He could only work at night and then only with the aid of litres of coffee.

While Guilbert's treachery caused a great scandal amongst the Water Drinkers, it was not the only reason why they were beginning to break up. Léon Noël had left to take up a teaching post in Orléans, and various others, worn down by privation, were spending half their time in hospital, or giving up the unequal contest and seeking a living in more conventional ways. The Desbrosses brothers strove mightily to keep the club together but to no avail. Even so, the friendships remained. Throughout this bitter winter, several, including Murger, suffered appalling hardship. In his view, however, life was worst of all for the Desbrosses. In December, he wrote to Noël: "They spend half the day fasting and the other half freezing. Even the cats avoid them, and as for heating, they have only their pipes – often without tobacco." The Desbrosses were sons of a cab driver who had thrown them out as wasters, and who was now apparently delighted to see them suffer.

At this time Murger was working on a grandiose verse drama called *Marie*. It was at best a very long-term investment. To eke out his salary from Tolstoi, he would submit verses, satires, or even jokes, to the smaller artistic magazines, but more often to trade journals which were less demanding. One in which he scored some success was *La Naiade*, the trade journal for public bath attendants. Of course, they paid very badly, "so many sous to the acre," he used to say. One of his most endearing qualities was his ability to turn adversity into a joke. Arsène Houssaye, who controlled *l'Artist* and other journals of interest to the Bohemians, used to refer to Murger and his friends as *"mes petits crétins"* – my little idiots. Perhaps he did exploit them but he kept them alive and kept their hope alive too. It was Houssaye who first proposed to Murger that he should write a story. The result was a fantasy called *The Loves of a Cricket and a Spark*.

Murger also wrote copy for commercial clients but he hated this. Angèle's father once gave him a commission to write an essay in praise of heating stoves, which he put off doing for so long that his uncle finally confiscated his clothes until he had finished it, an incident he later converted into a splendid story. There was also the dentist who had written a heroic poem entitled *Osanores or Dental Prosthesis*, and who was prepared to pay fifty sous for each line that was improved. This was a source of income for several Bohemians for several weeks. Best of all was when Tolstoi introduced Murger to a friend who needed help with his entry for a poetic competition to celebrate the marriage of one of the Tsar's daughters. This man's effort was so bad that Murger had more or less to rewrite it, and it was agreed that any prize should be shared between them. Their combined effort won, and in March 1842 Murger received the first instalment of his share of the prize. He wrote to Noël a delightful and much-quoted letter.

Carissimo!!!
    Imagine – if I am not using a liveried courier to send you this, it is only because you live too nearby – a mere thirty leagues! not worth the trouble since otherwise I have the wherewithal – I am swimming in a river of gold, in a sea of half-franc coins. It absolutely rains kings and queens of every country and countenance: I am washing my hands in the Pactolus – and almond soap. I have coloured gloves and likewise coats and trousers. How they deceive us, these poets who pretend the world is dark and bad. They know nothing, these miserere-chanters who cannot imagine what delights I am enjoying: they do not dream what pleasure can be had in offering a cabby a tip: they cannot appreciate the aroma of Havana smoke, the joy of sunshine, the creak of tight-fitting new boots. Well, well. All that is what I am feeling, seeing and tasting. You would not recognise your fat Fleming – he has disappeared into dust with his ancient coat and boots with rows of holes like a man-o'-war. The owl has died to return a phoenix. Not a bad line for a Latin couplet, eh? But so it is, dear friend. At this moment the great and powerful lord Viscount of la Tour d'Auvergne is radiant. Pedestrians line up to see him pass; the poor stretch out for alms and he tosses them a franc; the women are hushed but he grants

them a smile – and what a smile! Such, oh great one, is my condition and I conclude that life is beautiful. Now, you are going to ask me whence comes this cloudburst of five-franc coins. It is a whirlwind from the North, my dear, like the Aurora Borealis. [As my share of the prize], my employer has given me an advance of 350 francs with 150 francs to come in a few months. Imagine my joy when this staggering news broke; quivering from your threadbare cravat to my moribund boots, I rushed to Rothschild's to cash my draft; thence to the bookshop; thence to the tailor; then the restaurant; then the theatre; the café; until at last home once more, to slide between new sheets, to savour the aromatic smoke, to dream I am emperor of Morocco and married to the Bank of France. Thus do I live; I have done so much that I have to admit that I can already see the sandy floor of the Pactolus. Still, I'm now properly dressed and;

I have enough to live for a week! I will live it!

Thereafter, I shall return to writing for those infantile minds that read the papers edited by Lélioux[8] and Bouche, wasting my time of course, simply in order to have gloves and cigars for the coming summer. Indeed tomorrow, even, I shall re-dedicate myself to work; already I have wasted three months; let us hope that this month will be fruitful of *chefs d'oeuvres*. And so – good day, dear friend – I would give 10,000 louis for a railway between Paris and your home town so that I could see you and repay you – at any rate a two-franc dinner – sadly it will have to wait – *vale!*[9]

The Pactolus, in whose waters Midas is said to have washed away his golden touch, was all too apt a symbol of Bohème. Its citizens had great difficulty in holding on to money. It was not just that there were too many windows through which to throw it, but also that there were so many creditors to pacify. Murger once wrote: "I have been watering my creditors and they merely sprout with renewed vigour." Nevertheless, by the mid-forties things were slowly improving. It was about this time that Murger managed to obtain the editorship of two trade magazines – *Le Moniteur de la Mode* and *Le Castor*, the journal for milliners for which Rodolfo was trying to write when Mimi first knocks on his door. As editor, he made sure that their readers had the benefit of regular and learned theological articles by Jean Wallon, which may have improved their minds, but did nothing for the journals' circulation. But what was the point of being an editor if you could not help your friends?

Murger's disaster with Marie may have stunted his emotional growth, but it did not destroy his interest in women. He could not keep away from them, and all this time he was having affairs.

These still seem to have been rather quixotic, but, in 1842, he became very excited about a woman called Christine, enough to write lyrical letters about her to Léon Noël. Christine was Danish, fair-haired, blue-eyed, with a wonderful slender figure. Like Marie, she was discontented with her life. Murger probably met her at one of the public dances – the Opera Ball or La Mabille – and she soon consented to visit his attic, ostensibly for a little company and friendship. True to form, that was all she got, plus, of course, copious verses. After several barren visits, she had to leave Paris. He was furious with himself for having missed such a chance, but she soon came back and gave him another. Surmising that perhaps it was the poverty of his attic that had inhibited him, she suggested a walk in the woods. He accepted with alacrity, but when the day came, he was so broke that he could not redeem his only decent trousers from the pawnbroker. Murger was very clothes-conscious, and during their romantic stroll, he was too mortified by his appearance to think of anything else. Christine never bothered him again.

All through these years he had continued to work on his verse-drama *Marie*, certain that it was his destiny to be a great tragic poet. In 1843, however, he met Champfleury, a writer who observed Bohème with an altogether colder and more analytical eye. Champfleury has far the strongest claim to be the original of Marcello, if only because it was he who so loved Marietta/Musetta. At this time, on Wednesdays, Murger used to hold little "at homes" in his attic at la Tour d'Auvergne. Bright conversation and the host's latest verses were on offer – but not much else. Champfleury, who had recently arrived from the provinces, was brought to one of these. He and Murger liked each other at once.

Not long afterwards Murger went back to hospital and while he was there it seems that bailiffs removed his furniture. When he came out, he moved in with Champfleury in rue de Vaugirard. They pooled everything, and like Rodolfo and Marcello, they set out to live in perfect comradeship, but it did not last long. Champfleury could not adjust to Murger's nocturnal habits. Murger tried to change, even working by day in a darkened room, but to no avail. After three months, and still good friends, they agreed to split up; but already Champfleury had given Murger a vital piece of advice. This was to abandon tragic verse and try his hand at comic prose. Soon we hear no more of the verse-drama *Marie*. Perhaps it did indeed serve to warm some cold and fuelless winter's night.

Champfleury was right. Much of Murger's poetry was mawkish and sentimental. His prose on the other hand was amusing. His wit might be rather arch and facetious but he had a droll view of life and an indomitable ability to laugh at adversity. He was not by any means a great writer nor fluent. He would labour a whole night to produce a single page of prose. Furthermore, he seemed to lack a creative imagination since nearly all his work was an elaboration of his own daily experiences. He returned repeatedly to the main events of his life, changing the names of the characters and re-examining each incident from every angle until it was wrung dry of possibilities. He was really a reporter, but a most endearing one. He could be funny about people without being unkind, and this, he now discovered, was his true métier. Champfleury did not have this knack. Although he also wrote about Bohème, he saw things too clearly. He described the same people and the same episodes as Murger, but he was without charm. As one critic put it, Champfleury analysed Bohème while Murger sang about it. Despite his puns and hyperbole, Murger was a genuinely funny man. One evening at the Café Momus, he extemporised a satirical version of the *Iliad*, transposed into modern times and related to contemporary characters, a *tour de force* which held his audience spellbound for three hours. He could also produce a sharp one-liner. One evening when Champfleury was holding forth rather uncharitably about Victor Hugo, Murger was distinctly heard to murmur to his neighbour, "He reminds me of a dog pissing on Notre Dame." There was a moment of tense silence until Champfleury laughed.

It was at this time that another incident occurred which deeply affected Murger. In February 1844, Joseph Desbrosses, *le Christ*, died in the Hôpital de Saint-Louis in the ward which Murger himself knew so well. If Murger had ever needed a warning to escape from Bohème, this was it. It was already the third death in their circle that winter. At the cemetery, they discovered to their embarrassment that none of them had the money to tip the gravedigger.

"Never mind," said he, "you'll all be back soon enough." *Le Christ's* death hit Murger especially hard. He had been everything the Water Drinkers had admired and stood for, devoted to his art, but never bigoted like Lazare. No matter how famished himself, he would share his crust with a needy friend. Furthermore, there was no doubt about his talent. And where had it all got him? Not to the Academy but first to the Hôtel Dieu and then to the morgue. Murger realised that he must get off the raft while he still had the strength to swim. He had discovered where his talent lay. If his friends could not take a little gentle mockery, so much the worse for them. He resolved to make some money at their expense. But he did not mock *le Christ*, for whom he reserved a special story called *Francine's Muff*. It is set in Bohème, but does not involve Rodolfo and his friends. It is the story of the love of Jacques D., a struggling young sculptor, for the tubercular Francine, who dies leaving him inconsolable. Jacques D. dies in his turn, never having got over his loss. It is full of sweet fancy but very sentimental. It is to *Francine's Muff* that we owe the most famous scenes between the two lovers – their first meeting, the candles which blow out, the dropped key, the tiny frozen hand and, at the end, the muff that warms it. It is a simple love story, with none of the irony with which Murger treats Marcello, Mimi and Musetta, but with a feeling of reverence for its young hero. It is Murger's homage to his friend, *le Christ*, and he would no doubt have been horrified at the way the opera grafts it onto the story of Rodolfo and Mimi. This is what makes the opera so much more sentimental than the book. It also makes much of Mimi fictional, for Francine did not exist and these tender things did not happen. *Le Christ* did fall in love at the very end of his life, but appropriately, it was with one of the young nuns at the hospital.

About a year after *le Christ's* death, Murger first met Lucile Louvet – Mimi II. Like Mimi in the opera, Lucile made artificial flowers. Murger first saw her at a picnic in the spring of 1845, escorted by her current lover, an artist on the fringes of Bohème called Crampon. Murger was at once struck by her resemblance to Marie, and it was not long before he and Lucile were living together in the Hôtel Merciol in rue de Canettes. Several Bohemians were lodging at the Merciol at that time. It was owned by M.

Benoit who appears in the opera. The coming together of Mimi and Rodolfo is described in one of Murger's stories in *le Corsaire*. He wrote that one evening, on returning home, Rodolfo found that M. Benoit had locked him out and re-let his room. Hoping to recover some of his belongings Rodolfo knocked on the door of his old room to find that the new tenant was none other than Mimi. To M. Benoit's disgust, she promptly invited Rodolfo to move in with her.

Murger's own description of Lucile is perhaps not reliable since he could never get the memory of Marie out of his head. Anyway, he thought he was writing fiction. Another inmate of the Hôtel Merciol, the romantic poet Théodore de Banville, remembered her later as:

> One of those faded Parisian flowers, born and raised in the shadows, who became wild with joy to see the sun on a day out at Marlotte or Bougival. Very pale, with a dull ashen pallor, soft lips, mousy brown hair and blue-grey eyes, one could see that she had suffered and accepted her suffering with resignation, and that just to share a poet's privations seemed to her like paradise.

We have an alternative, much harsher description of her by another so-called friend of Murger, the young nobleman Charles d'Héricault. Too fastidious to enter, he hovered on the fringes of Bohème, half fascinated by and half loathing what he saw. He wrote that, calling one day on Murger:

> the door was opened by a pock marked housekeeper. It was Mimi! Pockmarked, oh! Pockmarked like a honeycomb. I'd like to believe she was as sweet. She seemed goodnatured but not very bright, something between a Parisian washerwoman and the housekeeper of a provincial apothecary. She was very pale, so often Nature's compensation for the scarred victims of the smallpox – and that was the extent of her beauty, that and the gentle expression I have mentioned. No hint of mischief nor of wit. It was on such an instrument that our poet had to make his music, like a deaf and dumb fiddler bowing on a broomstick. But then, he was a fountain of idealism, lavishing it on any filthy skirt.

Schanne in his memoirs steered a middle course, although he made it plain that he had not liked Lucile:

> As to Mimi, she was indeed a sickly plant grown in the shade, in the slums of Paris, and though she could sometimes look angelic, she was devoid of morals. A little flirt – she deceived Rodolphe as Marguerite would have

deceived Faust had there been another act. How many times did I and my friends lecture her and, heaven knows, we were hardly moralists. The good La Fontaine would have blushed to hear us. We used to say to her; 'Do what you want, that's your business, but keep up appearances; at least find pretexts to cover your scandals; tell him you've stayed with a sick relation or friend.' Ah! she would just laugh and pirouette and only did what she pleased. It seemed that it really gave her pleasure to enslave a man of superior intellect, and drive him mad with jealousy.

But Murger liked Lucile, and saw more in her than the others, who had never loved Marie. His friends were generally dismayed when, early in 1845, he set up house with her. After all, he could barely afford to live singly, let alone keep a mistress. No-one was to know that one day she would make his fortune. Perhaps it was Lucile's arrival in his life that stimulated him to send that first story to *Le Corsaire*, although it did not, of course, feature Mimi. Despite his friends' doubts, Lucile fitted in. As Rodolfo put it: "There was first a great outcry amongst the Bohemians when they learned of this union but, as Mademoiselle Mimi was very taking, not at all prudish and able to stand tobacco smoke and literary conversation without a headache, they became accustomed to her and treated her as a comrade."

This was the period when the Café Momus was much frequented by the Bohemians, who more or less monopolised a room on the second floor. They were not quite the same group that had formed the ragged Water Drinkers, although several, like Murger, had progressed from one to the other. They now found themselves mixing with men like Théodore de Banville, the painter Gustave Courbet and Charles Baudelaire, men whom Arsène Houssaye would hardly have dared call his *petits crétins*. The Momus was not in the Latin Quarter but on the right bank of the Seine, in the rue Saint Germain l'Auxerrois. It was very popular with the Bohemians because the coffee was good value and the landlord, Louvet, who had poetic ambitions himself, was quite happy for them to pass the whole evening there, chattering and arguing but spending as little as possible. Their technique was that the first to arrive would order nothing, saying that he was waiting for a friend. Each arrival would say the same, until someone arrived with enough money for a pot of coffee. That one pot would then become their excuse for a noisy evening, drinking water, monopolising the papers provided, playing on the only backgammon board, arguing about matters cultural, and generally taking advantage of M. Louvet's good nature. As their occupation of the second floor became more established, they even had the effrontery to demand that M. Louvet should subscribe to *Le Moniteur de la Mode, Le Castor* and other obscure journals edited by one or another of the company. In fact, they almost brought him to ruin by driving away his profitable customers, but realising at the last moment what they were doing, they concocted a rescue strategy. They ran a story in several of their journals stating that valuable documents had been found in the attic of the café, and saying that the landlord was uncertain what to do with them. This was pure invention, but it brought such a wave of custom that M. Louvet was able to pay his creditors.

In the opera, both Marcello's love for Musetta and her infidelities are already established features of Bohème by the time Mimi knocks on Rodolfo's door. In real life, both affairs probably started at about the same time. Marie-Christine Roux was a country girl, illiterate but pretty, high-spirited and popular. She made enough to provide for her mother and sister in Lyon by modelling for artists, amongst other activities. She is said to have sat for several leading artists including Gérôme, Pradier and Ingres. In due course, she brought her mother and sister to Paris, and set them up in the Ile St-Louis, living there herself when not otherwise involved. Champfleury was by no means the only one to fall in love with her, but seems to have done so particularly heavily, and she seems to have preferred him, but she was not to be pinned down. Perhaps he is not to be blamed if his book about her, *Les Aventures de Mlle Mariette*, strikes a sour note. It contains several characters recognisable from *Scenes de la Vie de Bohème* including Murger and Mimi, renamed Henry Streich and Rose. Streich is dismissed as able only to write about his own affairs with Rose who, though "pale and melancholy", supplies him with regular infidelities on which to base his stories. This is a jaundiced view of Murger's book.

Although Marie Roux seems to have had a fondness for Champfleury, she was even less faithful than Lucile. At this stage of her life she was as gay and carefree as she appears in the opera, being abundant with her fancy, provided her lovers were young and amusing. Murger quotes Molière to sum up her attitude: "You like me and I like you. It's agreed – let's make love." Everyone understood the rules and they accepted them, but she caused poor Champfleury much agony. The opera is truthful when it portrays two lovesick young men, consoling themselves with the thought that their mistresses are not betraying them for other young men so much as for a shawl, a bonnet or a pair of boots.

Marie was evidently very pretty. Nadar took her photograph twice. The earlier and more attractive picture shows her seated beside her lumpish sister, Antoinette, known as Anna but a dull girl whose company the Bohemians dreaded.[10] It hardly does Marie justice if Schanne is to be believed;

> A true daughter of la Bohème was this Mariette/Musette; but beautiful, really beautiful. Painters and sculptors competed for her and had to book her well in advance in order to be sure of a séance. In truth, this body, pure white with just a hint of rose around the joints was wonderfully proportioned; splendidly endowed, the sight of her filled one with that same spiritual peace that classical statues can inspire. Only her face, merry and slightly mocking, lacked perfect balance. At least, what gave it this look was a rather unusual feature; she smiled askew. Let me explain; the left corner of her mouth went slightly up whereas the right one stayed still which made us say, 'she squints with her mouth'.

Nadar's second study of her makes her look heavy, but if, as it is believed, it is the first photograph ever made of a nude woman, she can claim to have blazed a well-trodden trail. It is hard to think of anyone else more worthy of the honour, but she had her doubts about it, and hid her face from the camera.

Although Champfleury was Marie's favourite, he could never rely on her. About the only person never to touch her was Murger; at least he is at pains to say so in his book, no doubt to reassure his friend. "Rodolphe," he wrote, "was a friend of Musette's but never more than a friend – neither of them was quite sure why." Perhaps his relations with Lucile at this time were too intense to leave room for others, or perhaps Marie Roux did not remind him enough of Marie Vimal. But perhaps also, he remembered how he had suffered when a friend had stolen his girl. Or maybe he was just too shy.

His affair with Lucile seems to have had three phases; during the first two, they lived together as man and wife but not always in harmony. He still idolised women and endowed them with attributes more appropriate to *Le Roman de la Rose* than to *La Vie de Bohème*. At any rate the physical side of their love seems to have been a success, and perhaps she came quite to enjoy his rhapsodies and his fetish for her "little white hands that he would cover with kisses". But she was not adequate for the pedestal he placed under her, and their rows gradually became fiercer, and their reconciliations less sweet.

Lucile took to leaving home on a whim, and staying away a night or more without taking any trouble to protect Murger from the jealousy she knew this would cause. Schanne condemned her for this but she must have had her own preoccupations. Desperately poor, she knew she would only be young once. If she did not use her youth and beauty to good effect, what would become of her when they were gone? Once the novelty of an intellectual lover had worn off, she must have wondered whether he would ever be able to afford the silks and velvets she craved. She may also have suspected that, if he ever did achieve affluence, he would leave her behind anyway. She could not really understand his quixotry and may have wondered whether it was really her he loved or some beatified Marie Vimal, transported by romantic memory beyond all emulation. In his way, Murger was just as unfaithful to Lucile, but her rivals were an old domino, a pair of gloves and a withered bouquet.

After eight stormy months, Lucile and Murger had their first "divorce" as he called it in his book. It was on his initiative. After one row too many, he told her to find a new lover. She did not want to, but for once failed to cajole him out of his resolution. Two days later, Murger asked her how the search was going, and Lucile said that she had not even looked, but she had. It only took her a fortnight to find a new protector, and one, by all accounts, who was better off – but then it would have been hard to find another one so badly off as Murger. All Murger's friends congratulated him on his deliverance, although some did find his nonchalance a little too studied.

But separation brought no relief. As in Act III of the opera at the Barrière d'Enfer, after a short while they came together again, in the winter of 1846. Of course, all the old troubles started anew.

The next break came in the spring and was initiated by Lucile. In *Scènes de la Vie de Bohème*, Rodolfo says that Mimi has left him to live with a rich Viscount, but a letter of Murger's was recently found and published in 1959 for the first time. In it he wrote: I have moved to rue Mazarine . . . my woman has left me – and married a large soldier who wants to cut my throat, something to which I am opposed."[11]

Of course, as all opera-goers know, this was not the end of the story. In the depths of the winter of 1848, Lucile returned. Some time before, she had been dismissed by her soldier. If Murger is to be believed, it was because she found a poem he had written about her in *L'Artist*. This had so delighted her that her soldier, in an attack of jealousy, threw her out, forbidding her to take with her anything he had given her – which was, of course, virtually everything she had. She went back to making flowers, but this involved pressing down on a bobbin with her chest in order to leave both hands free to arrange the petals. Her chest was now too painful to do this. According to Murger, Lucile tried without success to commit suicide by drinking disinfectant. This, along with her advanced tuberculosis, left her so weak that she could no longer cope with life. In desperation, she returned to her former lover. Murger took her in and was able to look after her tolerably well at first so that she rallied a little, but by the beginning of March his money was gone, and Lucile was sinking fast. He had no way to help her.

It was apparently Lucile who took the initiative, and suggested that it would be better for them both if she went to hospital. On 6th March, 1848, Murger took her to La Pitié. As he left her, she suddenly panicked and cried out to him to take her home with him, but her condition had deteriorated too far. She had been too weak to walk down the stairs from his garret to the cab, and he had had to carry her. Nevertheless, she survived some five weeks. Murger has been accused of heartlessness during her illness. He does not seem to have visited her as often as he might have done. Visits were allowed on Thursdays and Sundays but he went only two or three times. His excuse was that he had no money, and knew that she would expect something from him. A few sous would enormously help her comfort in hospital, but he could not afford even that. It seems she missed him dreadfully when he did not come. On one occasion, however, he delighted her by going first to the woods of Aulnay and Fontenay and gathering a tiny bunch of early violets for her. She realised that he could not afford anything else.

Lucile died on 9th April. On the previous day Murger, having promised to do so, had started out to visit her, but on the way he met a friend who was a doctor under training at La Pitié. This man gave Murger to understand that Lucile was already dead. It was a terrible misunderstanding. The doctor thought he had seen her bed empty, and had jumped to conclusions. Murger turned back, only to learn next day that there had been a mistake. He rushed to the hospital, but it was too late. By this time, Lucile really was dead, and as was standard practice with dead paupers, her body had been used for dissection. What was left of it was in the wagon standing in the courtyard and about to leave for a communal grave. Murger had neither the means – nor perhaps the desire – to intervene. He was, at this time, going through one of his last and most acute periods of poverty.

With Lucile's death, we have reached the real-life equivalent of that last harrowing moment in the opera when Rodolfo turns back from the window and sees his friends all looking at him in anguish. Mimi is dead and, apart from one last cry of pain, the opera is over. In the best traditions of the nineteenth-century novel, however, a final chapter is needed to tidy up the loose ends, and discover what happened afterwards to the surviving characters.

In the February preceding Lucile's death, Paris had been convulsed by the revolution which overthrew the last king of France, Louis-Philippe, and which drew a symbolic line under the so-called Romantic Era. The new republic heralded a much more materialistic time and, as if in response, the survivors amongst the Bohemians were beginning to find, one by one, their various ways to escape. Already Champfleury, Tabar, Lélioux, Nadar and Murger himself, were beginning to enjoy some renown outside their own immediate circle. For those who were going to survive, the worst was nearly over. Others, like Schanne and Jean Wallon, were withdrawing more and more into safe bourgeois family retreats. But there were many who had neither success nor family to save them. Some, like *le Christ* and Privat d'Anglement, were already dead. Others disappeared from view.

Of the characters in *La Bohème*, Schanne lived the longest. He did not write his memoirs until 1887, when he claimed to be the last survivor. By this time, he had long given up any ambition to become an artist while, if his only engagement as a pianist had been to compete with a noisy parrot, he must have been an excruciatingly bad musician. In any case, he had had to take over the family toy business, but he still liked to hang around on the fringes of the artistic community, a life which never lost its seductions for him. He derived huge pleasure from coaching actors who sought his advice as to how to play Schaunard. In his memoirs, he ruefully lists his achievement in terms of published works. These number only six songs and one portrait which was accepted by the Salon in 1850. His real talent was to make himself agreeable.

Although Colline plays an important role in *La Bohème*, Jean Wallon was always on the fringes of the group. He loved to sit with them in the Café Momus, contentedly smoking his pipe and tossing an occasional pun or aphorism into the conversation. But he ate and slept with his well-to-do family on the Ile Saint-Louis. The others suspected him of leading a double life and, like Rigoletto, of hiding from them a secret lady-friend; but it was only his mother. Later he married a sensible middle-class girl with a small dowry, and settled down to write anti-Jesuit tracts, and earn his living as a civil servant. He became extremely respectable, but never quite lived down his raffish reputation as Rodolfo's friend, Colline. His wife once wrote to the papers complaining that they would not take her husband seriously in his own right but it was to no avail. It would have helped if his religious essays had been less boring. They are available in the Bibliothèque Nationale in Paris.

Marc Trapadoux's career was even more obscure than Wallon's. He became a teacher in a college in the suburbs of Paris. Although he came from a rich family in Lyons, he was arguably a more genuine Bohemian than Wallon. He was known as the "green giant" because of his exceptional strength and his voluminous green coat. It is this coat rather than its owner that is featured in *La Bohème*.

Champfleury died in 1886 after only a moderately successful life of letters. In addition to *Les Aventures de Mademoiselle Mariette*, he wrote several works about Bohème, notably *Les Souvenirs de Jeunesse* and *Les Confessions de Sylvius*. They are not very interesting and they always have a slightly bitter taste. He took himself too seriously, but Mariette's infidelities did not improve him. He eventually became a great expert on porcelain and the director of the factory at Sèvres. Perhaps that is his greatest claim to fame – apart from such second-hand immortality as he derives from Marcello. Marcello's other main constituent, Léopold Tabar, died in 1869 after a reasonably successful career. His entry in Bénézit reads; "Pupil of Delaroche. Salon début in 1842. Initially painter of historical subjects, but later also of landscapes, notably of Venice and Constantinople, where he painted *Portrait of the Sultan* [Salon 1869]. We owe him various scenes from the Italian Campaign. Awarded medal in 1867. This talented artist deserves more fame than he receives and often his works are attributed to better known artists." There follows a list of his paintings in various municipal galleries. Their titles reveal a taste for stirring and bloodthirsty subjects. *Attila massacring prisoners, Convoy of wounded, The wounded Padre, Joshua stopping the sun*, and so on. *Pharaoh engulfed in the Red Sea* would have been typical. He married Alexina Goury, a pupil.

Marie Roux came to a sad end. By the time Lucile died, she was already beginning to think more seriously about the future. She once said; "Tomorrow is just a trick of the calendar. It is a daily excuse that people have invented for not doing what should be done at once. Tomorrow there may be an earthquake; happily, today the earth is still." Nevertheless, nagged perhaps by her mother and sister, she began to worry more and more about tomorrow, and how they would all live when she was no longer the darling of the left bank. She came to the conclusion that the right bank might be less lively, but offered more security in the long run. She moved to rue Bréda, near to Nôtre Dame de la Lorette, which was the centre in those days for aristocratic whoring. She ceased to be a *grisette* and became a *lorette*, a slang term for a prostitute. Asked by one of her old friends what had become of her heart she replied; "It is so well covered in velvet that I cannot feel it." [Her comment is quoted verbatim in Act IV of the opera.] Unlike many prostitutes, and in contrast to her earlier insouciance, she became a fanatical hoarder. Schanne visited her in the early sixties and was shocked to find how miserly she had become. She showed him a carved ivory coffer in which she had amassed a small fortune of 40,000 francs. It was not so much the amount which shocked him, as the loving way she fingered the gold coins. He concluded sadly that all her high spirits and joyfulness had been hiding a calculating spirit. Perhaps he was right but she always loved and cared for her mother and sister, and perhaps it was they who contrived in the end to tether her wayward heart. She would have done better not to let them. Her tomorrow was overtaken, not by an earthquake, but by a storm at sea. In early 1863, with her mother, she embarked for Algiers aboard a ferry called the *Atlas*. It was never seen again. Somewhere in the Mediterranean hides Marie Roux, her ivory coffer and her little hoard of gold.

Finally, we must return to Murger. Perhaps preoccupied by Lucile's troubles, he took no part in the revolution in the spring of 1848. He had no sympathy with the working classes, whom he regarded as sentimental and pig-headed like his father. Nevertheless, it came as something of a surprise when the Tsarist files were opened in the 1920s, and revealed that Tolstoi had been a secret agent, who had been using Murger to gather intelligence. After the revolution of 1848, Tolstoi had no more need of Murger who thus lost his main source of income.

Worse still, Lucile was hardly buried before Murger himself had to go back to hospital: not, this time, to his familiar Saint-Louis, but to the more sinister Hôpital du Midi, which may indicate that his problem was venereal. Even so, he managed to write bravely cheerful letters suggesting that his friends might help him out with a little tobacco or, better still, some money, since even a small tip for the nurses would improve his situation greatly. One of these friends, cultivated perhaps for his wealth, was d'Héricault. Although Murger was still not yet thirty, d'Héricault gives us a picture of how his illness, privations and excesses had eroded his once rosy looks.

> He was extremely ugly in an absolutely vulgar way, very clumsy, small and filthy. A cracked voice, no hair, a long brown beard with a faded look to it, his lifeless eyes, which watered continuously, were large, soft and

timid, and somehow managed to be both bulging and hooded at the same time. Here was the poet of youth! He reminded me immediately of a portrait of Clément Marot except that Clément Marot retained a little hair, had decent clothes and was presumably reasonably clean.

These were dark days indeed for Murger. He wrote to Victor Hugo, an eminent republican well placed to benefit from the revolution, asking whether there was a chance of a position. He got a charming reply expressing the great man's shock that society did not value its talented members better, but offering no practical help. Worse and worse, at about this time there was a change of editor at *Le Corsaire* and the series on *La Vie de Bohème* came to an end. It had had a mild success. Murger had been noticed in artistic circles, and the stories might even have brought a little extra circulation to *Le Corsaire*, but since that was in any case tiny, it had not established him nor immediately opened any doors.

One day, early in 1849 however, a young man called Théodore Barrière came to see him. Barrière was well-off by Bohemian standards. He had been having some small successes writing for the theatre, converting known works for the stage, often in collaboration with the author. He lived an orderly life at home with well-to-do parents, by whose advice he set great store, and they were very anxious that he should not get mixed up with disreputable people. They also kept a parrot called Coco, whose opinion of strangers was considered important by the family.

Barrière was a little shocked to find Murger still in bed at midday, and became more so when he did not get up to greet a visitor, but he at once explained the purpose of his visit, a proposal jointly to turn *Scènes de la Vie de Bohème* into a play. Murger was enthusiastic and wanted to start straight away. Barrière invited him home, but Murger demurred. After some prevarication, he confessed that he was only in bed because he had no trousers, having lent his only pair to a friend in need. He hoped to have them back by the evening. The delay at least enabled him to do his best over his own appearance before his crucial encounter with Coco. Luckily that wise bird took to him straight away. The partnership was agreed, and they set about applying Barrière's theatrical expertise to Murger's raw material.

The result was a long way from Murger's book and, indeed,

from the real Bohème. The opera, although sentimental, is much more faithful to them both than is this play. Barrière invented a rich uncle, a ludicrous Monsieur Durandin, whose only topic of conversation seems to be stock exchange prices. Durandin wants his nephew and heir to marry a rich and pretty widow, Césarine de Rouvre, but Rodolphe is a poet, and wants to live in Bohème with his little *grisette*, Mimi. The scenes alternate between polite society and Bohème, with the rich characters coming out very badly as stupid and scheming people. Every duplicity is tried to poison Rodolphe's and Mimi's love, culminating in a visit to her by Durandin which is almost indistinguishable from Germont's visit to Violetta in *La Traviata*. Naturally, Mimi's purity and self-lessness shine through and melt even the cold hearts, first of Césarine and then of Durandin. Everyone ends up kneeling round Mimi's bed imploring her to get well, and promising that when she does, all obstacles to her happiness will have been removed – but she is already dead. "Ah, my youth!" cries Rodolphe, when this is discovered. "It is you that dies!"

Somewhat apprehensive, all the Bohemians were at the *Théâtre des Variétés* when the play opened that autumn. Their reactions were mainly of relief; but Nadar, in particular, objected to that last line. How could Rodolphe be so cynical as to think only of himself when Mimi lies not yet cold on her truckle bed? Murger shrugged. "Ah," he said, "but is that not the truth?"

The play was an instant success, and from that evening forward, Murger's days of hunger were over. Overnight he became what he had always wanted to be, a conventional bourgeois. How happy this would have made his mother! He now had no difficulty finding publishers, but he never became rich. Unbelievably, he sold the copyright of the stories in book form to the publisher Michel Lévy for a paltry 500 francs. Lévy's profits were enormous. Accused of exploitation, he later explained that, although he had not initially paid him much, Murger was forever asking him for loans which he never refused. Still, Murger should not have had to ask.

Murger was soon writing regularly for prestigious journals like the *Revue des Deux Mondes*. Nearly all his stories were still autobiographical, recounting over and again with different names and from different angles the main episodes of his life. *Les Amours d'Olivier* was about his first affair with Marie Vimal. In 1851, they met again and even set up house together but the magic had gone. Their reconciliation only lasted a fortnight, and he wrote about it in a bitter-sweet story called *Le Dernier Rendez-vous*. In it, the two former lovers spend the day revisiting their old haunts. At first, they are full of excitement and renewed passion, but slowly as the day goes on, they discover that too much has happened in the meanwhile. They are no longer the same, or rather, neither is the person cherished in the other's memory.

This disillusionment inspired Murger's finest poem. It is called *Le Chanson de Musette* but, like so much of his writing, it is really about Marie and it is charming. It ends:

> Musette, who has at last confessed
> The carnival of life has gone
> Came back, one morning, to the nest
> Whence like a wild bird she had flown
> But while I kissed the fugitive
> My heart no more emotion knew
> For, she had ceased for me to live
> And "You," she said, "are no more you.[12]

Dumas *fils* apparently once said he would gladly exchange all his works to have written *Le Chanson de Musette*. It was set to music by Vernier and became one of the most popular songs of the day.

Murger lived mostly outside Paris during his last decade, hiring a house in the small village of Marlotte near Fontainebleau. Here he became a wildly enthusiastic but incompetent hunter. He had several friends amongst the local fauna that he claimed to have shot at and missed so often that they no longer bothered to fly away when they saw him coming. He also had a mistress, Anaïs Latrasse, the so-called Mimi IV. Mimi III had been a girl named Juliette. He had taken up with Juliette soon after Lucile's death, but the affair had been short-lived. Perhaps Juliette was only a Mimi because she too died of tuberculosis.

Murger's health did not improve, despite his more orderly way of life. By the time of his death at the age of thirty-nine, he looked like an old man. His great ambition was to shake off all traces of his disreputable, Bohemian past, and to become accepted as a serious literary figure. The trouble was that in his best work he was always harking back to his youthful experiences; and no matter how much he might curse "that damned book", he could never escape it. Upper-class intellectuals, like Gérard de Nerval, simply ignored him in their literary commentaries. They felt he had brought Bohème into disrepute. Although he became adept at covering them up, the yawning gaps in his education too often revealed themselves. Considering he left school at thirteen, he did wonderfully well, but any true intellectual could tell at once that he was ill-bred and ignorant. The fact that Murger's writing was vastly more popular than theirs by no means mollified people such as d'Héricault and the brothers Goncourt, who poured scorn and vituperation upon him. An author who condoned free love and made jokes about not paying the rent was an easy target in the middle of the nineteenth century. One of these critics, Tybalt wrote:

> Murger glorified idleness, hypocrisy and the indolence of café society; the vulgar lechery and cheap ribaldry of a trooper; the spurious artist and the charlatan. He framed with lilac that terrible path of Bohemia that leads only to prison or the hospital. In so far as the banality of his nature allowed, he glorified in poetry, free love and the hatred of work. He extolled deceit. Fine examples indeed to set up as heroes for our students to emulate.

Such influential opponents denied Murger his greatest ambition which was to become an academician, but in 1859, he was made a member of the Legion of Honour. Knowing how much this would please him, his friends all went out to Marlotte to tell him, and celebrate the happy news. All went well until as his party piece, he tried to sing *Le Chanson de Musette* and broke down. He really was a very sentimental man.

In 1861, Murger was suddenly attacked by terrible pains in his legs, and was rushed to hospital. There was little the doctors could do, either to cure the problem or to alleviate the pain, but he still managed to joke with his visitors. Mercifully, after a week he died. His last words were: "Pas de musique, pas de bruit, pas de Bohème." He is buried in the Cemetery of Montmartre, not far from Alexandre Dumas *fils* and Marie Duplessis. Over his grave stands a statue of a graceful girl, said to be based on Marie Roux, scattering flowers and representing Youth. It bears the inscription: *La jeunesse n'a qu'un temps.* We are only young once.

D'Héricault was scandalised when no less than two Government ministers spoke at the funeral. He thought it altogether too much of a fuss for such a common little man. Nevertheless, he ~~himself, with over two thousand others, followed the cortège.~~ Later, his purpose in writing a book about Murger seems to have been mainly to give vent to his outrage that a monument should have been raised to the man in the Jardin du Luxembourg. The truth was that, notwithstanding his unappetising appearance and his modest talent, everyone liked Murger for his courage, his gentle irony, his good humour and his quest for a romantic ideal that did not really exist – not, that is, if we are to believe Mozart's don Alfonso. And, of course, we still like Murger today. In fact, *La Bohème* can only succeed if we like Rodolfo.

NOTES

1 Early in his career, Henri Murger decided to adopt the *nom-de-plume*, Henry Mürger, giving his real name a slightly foreign touch. He felt this might intrigue his readers, and also explain any lapses caused by his inadequate education.

   Names can be confusing when studying *La Bohème*. Several of the characters in real life had nick-names or used *noms-de-plume*. I have used the names that are most commonly used by historians and biographers – Henri Murger, Champfleury, Nadar, etc.

   I have also generally used the women's maiden names – Vimal and Louvet – rather than the surnames they had acquired through failed marriages. When referring to their real selves, I have used their actual names - Lucile and Marie – rather than their Bohemian nick-names – Mimi and Musetta.

   There is also a choice regarding the fictional names. I have used the operatic version – Rodolfo and Marcello rather than Rodolphe and Marcel – except where a passage from the book is being quoted or there is some other strong reason for using the French version.

2 The main hospital in any town was usually known as the Hôtel Dieu.

3 Harpagon was the miser in Molière's play *L'Avare*.

4 In July 1816, shortly after the restoration of the Bourbon monarchy, the *Medusa*, a frigate of the French navy, foundered off the coast of Senegal. It was a story of incompetence and cowardice. The crew, busy celebrating the crossing of the Equator, let their ship drift into dangerous waters. The *Medusa* had insufficient lifeboats, and these were taken by the captain and officers. A makeshift raft was constructed onto which 152 members of the crew clambered. The boats were supposed to tow it to safety but, when a sea got up, the officers cut the ropes and the raft was allowed to drift away. Twelve days later, when the raft was

found by another vessel, only fifteen of its crew were still alive.

The disaster became a great scandal and an indictment of the restored Bourbon monarchy, especially when it was revealed that the *Medusa's* captain had achieved his position through nepotism.

In 1817, the Romantic artist, Géricault, painted his famous picture of the raft just at the moment when the survivors see a sail on the horizon. Initially, it had to be exhibited as *Shipwreck Scene*, without reference to the *Medusa*, and it did not immediately cause a great sensation, but its subversive power grew as the Bourbon's popularity waned. By Murger's day, twenty years later, it was part of the iconography symbolising the bad days of the old régime.

5 Murger's preface is very long. This extract is much abridged.

6 Schanne had three nick-names, all in the punning fashion the Bohemians so enjoyed. As well as Schannard, which was short for Schannard-sauvage [wild duck], he was called Schanne–à-peche [fishing rod] and Schanne-en-jonc [malacca cane]. From all this, we can only conclude that, contrary to normal operatic usage, we should pronounce the sch in his name in the Flemish manner [sk] rather than the German [sh]

7 Pauvre Myosotis, lorsque je t'abandonne,
Lorsque tes blancs feuillets semblent me supplier;
Si je suis si cruel, oh! pardonne, pardonne!
Tu dis: N'oubliez pas – et je veux oublier.

8 Adrien Lélioux was, at this time, editor of a journal called *La Gazette de la Jeunesse*.

9 Léon Noël quotes this letter in full in his contribution to *Histoire de Murger par Trois Buveurs d'Eau*.

10 I had much trouble tracing the negative of this photograph because I was seeking a picture entitled 'Marie and Antoinette Roux', or perhaps 'The Roux Sisters'. In fact it is listed as 'Mariette Champfleury and Anna Roux'. Marie never married Champfleury so I pondered why his name was used. Did she come to regret their separation and indulge in a little wishful thinking? It is inconceivable that he would have approved. Most probably it was just a mistake by Philippe Nadar, who catalogued his father's negatives. Perhaps when asked who she was, the father simply said '*Oh, elle était la femme de Champfleury.*' *Femme* is ambiguous.

11 Quoted from R. Baldick's excellent book *The First Bohemians* [Hamish Hamilton, 1961]. The letter was discovered by Mr Baldick.

12 Musette, qui s'est souvenue
Le carnaval étant fini,
Un beau matin est revenue
Oiseau volage, à l'ancien nid:
Mais en embrassant l'infidèle
Mon coeur n'a plus senti d'émoi
Et Musette, qui n'est plus elle,
Disait que je n'étais plus moi.
[The translation in the text is taken from the 1887 English edition of *Scènes de la Vie de Bohème by Vizetelly.*]

Bibliography

SIMON BOCCANEGRA

ADAMS, N.B. *Romantic Dramas of G. Gutiérrez* (Inst. de las Españas en los Estados Unidos, 1922)

BALBI, G.P. *Simon Boccanegra e la Genova del '300* (Marietti, 1991)

BENT, J.T. *Genoa: How the Republic Rose and Fell* (Kegan Paul, 1881)

CAPPELLETTE *Dizionario Biografico degli Italiani* (Enciclopedia Italiana, 1970)

CARDEN, R.W. *City of Genoa* (Methuen, 1908)

DE BRÉGUIGNY, O.FEUDRIX. *History of Genoese Revolutions* (tr. Griffiths, 1751)

DE SISMONDI, J.V.L.S. *History of the Italian Republics* (Routledge, 1906)

DUFFY, B. *Tuscan Republics with Genoa* (Unwin, 1892)

GUTIÉRREZ, A. G. *Simon Boccanegra, the play* (Galería Dramatica, Madrid 1836)

MALLESON, G.B. *Studies from Genoese History* (Longmans, 1875)

VINCENS, E. *Histoire de Gênes* (Firmin Didot, 1842)

IL TROVATORE

ARAVENA, A.C. *Jorge Manrique y el Despuntar Renacenista* (Cancionero, 1929)

BALAGUER, V. *Historia de Cataluña* (Manuel Tello, 1886)

BISSON, T.N. *The Medieval Crown of Aragon* (Clarendon, 1986)

CHAYTOR, H.J. *A History of Aragon and Catalonia* (Methuen, 1933)

DE ENTRAMBASAGUAS, J. *La realidad de el Trovador* (Miscelanea Erudita)

DE GAMEZ, G.D. (trs. Evans, J.) *The Unconquered Knight* (Routledge, 1929)

DE GUZMAN, F.P. *Generaciones y Semblanzas* (Imprenta Real de la Gazeta, 1775)

DEYERMOND, A. *Jorge Manrique: A Spanish Poet of Death and Love* (Notes for an Exhibition, Westfield College, 1979)

EDKINS, A. *Verses which Jorge Manrique made on the death of don Rodrigo Manrique* (privately published, 1973)

GUTIÉRREZ, E.C. *Noticia de los Condes de Urgel* (Inst. de Estudíos Ilerdenses, 1973)

GUTIÉRREZ, A.G. *El Trovador* (Galéria Dramatica, 1836)

Don Carlos and Company

HILLGARTH, J.N. *The Spanish Kingdoms* (Clarendon, 1974)
MACDONALD, I.I. *don Fernando de Antequera* (Dolphin, 1984)
MANRIQUE, J. *Coplas que fizo por la muerte de su padre* (A. de Sancha, 1779)
PIDAL, R.M. *España y su Historia* (Ediciones Minotauro, 1957)
MONFAR *Historia de los Condes de Urgel* (Monfort, 1847)
SILVA, C.R. *Garcia Gutiérrez; Politica y Guerras Civiles*
SICILIANO, E.A. *La Verdadera Azucena de el Trovador*
SOLVEDILA, F. *Historia de Catalunya* (Alpha, 1962)
　　　　　　Sintesis de Historia de Cataluña (Destino, 1973)

RIGOLETTO

BERNIER, J. *Histoire de Blois* (Muguet, 1682)
BRABANT, L. van *Louise Labé et ses aventures amoureuses avec Clément Marot* (Coxyde, 1966)
BRANTÔME *Ouevres Complets* (Desrez, 1837)
CASTIGLIONE, B. (tr. Singleton) *Book of the Courtier* (Doubleday, New York 1959)
COLLETET, G *Notices sur les trois Marots* (Lemerre, 1871)
DE BEATIS, A. *Voyage du Cardinal d'Aragon* (Perrin, 1913)
DECRUE, F. *Le Cour de France* (Firmin et Didot, 1888)
DE LESCURE, M.F.A. *Les Amours de François Ier* (Achille Faure, 1864)
DE RADIER, J.F.D. *Des Fous en Titre d'Office* (Dentu, 1826)
DE RADIER, J.F.D. *Dictionnaire de l'Amour* (la Haye, 1741)
DESPERIERS, B. *Oeuvres Françoises* (Bibliotèque Elzevirienne, 1856)
DODU, G. *Les Amours et la Mort de François Ier* (Paris 1934)
DORAN, J. *History of Court Fools* (Bentley, 1858)
D'ORLIAC, J. (tr. Atkinson) *The Moon Mistress* (Harrap, 1931)
DU PERRON, D. *The Miscellaneous Remains of Cardinal Perron* (Butler, 1707)
HACKETT, F. *Francis the First* (Heinemann, 1934)
HUGO, V. *Le Roi s'Amuse* (Rendeul, 1832)
JACKSON, Lady *The Court of France* (Bentley, 1886)
JACOB, P.L. [Bibliophil Jaques] *Les Deux Fous* (Rendeul, 1830)
JOURDA, P. *Marot – l'homme et l'oeuvre* (Boivin, 1950)
　　　　　Marot – les lettres (Hatier, 1967)
　　　　　Une Princesse de la Renaissance (Paris 1932)
KNECHT, R.J. *Francis I & Absolute Monarchy* (London Historical Association, 1969)
KNECHT, R.J. *François Premier* (Cambridge University Press, 1972)
LALANNE, M.C.L. [ed.] *Journal d'un Bourgeois de Paris* [Renouard, 1854]
MAROT, C. *Oeuvres Completes* (Portaut, 1596)
MAROT, J. *Les Ouevres de Jean Marot* (Coustelier, 1723)
MORLEY, H. *Clément Marot* (Chapman & Hall, 1871)
NAVARRE, Marguerite de. *Le Heptameron* (1559)
PARIS, A.P. *Etudes sur François Ier* (Techener, 1885)

Bibliography

RABELAIS (tr. Urquhart) *Oeuvres, Book III* (Bohn, 1846)
REVUE HISTORIQUE *Un Traitre au XVI Siecle*
VARILLAS, A. *Histoire de François Ier* (Arnout Leers, 1684)

DON CARLOS

DAVIES, R.T. *The Golden Century of Spain* (MacMillan, 1937)
DE SAINT-REAL, V. *Don Carlos, a novel* (Herringman, 1674)
FREER, M. *Elizabeth de Valois* (Hurst and Blackett, 1857)
GACHARD, M. *Don Carlos et Philippe II* (Michel Lévy Frères, 1867)
HUME, M.A.S. *Philip II of Spain* (MacMillan, 1896)
KAMEN, H. *Spain 1496–1714* (Longman, 1983)
LLORENTE, J.A. *The Inquisition of Spain* (Whittaker, 1826)
LYNCH, J. *Spain under the Hapsburgs* (Blackwell 1964)
MARANON, G. *Antonio Perez* (Buenos Aires, Mexico 1947)
MARIEJOL, J.H. (tr. Wells) *Master of the Armada* (Hamish Hamilton, 1933)
MILLER, T. *The Castles and the Crown* (Gollancz, 1963)
MURO, G. (tr. A. Weil) *La Princesse d'Eboli* (Charpentier, 1878)
PARKER, G. *Philip II* (Hutchinson, 1979)
PETRIE, Sir C. *Philip II of Spain* (Eyre & Spottiswood, 1963)
PRESCOTT, W.H. *History of Spain* (Routledge, 1887)
SCHILLER, F. *Don Carlos, a play* (Bohn, London 1854)

LUCIA DI LAMMERMOOR

ANON *Memoirs of John, Earl of Stair by an Impartial Hand* (Booksellers of London and Westminster, 1695)
BREWSTER, D. *Second Daughter* (T.C. Farries & Co., 1989)
DOUGLAS, Sir R. *Peerage of Scotland* (Douglas 1911)
GRAHAM, J.M. *Annals of Viscount Stair* (Blackwood, 1875)
LAW, R. *Memorialls* (Constable, Edinburgh, 1818)
MACAULAY, Lord *Narratives from Macaulay* (MacMillan, 1905)
MACKAY, A.J.G. *Memoir of Sir James Dalrymple* (Edmonston and Douglas, 1873) 1818)
McGIBBON, D. *and* Ross, T. *Castellated and Domestic Architecture in Scotland* (Douglas, 1887)
McKERLIE, P. *History of the Lands and their Owners of Galloway* (Edinburgh 1870–79)
MURRAY, T. *Literary History of Galloway* (Waugh & Innes, 1822)
NAYLOR, I. *Historic Border Families and Houses* (Reiver Press, 1989)
SCOTT, Sir W. *Waverley Novels* (Cadell, Edinburgh 1851)
SOMERS, Lord *Tracts* (Cadell & Davies, 1809–15)
SYMSON, A. *A Large Description of Galloway* (Sibbald and Macfarlane, 1684)
WHYTE, D. *Kirkliston – A Parish History* (Dunfermline Press, 1991)

UN BALLO IN MASCHERA

ABERG, A. *A Concise History of Sweden* (Swedish Museums Assoc., 1958)
BAIN, R.N. *Gustavus III & his Contemporaries* (Kegan Paul, 1894)
BROWN, J. *Memoirs of the Courts of Sweden* (Grolier Society, 1904)
CRONIN, N.N. *History of Sweden* (privately printed, Chicago 1902)
HAGER, O. and VILLIUS, H. *Sammensvarjningen* (Swedish Radio, 1988)
OAKLEY, S. *The Story of Sweden* (Faber & Faber, 1966)
ROBERTS, M. *The Age of Liberty* (Cambridge University Press, 1986)
SAHLBERG, G. (tr. Austin, P.B.) *Murder at the Masked Ball* (Macdonald, 1974)
SCOBBIE, I. *Sweden* (Benn, 1966)

LA TRAVIATA

DUMAS, fils, A. *La Dame aux Camélias* (Calman-Lévy, 1852)
DU PLESSIX GRAY, F. *Splendour & Miseries* (New York Review of Books, July 1992)
GROS, J. *Une Courtisane Romantique* (Au Cabinet du Livre, 1929)
GROS, J. *Alexandre Dumas et Marie Duplessis* (Conard, 1923)
HENRIOT, E. *Portraits de Femmes* (Michel, Paris 1950)
HURE, P–A. *Liszt en son Temps* (Hachete, Paris, 1987)
ISSARTEL, Chr. *Les Dames aux Camélias* (Hachette, Paris 1981)
MME Judith (tr. Mrs Bell) *My Autobiography* (Nash, 1912)
PRASTEAU, J. (tr. Rodway, S.) *The Lady of the Camelias* (Hutchinson, 1965)
RAT, M. *La Dame aux Camélias* (del Duca, Paris 1960)
ROQUEPLAN, N. *Parisine* (Hetzel, 1868)
SAUNDERS, E. *La Dame aux Camélias et les Dumas* (Correa, Paris 1954)
SOREAU, G. *La Vie de la Dame aux Camélias* (La Revue de France, 1898)
VIENNE, R. *La Verité sur la Dame aux Camélias* (Paris-Ollendorf, 1888)
WEIL, Ct. *Les Dessous du Congrès de Vienne* (Payot, Paris 1917)

LA BOHÈME

BALDICK, R. *The First Bohemian* (Hamish Hamilton, 1961)
BEAUVALLET & NEUVILLE *Les Femmes de Murger* (Charlier & Huillery, 1861)
BOISSON, M. *Les Compagnons de la Vie de Bohème* (Tallendier, 1929)
CHAMPFLEURY *Les Aventures de Mlle Mariette* (Lecou, 1853)
            Souvenirs de Jeunesse (Dentu, 1872)
DELVAU, A. H. *Murger et la Bohème* (Backelin, 1866)
DE NERVAL, G. *La Bohème Galante* (Levy, 1855)
DESCAVES, L. *La Conversion de Murger* (L'Intransigeant, March 1922)
D'HERICAULT, Ch. *Murger et son Coin* (Tremaux, 1896)
DUFAY, P. *Buveurs d'eau à la Vie de Bohème* (Mercure de France, April 1992)
GROS, J. *Marie ou le Premier Amour de Murger* (Elzevier, Dijon 1934)

Bibliography

GROS, J. *Le Premier Amour d'Henry Murger* (Grand Revue, March 1929)
HOUSSAYE, A. *Souvenirs de Jeunesse, 1830–1850* (Flammarion, 1896)
MAILLARD, F. *Les Derniers Bohèmes* (Sartorius, 1874)
MONTORGUEIL, G. *A la Maison de Murger* (Temps, March 1992)
MOSS & MARVAL *The Legend of the Latin Quarter* (W.H. Allen, 1947)
MURGER, H. *Bohemians of the Latin Quarter* (Vizatelly, 1887)
    Le Dernier Rendez-vous (Lévy, 1856)
    Le Roman de Toutes les Femmes (Lagny, 1875)
    Les Buveurs d'Eau (Lévy, 1855)
    Les Nuits d'Hiver (Lévy, 1861)
    Les Vacances de Camille (Lévy, 1857)
    Scènes de la Vie de Bohème (Lévy, 1851)
    Scènes de la Vie de Jeunesse (Lévy, 1851)
MURGER, H. & BARRIER, Th. *La Vie de Bohème* (Dondey, 1852)
PELLOQUET, Th. *Henry Murger* (Bourdilliat, 1861)
SCHANNE, A. *Les Souvenirs de Schaunard* (Charpentier, Paris 1887)
SEE, E. *A Propos du Centennaire de Murger* (Excelsior, March 1922)
TROIS BUVEURS d'EAU [Lélioux, Noël, Nadar] *Histoire de Murger* (Hetzel, 1862)
WARNOD, A. *La Vraie Bohème d'Henry Murger* (Dupont, 1947)

Index

Names of fictional characters
are in *italics* throughout

254

Index

Index

Index

Index

Index